PLAYS BY

Edward Albee

(DATES OF COMPOSITION)

ADAPTATIONS

EDWARD ALBEE

THE PLAYS

EDWARD ALBEE

VOLUME TWO
Tiny Alice
A Delicate Balance
Box AND *Quotations from*
Chairman Mao Tse-tung

THE PLAYS

Atheneum
NEW YORK 1981

Library of Congress Cataloging in Publication Data

Albee, Edward, 1928-
    The plays.

        Contents: —v. 2. Tiny Alice, A delicate balance. Box and Quotations from Chairman Mao Tse-Tung—v. 3. Everything in the garden. Malcolm. The ballad of the sad café—v. 4. Seascape. Counting the ways. Listening. All over.
    I. Title.
PS3551.L25A19   1981   812'.54   81-3616
ISBN 0-689-70614-6 (pbk. : v. 2)   AACR2

Tiny Alice

FOR

NOEL FARRAND

AUTHOR'S NOTE

It has been the expressed hope of many that I would write a preface to the published text of *Tiny Alice*, clarifying obscure points in the play—explaining my intention, in other words. I have decided against creating such a guide because I find —after reading the play over—that I share the view of even more people: that the play is quite clear. I will confess, though, that *Tiny Alice* is less opaque in reading than it would be in any single viewing. One further note: this printed text of *Tiny Alice* represents the complete play. Some deletions—mainly in the final act—were made for the New York production; and while I made the deletions myself, and quite cheerfully, realizing their wisdom in the particular situation, I restore them here with even greater enthusiasm.

EDWARD ALBEE

FIRST PERFORMANCE

December 29, 1964, New York City, Billy Rose Theatre

LAWYER	*William Hutt*
CARDINAL	*Eric Berry*
JULIAN	*John Gielgud*
BUTLER	*John Heffernan*
MISS ALICE	*Irene Worth*

DIRECTED BY *Alan Schneider*

SETS BY *William Ritman*
GOWNS BY *Mainbocher*
LIGHTING BY *Martin Aronstein*

ACT ONE

SCENE ONE

(The CARDINAL'S *garden. What is needed . . . ? Ivy climbing a partial wall of huge stones? An iron gate? Certainly two chairs—one, the larger, obviously for His Eminence; the other, smaller—and certainly an elaborate birdcage, to stage left, with some foliage in it, and two birds, cardinals . . . which need not be real. At rise, the* LAWYER *is at the birdcage, talking to the birds)*

LAWYER

Oomm, yoom, yoom, um? Tick-tick-tick-tick-tick. Um? You do-do-do-do-do-um? Tick-tick-tick-tick-tick-tick-tick-um? *(He raises his fingers to the bars)* Do-do-do-do-do-do-do? Aaaaa-awwwww! Oomm, yoom, yoom, um?
   (The CARDINAL *enters from stage right—through the iron gates?—unseen by the* LAWYER, *who repeats some of the above as the* CARDINAL *moves toward center)*

CARDINAL
(Finally. Quietly amused)

Saint Francis?

LAWYER
(Swinging around; flustered; perhaps more annoyed than embarrassed at being discovered)

Your Eminence!

CARDINAL

Our dear Saint Francis, who wandered in the fields and forests, talked to all the . . .

LAWYER
(Moving to kiss the ring)
Your Eminence, we appreciate your kindness in taking the
time to see us; we know how heavy a schedule you . . .

CARDINAL
(Silencing him by waving his ring at him. The LAW-
YER *kneels, kisses the ring, rises)*
We are pleased . . . *we* are pleased to be your servant *(Trail-
ing off)* . . . if . . . we can be your servant. We addressed
you as Saint Francis . . .

LAWYER *(Properly mumbling)*
Oh, but surely . . .

CARDINAL
. . . as Saint Francis . . . who did talk to the birds so, did
he not. And here we find *you*, who talk not only to the birds
but to *(With a wave at the cage)*—you must forgive us—to
cardinals as well. *(Waits for reaction, gets none, tries again)*
. . . To cardinals? As well?

LAWYER *(A tight smile)*
We . . . we understood.

CARDINAL *(He, too)*
Did we.
(A brief silence, as both smiles hold)

LAWYER
(To break it, moving back toward the cage)
We find it droll—if altogether appropriate in this setting—
that there should be two cardinals . . . uh, together . . .
(Almost a sneer) . . . in conversation, as it were.

CARDINAL *(The smile again)*

Ah, well, they are a comfort to each other . . . companion-
ship. And they have so much to say. They . . . understand
each other so much better than they would . . . uh, *other*
birds.

LAWYER

Indeed. And so much better than they would understand
saints?

CARDINAL
(Daring him to repeat it, but still amused)
Sir?

LAWYER *(Right in)*
That cardinals understand each *other* better than they understand saints.

CARDINAL *(Not rising to it)*
Who is to say? Will you sit?

LAWYER *(Peering into the cage)*
They are extraordinary birds . . . cardinals, if I may say
so. . . .

CARDINAL *(Through with it)*
You push it too far, sir. Will you join us?
(He moves to his chair, sits in it)

LAWYER
*(Brief pause, then surrender; moves to the other
chair)*
Of course.

CARDINAL *(A deep sigh)*
Well. What should we do now? *(Pause)* Should we clap our
hands *(Does so, twice)* . . . twice, and have a monk appear?

A very old monk? With just a ring of white hair around the
base of his head, stooped, fast-shuffling, his hands deep in his
sleeves? Eh? And should we send him for wine? Um? Should
we offer you wine, and should we send him scurrying off after
it? Yes? Is that the scene you expect now?

LAWYER
(*Very relaxed, but pointed*)
It's so difficult to know what to expect in a Cardinal's garden,
Your Eminence. An old monk would do . . . or—who is to
say?—perhaps some good-looking young novice, all freshly
scrubbed, with big working-class hands, who would . . .

CARDINAL (*Magnanimous*)
We have both in our service; if a boy is more to your pleasure . . .

LAWYER
I don't drink in the afternoon, so there is need for neither
. . . unless Your Eminence . . . ?

CARDINAL
(*His eyes sparkling with the joke to come about his
nature*)
We are known to be . . . ascetic, so we will have none of it.
Just . . . three cardinals . . . and Saint Francis.

LAWYER
Oh, not Saint Francis, not a saint. Closer to a king; closer
to Croesus. That was gibberish I was speaking to the cardinals
—and it's certainly not accepted that Saint Francis spoke
gibberish to his . . . parishioners . . . intentional gibberish
or otherwise.

CARDINAL
It is not accepted; no.

LAWYER

No. May I smoke?

CARDINAL

Do.

LAWYER *(Lights up)*
Closer to Croesus; to gold; closer to wealth.

CARDINAL *(A heavy, weary sigh)*
Aahhhh, you *do* want to talk business, don't you?

LAWYER *(Surprisingly tough)*
Oh, come on, Your Eminence: *(Softer)* Do you want to spend
the afternoon with me, making small talk? Shall we . . .
shall we talk about . . . times gone by?

CARDINAL
(Thinks about it with some distaste)
No. No no; we don't think so. It wouldn't do. It's not chari-
table of us to say so, but when we were at school we did
loathe you so.
(Both laugh slightly)

LAWYER
Your Eminence was not . . . beloved of everyone himself.

CARDINAL
(Thinking back, a bit smugly)
Ah, no; a bit out of place; out of step.

LAWYER
A swine, I thought.

CARDINAL
And we you.
(Both laugh a little again)

LAWYER

Do you ever slip?

CARDINAL

Sir?

LAWYER

Mightn't you—if you're not careful—*(Tiny pause)* lapse . . .
and say *I* to me . . . not we?

CARDINAL
(Pretending sudden understanding)
Ah *ha!* Yes, we under*stand.*

LAWYER

Do we, do we.

CARDINAL

We do. We—and here we speak of our*selves* and not of our
station—we . . . *we* reserve the first-person singular for intimates . . . and equals.

LAWYER

. . . And your superiors.

CARDINAL
(Brushing away a gnat)
The case does not apply.

LAWYER
(Matter-of-factly; the vengeance is underneath)
You'll grovel, Buddy. *(Slaps his hip hard)* As automatically
and naturally as people slobber on that ring of yours. As naturally as that, I'll have you do your obeisance. *(Sweetly)* As
you used to, old friend.

CARDINAL
We . . . *(Thinks better of what he was about to say)* You

were a swine at school. *(More matter-of-factly)* A cheat in your examinations, a liar in all things of any matter, vile in your personal habits—unwashed and indecent, a bully to those you could intimidate and a sycophant to everyone else. We remember you more clearly each moment. It is law you practice, is it not? We find it fitting.

LAWYER
(A mock bow, head only)
We are of the same school, Your Eminence.

CARDINAL
And in the same class . . . but not *of*. You have come far—in a worldly sense . . . from so little, we mean. *(Musing)* The law.

LAWYER
I speak plainly.

CARDINAL
You are plain. As from your beginnings.

LAWYER *(Quietly)*
Overstuffed, arrogant, pompous son of a profiteer. And a whore. You are in the Church, are you not? We find it fitting.

CARDINAL
(A burst of appreciative laughter)
You're *good!* You *are! Still!* Gutter, but good. But, in law . . . *(Leaves it unfinished with a gesture)* Ah! It comes back to us; it begins to. What did we call you at school? What name, what nickname did we have for you . . . all of us? What term of simple honesty and . . . rough affection did we have for you? *(Tapping his head impatiently)* It comes back to us.

LAWYER *(Almost a snarl)*
We had a name for you, too.

CARDINAL *(Dismissing it)*
Yes, yes, but we forget it.

LAWYER
Your Eminence was not always so . . . eminent.

CARDINAL *(Remembering)*
Hy-e . . . *(Relishing each syllable)* Hy-e-na. Hy. E. Na. We
recall.

LAWYER
(Close to break-through anger)
We are close to Croesus, Your Eminence. I've brought gold
with me . . . *(Leans forward)* money, Your Eminence.

CARDINAL *(Brushing it off)*
Yes, yes; later. Hy-e-na.

LAWYER *(A threat, but quiet)*
A great deal of money, Your Eminence.

CARDINAL
We hear you, and we will discuss your business shortly. And
why did we call you hyena . . . ?

LAWYER *(Quiet threat again)*
If Croesus goes, he takes the gold away.

CARDINAL *(Outgoing)*
But, Hyena, you are not Croesus; you are Croesus' emissary.
You will wait; the gold will wait.

LAWYER
Are you certain?

CARDINAL *(Ignoring the last)*
Ah, yes, it was in natural-science class, was it not? *(The* LAW-
YER *rises, moves away a little)* Was it not?

LAWYER

Considering your mother's vagaries, you were never certain of
your true father . . . were you?

CARDINAL

Correct, my child: considering one's mother's vagaries, one
was never certain of one's true father . . . was one? But then,
my child, we embraced the Church; and we *know* our true
father. *(Pause; the* LAWYER *is silent)* It was in natural-science
class, eleven-five until noon, and did we not discover about
the hyena . . .

LAWYER

More money than you've ever seen!

CARDINAL *(Parody; cool)*

Yum-yum. *(Back to former tone)* Did we not discover about
the hyena that it was a most resourceful scavenger? That, failing all other food, it would dine on offal . . .

LAWYER *(Angrier)*

Millions!

CARDINAL *(Pressing on)*

. . . and that it devoured the wounded and the dead? We
found that last the most shocking: the dead. But we were
young. And what horrified us most—and, indeed, what gave
us all the thought that the name was most fitting for yourself—

LAWYER *(Ibid.)*

Money!

CARDINAL

. . . was that to devour its dead, scavenged prey, it would
often chew into it . . .

LAWYER

MONEY, YOU SWINE!

CARDINAL
(Each word rising in pitch and volume)
. . . chew into it THROUGH THE ANUS????
(Both silent, breathing a little hard)

LAWYER *(Finally; softly)*

Bastard.

CARDINAL *(Quietly, too)*
And now that we have brought the past to mind, and remembered what we could not exactly, shall we . . . talk business?

LAWYER *(Softly; sadly)*
Robes the color of your mother's vice.

CARDINAL *(Kindly)*
Come. Let us talk business. You are a businessman.

LAWYER *(Sadly again)*
As are you.

CARDINAL
(As if reminding a child of something)
We are a Prince of the Church. Do you forget?

LAWYER
(Suddenly pointing to the cage; too offhand)
Are those two lovers? Do they mate?

CARDINAL
(Patronizing; through with games)
Come; let us talk business.

LAWYER *(Persisting)*
Is it true? Do they? Even cardinals?

CARDINAL (*A command*)
If you have money to give us . . . sit down and give it.

LAWYER
To the lay mind—to the cognoscenti it may be fact, accepted
and put out of the head—but to the lay mind it's speculation
. . . voyeuristic, perhaps, and certainly anti-Rome . . . mere
speculation, but whispered about, even by the school children
—indeed, as you must recall, the more . . . urbane of us
wondered about the Fathers at school . . .

CARDINAL
. . . the more wicked . . .

LAWYER
. . . about their vaunted celibacy . . . among one another.
Of course, we were at an age when everyone diddled everyone
else . . .

CARDINAL
Some.

LAWYER
Yes, and I suppose it was natural enough for us to assume
that the priests did too.

CARDINAL
(*As if changing the subject*)
You have . . . fallen away from the Church.

LAWYER
And into the arms of reason.

CARDINAL
(*Almost thinking of something else*)
An unsanctified union: not a marriage: a whore's bed.

LAWYER

A common-law marriage, for I am at law and, as you say, common. But it is quite respectable these days.

CARDINAL
(Tough; bored with the church play-acting; heavy and tired)
All right; that's enough. What's your business?

LAWYER
(Pacing a little, after an appreciative smile)
My employer . . . wants to give some of her money to the Church.

CARDINAL
(Enthusiastic, but guarded)
Does she!

LAWYER

Gradually.

CARDINAL *(Understanding)*
Ah-ha.

LAWYER *(Offhand)*
A hundred million now.

CARDINAL *(No shown surprise)*
And the rest gradually.

LAWYER

And the same amount each year for the next twenty—a hundred million a year. She is not ill; she has no intention of dying; she is quite young, youngish; there is no . . . rush.

CARDINAL

Indeed not.

LAWYER

It is that she is . . . overburdened with wealth.

CARDINAL

And it weighs on her soul.

LAWYER

Her soul is in excellent repair. If it were not, I doubt she'd be making the gesture. It is, as I said, that she is overburdened with wealth, and it . . . uh . . .

CARDINAL
(Finding the words for him)

. . . piles up.

LAWYER *(A small smile)*

. . . and it is . . . wasted . . . lying about. It is one of several bequests—arrangements—she is making at the moment.

CARDINAL
(Not astonishment, but unconcealed curiosity)

One of several?

LAWYER

Yes. The Protestants as well, the Jews . . . hospitals, universities, orchestras, revolutions here and there . . .

CARDINAL

Well, we think it is a . . . responsible action. She is well, as you say.

LAWYER

Oh, yes; very.

CARDINAL

We are . . . glad. *(Amused fascination)* How did you become her . . . lawyer, if we're not intruding upon . . . ?

LAWYER *(Brief pause; tight smile)*
She had a dossier on me, I suppose.

CARDINAL
It must be a great deal less revealing than ours . . . than our dossier on you.

LAWYER
Or a great deal *more* revealing.

CARDINAL
For her sake, and yours, we hope so.

LAWYER
To answer your question: I am a very good lawyer. It is as simple as that.

CARDINAL *(Speculating on it)*
You *have* escaped prison.

LAWYER
I've done nothing to be imprisoned for.

CARDINAL
Pure. You're pure. You're ringed by stench, but you're pure. There's an odor that precedes you, and follows after you're gone, but you walk in the eye of it . . . pure.

LAWYER *(Contemptuous)*
Look, pig, I don't enjoy you.

CARDINAL
(Mockingly; his arms wide as if for an embrace)
School chum!

LAWYER
If it were not my job to . . .

CARDINAL *(Abruptly)*

Well, it is! Do it!

LAWYER
(A smile to a hated but respected adversary)
I've given you the facts: a hundred million a year for twenty years.

CARDINAL

But . . . ?

LAWYER *(Shrugs)*

That's all.

CARDINAL
(Stuttering with quiet excitement)
Y-y-y-y-yes, b-b-but shall I just go to the *house* and pick it up in a *truck?*

LAWYER *(Great, heavy relief)*

ᴧᴧᴧᴧᴧᴧᴧᴧHHHHHHHHhhhhhhhhhh.

CARDINAL *(Caught up short)*

Hm? *(No reply)* ʜᴍ???

LAWYER

Say it again. Say it once again for me.

CARDINAL *(Puzzled; suspicious)*

What? Say what?

LAWYER *(Leaning over him)*

Say it again; repeat what you said. It was a sweet sound.

CARDINAL *(Shouting)*

SAY WHAT!

LAWYER (*Cooing into his ear*)

"Yes, but shall I just go to the house and pick it up in a truck?"

CARDINAL

(*Thinks on it a moment*)

Well, perhaps there was a bit . . . perhaps there was too much levity there . . . uh, if one did not know one . . .

LAWYER (*Coos again*)

. . . "But shall *I* just go to the house . . ."

CARDINAL

Wh . . . NO!

LAWYER (*Sings it out*)

Shall IIIIIIII just go!

CARDINAL (*Cross*)

No! We . . . we did not say that!

LAWYER

IIIIIIIIIIIIIII.

CARDINAL (*A threat*)

We did not say "I."

LAWYER (*Almost baby talk*)

We said I. Yes, we did; we said I. (*Suddenly loud and tough*) We said I, and we said it straight. I! I! I! By God, we picked up our skirts and lunged for it! IIIIIII! Me! Me! Gimme!

CARDINAL (*Full shout*)

WE SAID NO SUCH THING!

LAWYER (*Oily imitation*)

We reserve the first-person singular, do we not, for . . . for intimates, equals . . . or superiors. *(Harsher)* Well, my dear, you found all three applying. Intimate. How close would we rub to someone for all that wealth? As close as we once did?

CARDINAL
(Not wanting to hear, but weak)
Leave . . . leave off.

LAWYER *(Pressing)*
Equals? Oh, money equals anything you want. Levels! LEVELS THE EARTH! AND THE HEAVENS!

CARDINAL
ENOUGH!!

LAWYER *(The final thrust)*
. . . Or superiors. Who is superior, the one who stands on the mount of heaven? We think not! We have come down off our plural . . . when the stakes are high enough . . . and the hand, the kissed hand palsies out . . . FOR THE LOOT!!

CARDINAL *(Hissed)*
Satan!

LAWYER *(After a pause)*
Satan? You would believe it . . . if you believed in God. *(Breaks into—for lack of a better word—Satanic laughter, subsides. Patronizing now)* No, poor Eminence, you don't have to drive a truck around to the back door for it. We'll get the money to you . . . to your . . . people. Fact, I don't want you coming 'round . . . at all. Clacketing through the great corridors of the place, sizing it up, not content with enough wealth to buy off the first two hundred saints picked out of a bag, but wondering if *it* mightn't get thrown into the bargain as a . . . summer residence, perhaps . . . uh, after she dies and scoots up to heaven.

CARDINAL
(On his feet, but shaky, uncertain)
This . . . uh . . .

LAWYER
. . . interview is terminated?

CARDINAL (Quietly)
This is unseemly talk.

LAWYER (Vastly, wryly amused)
Oh? Is it?

CARDINAL
(A mechanical toy breaking down)
We will . . . we will forgive your presumption, your . . .
excess . . . excuse, yes . . . excuse? . . . We will . . . over-
look your . . . (A plea is underneath) Let us have no more
of this talk. It is unseemly.

LAWYER
(Businesslike; as if the preceding speech had not
happened)
As I said, I don't want you coming 'round . . . bothering
her.

CARDINAL (Humble)
I would not bother the lady; I have not met her. Of course,
I would very much like to have the pleasure of . . .

LAWYER
We slip often now, don't we.

CARDINAL (Very soul-weary)
Pardon?

LAWYER
The plural is gone out of us, I see.

CARDINAL

Ah. Well. Perhaps.

LAWYER

Regird yourself. We *are* about terminated. *(Quick, insulting finger-snaps)* Come! Come! Back up; back on your majesty! Hup!

CARDINAL

(Slowly, wearily coming back into shape)

Uh . . . yes . . . of—of course. We, uh, we shall make any arrangements you wish . . . naturally. We . . . we have no desire to intrude ourselves upon . . . uh . . . upon . . .

LAWYER

Miss Alice.

CARDINAL

Yes; upon Miss Alice. If she . . . if Miss Alice desires privacy, certainly her generosity has earned it for her. We . . . would not intrude.

LAWYER

You *are* kind. *(Fishing in a pocket for a notebook)* What . . . is . . . your . . . secretary's . . . name . . . I think I have it . . . right . . . *(Finds notebook)*

CARDINAL

Brother . . .

LAWYER

Julian! Is that not right?

CARDINAL

Yes, Brother Julian. He is an old friend of ours; we . . .

LAWYER

Rather daring of you, wasn't it? Choosing a lay brother as

your private secretary?

CARDINAL
(A combination of apology and defiance)
He is an old friend of ours, and he has served the . . .

LAWYER (Praising a puppy)
You are adventurous, are you not?

CARDINAL
He has been assigned many years to the . . .

LAWYER
(Waving his notebook a little)
We have it; all down; we know.

CARDINAL (A little sadly)
Ah-ha.

LAWYER
Yes. Well, we will send for your . . . Brother Julian. . . .
To clear up odds and ends. Every bank has its runners. We
don't ask vice presidents to . . . fetch and carry. Inform
Your Brother Julian. We will send for him.
(LAWYER exits)

CARDINAL (To the exiting figure)
Yes, we . . . will.
(Stands still, looks at the ground, tired, looks at his
sleeves, his fingernails, his ring, up, out, over. Sighs,
looks at the cage. Smiles slightly, moves to the cage,
the fingers of his left hand fluttering at it)
Do . . . do you . . . do you have much to say to one another,
my dears? Do you? You find it comforting? Hmmmmmmmm?
Do you? Hmmmm? Do-do-do-do-do-do-do-do? Hmmmmmmm?
Do?

CURTAIN

SCENE TWO

(*The library of a mansion—a castle. Pillared walls, floor-to-ceiling leather-bound books. A great arched doorway, rear center. A huge reading table to stage left—practical. A phrenological head on it. To stage right, jutting out of the wings, a huge doll's-house model of the building of which the present room is a part. It is as tall as a man, and a good deal of it must be visible from all parts of the audience. An alternative —and perhaps more practical—would be for the arched doorway to be either left or right, with bookshelves to both sides of the set, coming toward the center, and to have the entire doll's house in the rear wall, in which case it could be smaller —say, twelve feet long and proportionately high. At any rate, it is essential. At rise,* JULIAN *is alone on stage, looking at the house*)

JULIAN
(*After a few moments of head-shaking concentration*)
Extraordinary . . . extraordinary.

BUTLER
(*After entering, observing* JULIAN, *not having heard him*)
Extraordinary, isn't it?

JULIAN (*Mildly startled*)
Uh . . . yes, unbelievable . . . (*Agreeing*) Extraordinary.

BUTLER
(*Who moves about with a kind of unbutlerlike ease*)
I never cease to wonder at the . . . the fact of it, I suppose.

JULIAN

The workmanship . . .

BUTLER *(A mild correction)*

That someone would do it.

JULIAN *(Seeing)*

Yes, yes.

BUTLER

That someone would . . . well, for heaven's sake, that someone would build . . . *(Refers to the set)* . . . *this* . . . castle? . . . and then . . . duplicate it in such precise miniature, so exactly. Have you looked through the windows?

JULIAN

No, I . . .

BUTLER

It is exact. Look and see.

JULIAN
*(Moves even closer to the model, peers through a
tiny window)*
Why . . . why, YES. I . . . there's a great . . . baronial dining room, even with tiny candlesticks on the tables!

BUTLER
(Nodding his head, a thumb back over his shoulder)
It's down the hall, off the hallway to the right.

JULIAN
(The proper words won't come)
It's . . . it's . . .

BUTLER

Look over here. There; right there.

JULIAN *(Peers)*
It's . . . it's this *room!* This room we're *in!*

BUTLER
Yes.

JULIAN
Extraordinary.

BUTLER
Is there anyone there? Are we there?

JULIAN
(Briefly startled, then laughs, looks back into the model)
Uh . . . no. It seems to be quite . . . empty.

BUTLER *(A quiet smile)*
One feels one should see one's self . . . almost.

JULIAN
(Looks back to him; after a brief, thoughtful pause)
Yes. That would be rather a shock, wouldn't it?

BUTLER
Did you notice . . . did you notice that there is a model within that room in the castle? A model of the model?

JULIAN
I . . . I did. But . . . I didn't register it, it seemed so . . . continual.

BUTLER *(A shy smile)*
You don't suppose that within that tiny model in the model there, there is . . . another room like this, with yet a tinier model within it, and within . . .

JULIAN (*Laughs*)
. . . and within and within and within and . . . ? No, I
. . . rather doubt it. It's remarkable craftsmanship, though.
Remarkable.

BUTLER

Hell to clean.

JULIAN
(*Conversational enthusiasm*)
Yes! I should think so! Does it open from . . .

BUTLER

It's sealed. Tight. There is no dust.

JULIAN
(*Disappointed at being joked with*)

Oh.

BUTLER

I was sporting.

JULIAN

Oh.

BUTLER (*Straight curiosity*)

Did you mind?

JULIAN (*Too free*)

I? No!

BUTLER (*Doctrine, no sarcasm*)
It would almost be taken for granted—one would think—
that if a person or a person's surrogate went to the trouble,
and expense, of having such a dream toy made, that the person *would* have it sealed, so that there'd be no dust. Wouldn't
one think.

JULIAN
(Sarcasm and embarrassment together)
One would think.

BUTLER *(After a pause, some rue)*
I have enough to do as it is.

JULIAN
(Eager to move on to something else)
Yes, yes!

BUTLER
It's enormous . . . *(A sudden thought)* even for a castle, I suppose. *(Points to the model)* Not that. *(Now to the room)* This.

JULIAN
Endless! You . . . certainly you don't work alone.

BUTLER
Oh, Christ, no.

JULIAN *(Reaffirming)*
I would have *thought*.

BUTLER
(Almost daring him to disagree)
Still, there's enough work.

JULIAN *(Slightly testy)*
I'm *sure*.

(A pause between them)

BUTLER
(For no reason, a sort of "Oh, what the hell")
Heigh-ho.

JULIAN

Will there be . . . someone? . . . to see me? . . . soon?

BUTLER

Hm?

JULIAN

Will there be someone to see me soon! (*After a blank stare from the other*) You announced me? I trust?

BUTLER (*Snapping to*)

Oh! Yes! (*Laughs*) Sorry. Uh . . . yes, there will be someone to see you soon.

JULIAN
(*Attempt at good-fellowship*)

Ah, good!

BUTLER

Are you a priest?

JULIAN (*Self-demeaning*)

I? No, no . . .

BUTLER

If not Catholic, Episcopal.

JULIAN

No . . .

BUTLER

What, then?

JULIAN

I am a lay brother. I am not ordained.

BUTLER

You are *of* the cloth but have not taken it.

JULIAN (None too happy)

You *could* say that.

BUTLER (No trifling)

One *could* say it, and quite accurately. May I get you some ice water?

JULIAN (Put off and confused)

No!

BUTLER (Feigns apology)

Sorry.

JULIAN

You must forgive me. *(Almost childlike enthusiasm)* This is rather a big day for me.

BUTLER (Nods understandingly)

Iced *tea.*

JULIAN (Laughs)

No . . . nothing, thank you . . . uh . . . I don't have your name.

BUTLER

Fortunate.

JULIAN

No, I meant that . . .

BUTLER

Butler.

JULIAN

Pardon?

BUTLER

Butler.

JULIAN

Yes. You. . . you *are* the butler, are you not, but . . .

BUTLER

Butler. My name is Butler.

JULIAN *(Innocent pleasure)*

How extraordinary!

BUTLER *(Putting it aside)*

No, not really. Appropriate: Butler . . . butler. If my name
were Carpenter, and I were a butler . . . or if I *were* a carpenter, and my name were Butler . . .

JULIAN

But *still* . . .

BUTLER

. . . it would not be so appropriate. And think: if I were
a woman, and had become a chambermaid, say, and my name
were Butler . . .

JULIAN *(Anticipating)*

. . . you would be in for some rather tiresome exchanges.

BUTLER *(Cutting, but light)*

None more than this.

JULIAN *(Sadly)*

Aha.

BUTLER *(Forgiving)*

Coffee, then.

JULIAN *(As if he can't explain)*

No. Nothing.

BUTLER *(Semi-serious bow)*

I am at your service.

(LAWYER enters)

LAWYER

I, too.

JULIAN

Ah!

LAWYER

I'm sorry to have kept you waiting, but . . .

JULIAN

Oh, no, no . . .

LAWYER

. . . I was conferring with Miss Alice.

JULIAN

Yes.

LAWYER *(To BUTLER; no fondness)*

Dearest.

BUTLER *(To LAWYER; same)*

Darling.

LAWYER *(To JULIAN)*

Doubtless, though, you two have . . . *(Waves a hand about)*

JULIAN

Oh, we've had a most . . . unusual . . .

LAWYER

(To BUTLER, ignoring JULIAN's answer)

You've offered our guest refreshments?

JULIAN

Brother Julian.

BUTLER

Ice water, iced tea, and coffee—hot assumed, I imagine—none taken.

LAWYER

Gracious! *(Back to* JULIAN*)* Port, perhaps. Removed people take port, I've noticed.

JULIAN
(More to please than anything)

Yes. Port. Please.

LAWYER *(To* BUTLER*)*

Port for . . .

JULIAN

Julian—Brother Julian.

LAWYER *(Slightly patronizing)*

I *know.* (BUTLER *goes to a sideboard*) I would join you, but it is not my habit to drink before sundown. Not a condemnation, you understand. One of my minor disciplines.

BUTLER
(Generally, looking at the bottle)

The port is eighteen-oh-six. *(To the* LAWYER*)* How do they fortify wines, again?

JULIAN

Alcohol is added, more alcohol . . . at the time of casking. Fortify . . . strengthen.

BUTLER

Ah, yes.

LAWYER (*To* JULIAN)

Of course, your grandfather was a vintner, was he not.

JULIAN

Goodness, you . . . you have my history.

LAWYER

Oh, we do. Such a mild life . . . save those six years in your thirties which are . . . blank . . . in our report on you.

JULIAN (*A good covering laugh*)

Oh, they were . . . mild, in their own way. Blank, but not black.

LAWYER

Will you fill them for us? The blank years?

JULIAN
(*Taking the glass from* BUTLER)

Thank you. (*The laugh again*) They were nothing.

LAWYER (*Steelier*)

Still, you will fill them for us.

JULIAN (*Pleasant, but very firm*)

No.

BUTLER

Gracious!

LAWYER

Recalcitrance, yes . . . well, we must have our people dig further.

JULIAN

You'll find nothing interesting. You'll find some . . . upheaval, but . . . waste, mostly. Dull waste.

LAWYER

The look of most of our vices in retrospect, eh?

BUTLER *(Light)*

I have fleshpot visions: carousals, thighs and heavy perfume. . . .

LAWYER *(To BUTLER)*

It's in your mind, fitting, a mind worthy of your name. *(To JULIAN)* Did you two . . . did he tell you his name, and did you two have a veritable badminton over it? Puns and chuckles?

JULIAN

We . . . labored it a bit, I more than . . . Butler, it would appear.

BUTLER

I was churlish, I'm sorry. If there weren't so many of *you* and only one of *me* . . .

JULIAN

Oh, now . . .

LAWYER *(Still on it)*

You're not going to tell me about those six years, eh?

JULIAN
(Stares at him for a moment, then says it clearly, enunciating)

No.

(LAWYER shrugs)

BUTLER

May I have some port?

LAWYER *(Slightly incredulous)*

Do you *like* port?

BUTLER

Not very, but I thought I'd keep him company while you play police.

LAWYER *(Shrugs again)*

It's not my house. *(Turns to* JULIAN*)* One can't say, "It's not my castle," can one? *(Back to* BUTLER*)* If you think it's proper.

BUTLER *(Getting himself some)*

Well, with the wine cellar stacked like a munitions dump, and you "never having any" until the barn swallows start screeping around . . .

LAWYER

There's no such word as screep.

BUTLER *(Shrugs)*

Fit.

JULIAN

I think it has a nice onomatopoetic ring about it . . .

LAWYER
(Down to business, rather rudely)

Your buddy told you why we sent for you?

JULIAN
(Offended, but pretending confusion)

My . . . buddy?

LAWYER

Mine, really. We were at school together. Did he tell you that? *(As* JULIAN *intentionally looks blank)* His Eminence.

JULIAN

Ah!

LAWYER *(Imitation)*

Ah! *(Snapped)* Well? Did he?

JULIAN

(Choosing his words carefully, precisely)

His Eminence informed me . . . generally. He called me into
his . . .

LAWYER

. . . garden . . .

JULIAN

. . . garden . . . which is a comfortable office in summer . . .

BUTLER

Ninety-six today.

JULIAN *(Interested)*

Indeed!

BUTLER

More tomorrow.

LAWYER *(Impatiently)*

Called you into his garden.

JULIAN

And—sorry—and . . . told me of the high honor which he
had chosen for me.

LAWYER *(Scoffing)*

He. Chosen. You.

JULIAN

Of . . . your lady's most . . .

LAWYER

Miss Alice.

JULIAN

Of Miss Alice's—sorry, I've not met the lady yet, and first names—of her overwhelming bequest to the Church . . .

LAWYER

Not a bequest; a bequest is made in a will; Miss Alice is not dead.

JULIAN

Uh . . . grant?

LAWYER

Grant.

JULIAN *(Taking a deep breath)*

Of her overwhelming grant to the Church, and of my assignment to come here, to take care of . . .

LAWYER

Odds and ends.

JULIAN *(Shrugs one shoulder)*

. . . if you like. "A few questions and answers" was how it was put to me.

BUTLER *(To* LAWYER, *impressed)*

He's a lay brother.

LAWYER *(Bored)*

We *know. (For* JULIAN's *benefit)* His Eminence—buddy . . .

JULIAN *(Natural, sincere)*

Tch–tch–tch–tch–tch . . .

LAWYER

He was my buddy at school . . . if you don't mind. *(Beginning, now, to* BUTLER, *but quickly becoming general)* His Eminence—though you have never met him, Butler, seen him, perhaps—is a most . . . eminent man; and bold, very bold; behind—or, underneath—what would seem to be a solid rock of . . . pomposity, sham, peacocking, there is a . . . flows a secret river . . . of . . .

BUTLER *(For* JULIAN's *benefit)*

This is an endless metaphor.

LAWYER

. . . of unconventionality, defiance, even. Simple sentences? Is that all you want? Did you know that Brother Julian here is the only lay brother in the history of Christendom assigned, chosen, as secretary and confidant to a Prince of the Church? Ever?

JULIAN *(Mildly)*

That is not known as fact.

LAWYER

Name others!

JULIAN

I say it is not known as fact. I grant it is not usual—my appointment as secretary to His Eminence. . . .

LAWYER *(Faint disgust)*

An honor, at any rate, an unusual honor for a lay brother, an honor accorded by a most unusual Prince of the Church— a prince of a man, in fact—a prince whose still waters . . . well, you finish it.

BUTLER
(Pretending puzzlement as to how to finish it)

. . . whose still waters . . .

JULIAN

His Eminence is, indeed, a most unusual man.

LAWYER *(Sourly)*

I said he was a prince.

BUTLER

(Pretending to be talking to himself)
. . . run quiet? Run deep? Run *deep! That's* good!

LAWYER

Weren't there a few eyebrows raised at your appointment?

JULIAN

There . . . I was not informed of it . . . if there were. His
Eminence would not burden me. . . .

LAWYER

(Still to JULIAN, *patronizing)*
He is really Santa Claus; we know.

JULIAN *(Rising to it)*

Your animosity toward His Eminence must make your task
very difficult for you. I must say I . . .

LAWYER

I have learned . . . *(Brief pause before he says the name
with some distaste)* Brother Julian . . . never to confuse the
representative of a . . . thing with the thing itself.

BUTLER

. . . though I wonder if you'd intended to get involved in
two watery metaphors there: underground river, and still
waters.

LAWYER *(To BUTLER)*

No, I had not. *(Back to* JULIAN*)* A thing with its representative. Your Cardinal and I loathe one another, and I find him unworthy of contempt. *(A hand up to stop any coming objection)* A cynic and a hypocrite, a posturer, but all the same the representative of an august and revered . . . body.

JULIAN *(Murmured)*

You are most unjust.

LAWYER

(As if he were continuing a prepared speech)
Uh . . . revered body. And Rome, in its perhaps wily—though *certainly* inscrutable—wisdom, Rome has found reason to appoint that wreckage as its representative.

JULIAN

Really, I can't permit you to talk that way.

LAWYER

You will permit it, you're under instructions, you have a job to do. In fact, you have this present job be*cause* I cannot stand your Cardinal.

JULIAN

He . . . he did not tell me so.

LAWYER

W*e* tell you so.
*(*JULIAN *dips his head to one side in a "perhaps it is true" gesture)*
And it is so.

JULIAN

I will not . . . I will not concern myself with . . . all this.

BUTLER *(Quite to himself)*

I don't *like* port.

LAWYER (*To* BUTLER)

Then don't drink it. (*To* JULIAN) You're quite right: bow
your head, stop up your ears and do what you're told.

JULIAN

Obedience is not a fault.

LAWYER

Nor always a virtue. See Fascism.

JULIAN (*Rather strong for him*)

Perhaps we can get on with our business. . . .

LAWYER (*He, too*)

You don't want to take up my time, or your own.

JULIAN

Yes.

BUTLER (*Putting down glass*)

Then I won't drink it.

LAWYER
(*To* JULIAN, *briskly, as to a servant*)

All right! I shall tell Miss Alice you've come—that the drab
fledgling is pecking away in the library, impatient for . . .
food for the Church.

JULIAN
(*A tight smile, a tiny formal bow*)

If you would be so kind.

LAWYER (*Twisting the knife*)

I'll find out if she cares to see you today.

JULIAN (*Ibid.*)

Please.

LAWYER
(*Moving toward the archway*)
And, if she cares to, I will have you brought up.

JULIAN
(*Mild surprise, but not a question*)
Up.

LAWYER
(*Almost challenging him*)
Up. (*Pause*) You will not tell us about the six years—those years blank but not black . . . the waste, the dull waste.

JULIAN (*Small smile*)
No.

LAWYER (*He, too*)
You will . . . in time. (*To* BUTLER) Won't he, Butler? Time? The great revealer?

(LAWYER *exits*)

JULIAN
(*After the* LAWYER *is gone; no indignation*)
Well.

BUTLER (*Offhand*)
Nasty man.

JULIAN
(*Intentionally feigning surprise*)
Oh? (HE *and* BUTLER *laugh*) Up.

BUTLER
Sir?

JULIAN
Up.

BUTLER

Oh! Yes! She . . . *(Moves to the model)* has her apartments
up . . . here. *(He points to a tower area)* Here.

JULIAN

A-ha.

BUTLER
(Straightening things up)
About those six years . . .

JULIAN
(Not unfriendly, very matter-of-fact)
What of them?

BUTLER

Yes, what of them?

JULIAN
Oh . . . *(Pause)* I . . . I lost my faith. *(Pause)* In God.

BUTLER
Ah. *(Then a questioning look)*

JULIAN

Is there more?

BUTLER

Is there more?

JULIAN
Well, nothing . . . of matter. I . . . declined. I . . . shriv-
eled into myself; a glass dome . . . descended, and it seemed
I was out of reach, unreachable, finally unreaching, in this
. . . paralysis, of sorts. I . . . put myself in a mental home.

BUTLER
(Curiously noncommittal)

Ah.

JULIAN

I could not reconcile myself to the chasm between the nature
of God and the use to which men put . . . God.

BUTLER

Between your God and others', your view and theirs.

JULIAN

I said what I intended: *(Weighs the opposites in each hand)*
It is God the mover, not God the puppet; God the creator,
not the God created by man.

BUTLER *(Almost pitying)*

Six years in the loony bin for semantics?

JULIAN *(Slightly flustered, heat)*

It is not semantics! Men create a false God in their own
image, it is easier for them! . . . It is not . . .

BUTLER

Levity! Forget it!

JULIAN

I . . . yes.

(A chime sounds)

BUTLER

Miss Alice will see you. I will take you up.

JULIAN

Forgive me . . . I . . .

BUTLER *(Moves toward archway)*

Let me show you up.

JULIAN

You *did* ask me.

BUTLER *(Level)*

Yes, and you told me.

JULIAN
(An explanation, not an apology)
My faith and my sanity . . . they are one and the same.

BUTLER

Yes? *(Considers it)* A-ha. *(Smiles noncommittally)* We must
not keep the lady waiting.
(They begin exiting, BUTLER *preceding* JULIAN*)*

CURTAIN

SCENE THREE

(An *upstairs sitting room of the castle. Feminine, but not frilly. Blues instead of pinks. Fireplace in keeping with the castle. A door to the bedroom in the rear wall, stage left; a door from the hallway in the side wall, stage left.*
At rise, MISS ALICE *is seated in a wing chair, facing windows, its back to the audience; the* LAWYER *is to one side, facing her*)

LAWYER
(*Pause, he has finished one sentence, is pondering another*)
. . . Nor is it as simple as all that. The instinct of giving may die out in our time—if you'll grant that giving is an instinct. The government is far more interested in taking, in regulated taking, than in promoting spontaneous generosity. Remember what I told you—what we discussed—in reference to the charitable foundations, and how . . . (*A knock on the hall door*) That will be our bird of prey. Pray. P-R-A-Y. What a pun I could make on that; bird of pray. Come in.
(*The hall door opens;* BUTLER *precedes* JULIAN *into the room*)

BUTLER
Brother Julian, who *was* in the library, is now here.

LAWYER
So he is. (*To* JULIAN, *impatiently*) Come in, come in.

JULIAN (*Advancing a little*)
Yes . . . certainly.

BUTLER

May I go? I'm tired.

LAWYER *(Grandly)*

By all means.

BUTLER *(Turns to go)*

Thank you. *(To* JULIAN*)* Goodbye.

JULIAN

Goodb . . . I'll . . . we'll see one another again?

BUTLER

Oh. Yes, probably. *(As he exits)* Goodbye, everybody.

LAWYER

(After BUTLER *exits, chuckles)*

What is it the nouveaux riches are always saying? "You can't get good servants nowadays"?

JULIAN

He seems . . .

LAWYER *(Curt)*

He is very good. *(Turns to the chair)* Miss Alice, our Brother Julian is here. *(Repeats it, louder)* OUR BROTHER JULIAN IS HERE. *(To* JULIAN*)* She's terribly hard of hearing. *(To* MISS ALICE*)* DO YOU WANT TO SEE HIM? *(To* JULIAN*)* I think she's responding. Sometimes . . . well, at her age and condition . . . twenty minutes can go by . . . for her to assimilate a sentence and reply to it.

JULIAN

But I thought . . . His Eminence said she was . . . young.

LAWYER

SHHHHHHHH! She's moving.

(MISS ALICE *slowly rises from her chair and comes*
around it. Her face is that of a withered crone, her
hair gray and white and matted; she is bent; she
moves with two canes)

MISS ALICE
(Finally, with a cracked and ancient voice, to JULIAN)
Hello there, young man.

LAWYER
(As JULIAN *takes a step forward)*
Hah! Don't come too close, you'll unnerve her.

JULIAN
But I'm terribly puzzled. I was led to believe that she was a
young woman, and . . .

MISS ALICE
Hello there, young man.

LAWYER
Speak to her.

JULIAN
Miss . . . Miss Alice, how do you do?

LAWYER
Louder.

JULIAN
HOW DO YOU DO?

MISS ALICE *(To* LAWYER)
How do I do *what?*

LAWYER
It's a formality.

MISS ALICE

WHAT!?

LAWYER

IT IS A FORMALITY, AN OPENING GAMBIT.

MISS ALICE

Oh. *(To* JULIAN*)* How do *you* do?

JULIAN

Very well . . . thank you.

MISS ALICE

WHAT!?

JULIAN

VERY WELL, THANK YOU.

MISS ALICE

Don't you scream at me!

JULIAN *(Mumbled)*

Sorry.

MISS ALICE

WHAT!?

JULIAN

SORRY!

MISS ALICE *(Almost a pout)*

Oh.

LAWYER *(Who has enjoyed this)*

Well, I think I'll leave you two now . . . for your business.
I'm sure you'll have a . . .

JULIAN
(An attempted urgent aside to the LAWYER*)*
Do you think you . . . shouldn't you be here? You've . . .
you've had more experience with her, and . . .

LAWYER *(Laughing)*
No, no, you'll get along fine. *(To* MISS ALICE*)* I'LL LEAVE YOU
TWO TOGETHER NOW. *(*MISS ALICE *nods vigorously)* HIS NAME
IS BROTHER JULIAN, AND THERE ARE SIX YEARS MISSING FROM
HIS LIFE. *(She nods again)* I'LL BE DOWNSTAIRS. *(Begins to
leave)*

MISS ALICE
(When the LAWYER *is at the door)*
Don't steal anything.

LAWYER *(Exiting)*
ALL RIGHT!

JULIAN
(After a pause, begins bravely, taking a step forward)
Perhaps you should sit down. Let me . . .

MISS ALICE
WHAT!?

JULIAN
PERHAPS YOU SHOULD SIT DOWN!

MISS ALICE
(Not fear; malevolence)
Keep away from me!

JULIAN
Sorry. *(To himself)* Oh, really, this is impossible.

MISS ALICE
WHAT!?

JULIAN

I SAID THIS WAS IMPOSSIBLE.

MISS ALICE
(Thinks about that for a moment, then)
If you're a defrocked priest, what're you doing in all that?
(Pointing to JULIAN's *garb)*

JULIAN

I AM NOT A DEFROCKED PRIEST, I AM A LAY BROTHER. I HAVE
NEVER BEEN A PRIEST.

MISS ALICE
What did you drink downstairs?

JULIAN
I had a glass of port . . . PORT!

MISS ALICE
(A spoiled, crafty child)
You didn't bring *me* one.

JULIAN
I had no idea you . . .

MISS ALICE
WHAT!?

JULIAN
SHALL I GET YOU A GLASS?

MISS ALICE
A glass of *what*.

JULIAN
PORT. A GLASS OF PORT.

MISS ALICE *(As if he were crazy)*

What for?

JULIAN

BECAUSE YOU . . . *(To himself again)* Really, this *won't* do.

MISS ALICE

(Straightening up, ridding herself of the canes, assuming a normal voice)

I agree with you, it won't do, really.

JULIAN *(Astonishment)*

I beg your pardon?

MISS ALICE

I said it won't do at all.

> *(SHE unfastens and removes her wig, unties and takes off her mask, becomes herself, as JULIAN watches, openmouthed)*

There. Is that better? And you needn't yell at me any more; if anything, my hearing is *too* good.

JULIAN *(Slightly put out)*

I . . . I don't understand.

MISS ALICE

Are you annoyed?

JULIAN

I suspect I will be . . . might be . . . after the surprise leaves me.

MISS ALICE *(Smiling)*

Don't be; it's only a little game.

JULIAN

Yes, doubtless. But why?

MISS ALICE
Oh, indulge us, please.

JULIAN
Well, of course, it would be my pleasure . . . but, considering the importance of our meeting . . .

MISS ALICE
Exactly. Considering the importance of our meeting.

JULIAN
A . . . a test for me.

MISS ALICE *(Laughs)*
No, not at all, a little lightness to counter the weight. *(Mock seriousness)* For we are involved in weighty matters . . . the transfer of millions, the rocking of empires. *(Normal, light tone again)* Let's be comfortable, shall we? Swing my chair around. *(JULIAN moves to do so)* As you can see—you *can*, I trust—I'm *not* a hundred and thirteen years old, but I *do* have my crotchets, even now: I have chairs everywhere that are mine—in each room . . . a chair that is mine, that I alone use.

JULIAN *(Moving the chair)*
Where would you . . .

MISS ALICE *(Lightly)*
Just . . . swing it . . . around. You needn't move it. Good. Now, sit with me. *(They sit)* Fine. In the dining room, of course, there is no question—I sit at the head of the table. But, in the drawing rooms, or the library, or whatever room you wish to mention, I have a chair that I consider my possession.

JULIAN
But you possess the entire . . . *(Thinks of a word)* establishment.

MISS ALICE

Of course, but it is such a large . . . establishment that one needs the feel of specific possession in every . . . area.

JULIAN
(Rather shy, but pleasant)

Do you become . . . cross if someone accidentally assumes your chair, one of your chairs?

MISS ALICE
(Thinks about it, then)

How odd! Curiously, it has never happened, so I cannot say. Tell me about yourself.

JULIAN

Well, there isn't much to say . . . much that isn't already known. Your lawyer would seem to have assembled a case book on me, and . . .

MISS ALICE

Yes, yes, but not the things that would interest him, the things that would interest me.

JULIAN *(Genuine interest)*

And what are they?

MISS ALICE *(Laughs again)*

Let me see. Ah! Do I terrify you?

JULIAN

You *did,* and you are still . . . awesome.

MISS ALICE *(Sweetly)*

Thank you. Did my lawyer intimidate you?

JULIAN

It would seem to be his nature—or his pleasure—to intimidate, and . . . well, I am, perhaps, more easily intimidated than some.

MISS ALICE

Perhaps you are, but he *is* a professional. And how did you find Butler?

JULIAN

A gentle man, quick . . . but mostly gentle.

MISS ALICE

Gentle, yes. He was my lover at one time. (*As* JULIAN *averts his head*) Oh! Perhaps I shouldn't have told you.

JULIAN

No, forgive me. Things sometimes . . . are so unexpected.

MISS ALICE

Yes, they are. I am presently mistress to my lawyer—the gentleman who intimidated you so. He is a pig.

JULIAN (*Embarrassed*)

Yes, yes. You have . . . never married.

MISS ALICE (*Quiet amusement*)

Alas.

JULIAN

You are . . . not Catholic.

MISS ALICE (*The same*)

Again, alas.

JULIAN

No, it is fortunate you are not.

MISS ALICE

I am bored with my present lover.

JULIAN

I . . . (Shrugs)

MISS ALICE

I was not soliciting advice.

JULIAN (Quiet laugh)

Good, for I have none.

MISS ALICE

These six years of yours.

JULIAN
(Says it all in one deep breath)
There is no mystery to it, my faith in God left me, and I
committed myself to an asylum. (Pause) You see? Nothing
to it.

MISS ALICE

What an odd place to go to look for one's faith.

JULIAN

You misunderstand me. I did not go there to look for my
faith, but because it had left me.

MISS ALICE

You tell it so easily.

JULIAN (Shrugs)

It is easy to tell.

MISS ALICE

Ah.

JULIAN (Giggles a little)

However, I would not tell your present . . . uh, your lawyer.

And that made him quite angry.

MISS ALICE

Have you slept with many women?

JULIAN *(Carefully)*

I am not certain.

MISS ALICE *(Tiny laugh)*

It is an easy enough thing to determine.

JULIAN

Not so. For one, I am celibate. A lay brother—you must know
—while not a priest, while not ordained, is still required to
take vows. And chastity is one of them.

MISS ALICE

A dedicated gesture, to be sure, celibacy without priesthood
. . . but a melancholy one, for you're a handsome man . . .
in your way.

JULIAN

You're kind.

MISS ALICE

But, tell me: why did you not become a priest? Having gone
so far, I should think . . .

JULIAN

A lay brother serves.

MISS ALICE

. . . but is not ordained, is more a servant.

JULIAN

The house of God is so grand . . . *(Sweet apologetic smile)*
it needs many servants.

MISS ALICE

How humble. But is that the only reason?

JULIAN

I am not wholly reconciled. Man's God and mine are not
. . . close friends.

MISS ALICE

Indeed. But, tell me, how are you not certain that you have
slept with a woman?

JULIAN (With curiosity)

Shall I tell you? We have many more important matters. . . .

MISS ALICE

Tell me, please. The money will not run off. Great wealth
is patient.

JULIAN

I would not know. Very well. It's good for me, I think, to talk
about it. The institution . . . to which I committed myself—
it was deep inland, by the way—was a good one, good enough,
and had, as I am told most do, sections—buildings, or floors
of buildings—for patients in various conditions . . . some for
violent cases, for example, others for children. . . .

MISS ALICE

How sad.

JULIAN

Yes. Well, at any rate . . . sections. Mine . . . my section
was for people who were . . . mildly troubled—which I
found ironic, for I have never considered the fleeing of faith
a mild matter. Nonetheless, for the mildly troubled. The
windows were not barred; one was allowed utensils, and one's
own clothes. You see, escape was not a matter of urgency, for
it was a section for mildly troubled people who had com-

mitted themselves, and should escape occur, it was not a danger for the world outside.

MISS ALICE

I understand.

JULIAN

There was a period during my stay, however, when I began to . . . hallucinate, and to withdraw, to a point where I was not entirely certain when my mind was tricking me, or when it was not. I believe one would say—how is it said?—that my grasp on reality was . . . tenuous—occasionally. There was, at the same time, in my section, a woman who, on very infrequent occasions, believed that she was the Virgin Mary.

MISS ALICE *(Mild surprise)*

My goodness.

JULIAN

A quiet woman, plain, but soft features, not hard; at forty, or a year either side, married, her husband the owner of a dry-goods store, if my memory is correct; childless . . . the sort of woman, in short, that one is not aware of passing on the street, or in a hallway . . . unlike you—if you will permit me.

MISS ALICE *(Smiles)*

It may be I am . . . noticeable, but almost never identified.

JULIAN

You shun publicity.

MISS ALICE

Oh, indeed. And I have few friends . . . that, too, by choice. *(Urges him on with a gesture)* But please . . .

JULIAN

Of course. My hallucinations . . . were saddening to me. I

suspect I should have been frightened of them—as well as
by them—most people are, or would be . . . by hallucinations. But I was . . . saddened. They were, after all, pro-
voked, brought on by the departure of my faith, and this in
turn was brought on by the manner in which people mock
God. . . .

MISS ALICE

I notice you do not say you lost your faith, but that it aban-
boned you.

JULIAN

Do I. Perhaps at bottom I had lost it, but I think more that
I was confused . . . *and* intimidated . . . by the world
about me, and let slip contact with it . . . with my faith.
So, I was *sad*dened.

MISS ALICE

Yes.

JULIAN

The periods of hallucination would be announced by a ringing in the ears, which produced, or was accompanied by, a
loss of hearing. I would hear people's voices from a great distance and through the roaring of . . . surf. And my body
would feel light, and not mine, and I would float—no, glide.

MISS ALICE

There was no feeling of terror in this? I would be beside myself.

JULIAN

No, as I said, sadness. Aaaaahhh, I would think, I am going
from myself again. How very, very sad . . . everything. Loss,
great loss.

MISS ALICE

I understand.

JULIAN

And when I was away from myself—never far enough, you know, to . . . blank, just to . . . fog over—when I was away from myself I could not sort out my imaginings from what was real. Oh, sometimes I would say to a nurse or one of the attendants, "Could you tell me, did I preach last night? To the patients? A fire-and-brimstone lesson. Did I do that, or did I imagine it?" And they would tell me, if they knew.

MISS ALICE

And did you?

JULIAN

Hm? . . . No, it would seem I did not . . . to their knowledge. But I was never sure, you see.

MISS ALICE *(Nodding)*

No.

JULIAN *(A brief, rueful laugh)*

I imagined so many things, or . . . did so many things I thought I had imagined. The uncertainty . . . you know?

MISS ALICE *(Smiles)*

Are you sure you're not describing what passes for sanity?

JULIAN *(Laughs briefly, ruefully)*

Perhaps. But one night . . . now, there! You see? I said "one night," and I'm not sure, even now, whether or not this thing happened or, if it did not happen, it did or did not happen at noon, or in the morning, much less at night . . . yet I say night. Doubtless one will do as well as another. So. One *night* the following either happened or did not happen. I was walking in the gardens—or I imagined I was walking in the gardens—walking in the gardens, and I heard a sound . . . sounds from near where a small pool stood, with rosebushes, rather overgrown, a formal garden once, the . . . the place had been an estate, I remember being told. Sounds . . . sobbing? Low cries. And there was, as well, the ringing in my ears, and . . . and fog, a . . . a milkiness, between myself and . . . everything. I went toward the cries, the sounds, and . . . I, I fear my description will become rather . . . vivid now. . . .

MISS ALICE

I am a grown woman.

JULIAN *(Nods)*

Yes. *(A deep breath)* The . . . the woman, the woman I told you about, who hallucinated, herself, that she was the Virgin . . .

MISS ALICE

Yes, yes.

JULIAN

. . . was . . . was on a grassy space by the pool—or this is what I imagined—on the ground, and she was in her . . . a nightdress, a . . . gossamer, filmy thing, or perhaps she was not, but there she was, on the ground, on an incline, a slight incline, and when she saw me—or sensed me there—she raised her head, and put her arms . . . *(Demonstrates)* . . . out, in a . . . supplication, and cried, "Help me, help me . . . help me, oh God, God, help me . . . oh, help, help." This, over and over, and with the sounds in her throat between. I . . . I came closer, and the sounds, her sounds, her words, the roaring in my ears, the gossamer and the milk film, I . . . a ROAR, AN OCEAN! Saliva, perfume, sweat, the taste of blood and rich earth in the mouth, sweet sweaty slipping . . . *(Looks to her apologetically, nods)* . . . ejaculation. *(She nods)* The sound cascading away, the rhythms breaking, everything slowly, limpid, quieter, damper, soft . . . soft, quiet . . . done.

(They are both silent. MISS ALICE is gripping the arms of her chair; JULIAN continues softly)

I have described it to you, as best I can, as it . . . happened, or did not happen.

MISS ALICE
(Curiously . . . dispassionately)
I . . . am a very beautiful woman.

JULIAN
(After a pause which serves as reply to her statement)
I must tell you more, though. You *have* asked me for an entirety.

MISS ALICE
And a very rich one.

JULIAN *(Brief pause, nods)*
As I mentioned to you, the woman was given to hallucinations as well, but perhaps I should have said that being the Virgin Mary was merely the strongest of her . . . delusions; she . . . hallucinated . . . as well as the next person, about perfectly mundane matters, too. So it may be that now we come to coincidence, or it may not. Shortly—several days— after the encounter I have described to you—the encounter which did or did not happen—the woman . . . I do not know which word to use here, either descended or ascended into an ecstasy, the substance of which was that she was with child . . . that she was pregnant with the Son of God.

MISS ALICE
And I live here, in all these rooms.

JULIAN
You don't laugh? Well, perhaps you will, at *me*. I was . . . beside myself, for I assumed the piling of delusion upon delusion, though the chance of there being fact, happening, there somewhere . . . I went to my . . . doctor and told

him of my hallucination—if indeed that is what it was. He
told me, then . . . that the woman had been examined, that
she was suffering from cancer of the womb, that it was advanced, had spread. In a month, she died.

MISS ALICE

Did you believe it?

JULIAN *(Small smile)*

That she died?

MISS ALICE

That you spoke with your doctor.

JULIAN *(Pause)*

It has never occurred to me until this moment to doubt it. He
has informed me many times.

MISS ALICE

Ah?

JULIAN

I *do see* him . . . in reality. We have become friends, we talk
from time to time. Socially.

MISS ALICE

Ah. And was it he who discharged you from . . . your
asylum?

JULIAN

I was persuaded, eventually, that perhaps I was . . . over-
concerned by hallucination; that some was inevitable, and a
portion of that—even desirable.

MISS ALICE

Of course.

JULIAN *(Looking at his hands)*
Have I answered your question? That I am not . . . sure
that I have slept with a woman.

MISS ALICE
(Puzzling . . . slowly)
I don't . . . know. Is the memory of something having hap-
pened the same as it having happened?

JULIAN
It is not the nicest of . . . occurrences—to have described to
you.

MISS ALICE *(Kindly)*
It was many years ago. *(Then, an afterthought)* Was it not?

JULIAN
Yes, yes, quite a while ago.

MISS ALICE *(Vaguely amused)*
I am rich and I am beautiful and I live here in all these rooms
. . . without relatives, with a . . . *(Wry)* companion, from
time to time . . . *(Leans forward, whispers, but still amused)*
. . . and with a secret.

JULIAN
Oh? *(Trying to be light, too)* And may I know it? The secret?

MISS ALICE
I don't know yet.

JULIAN *(Relaxing)*
Ah-ha.

MISS ALICE
(Sudden change of mood, to brisk, official, cool)
Well then. You're here on business, not for idle conversation,
I believe.

JULIAN
(Confused, even a little hurt)
Oh . . . yes, that's . . . that's right.

MISS ALICE
You have instruction to give me—not formal, I'm not about
to settle in your faith. Information, facts, questions and answers.

JULIAN *(Slightly sour)*
Odds and ends, I believe.

MISS ALICE *(Sharp)*
To you, perhaps. But important if you're to succeed, if you're
not to queer the whole business, if you're not to . . .

JULIAN
Yes, yes!

MISS ALICE
So you'll be coming back here . . . when I wish to see you.

JULIAN
Yes.

MISS ALICE
Several times. It might be better if you were to move in. I'll
decide it.

JULIAN
Oh . . . well, of course, if you think . . .

MISS ALICE
I think. (JULIAN *nods acquiescence*) Very good. (SHE *rises*) No
more today, no more now.

JULIAN
(Up, maybe retreating a little)
Well, if you'll let me know when . . .

MISS ALICE
Come here.
*(JULIAN goes to her; she takes his head in her hands,
kisses him on the forehead, he registers embarrassment, she laughs, a slightly mocking, unnerving
laugh)*
Little recluse. *(Laughs again)*

JULIAN
If you'll . . . advise me, or His Eminence, when you'd like
me to . . .

MISS ALICE
Little bird, pecking away in the library. *(Laughs again)*

JULIAN
I'm . . . disappointed you find me so . . . humorous.

MISS ALICE
(Cheerful, but not contrite)
Oh, forgive me, I live so alone, the oddest things cheer me
up. You . . . cheer me up. *(Holds out her hand to be kissed)*
Here. *(JULIAN hesitates)* Ah-ah-ah, he who hesitates loses all.
*(JULIAN hesitates again, momentarily, then kisses her
hand, but kneeling, as he would kiss a Cardinal's
ring. MISS ALICE laughs at this)*
Do you think I am a Cardinal? Do I look like a Prince? Have
you never even kissed a woman's hand?

JULIAN *(Back on his feet, evenly)*
No. I have not.

MISS ALICE *(Kindlier now)*

I'll send for you, we'll have . . . pleasant afternoons, you
and I. Goodbye.

(MISS ALICE *turns away from* JULIAN, *gazes out a win-*
dow, her back to the audience. JULIAN *exits. The*
LAWYER *enters the set from the bedroom door)*

LAWYER
(To MISS ALICE, *a bit abruptly)*

How did it go, eh?

MISS ALICE
(Turns around, matter-of-factly)

Not badly.

LAWYER

You took long enough.

(MISS ALICE *shrugs)*

When are you having him again?

MISS ALICE *(Very wickedly)*

On business, or privately?

LAWYER

Don't be childish.

MISS ALICE

Whenever you like, whenever you say. *(Seriously)* Tell me
honestly, do you really think we're wise?

LAWYER

Wise? Well, we'll see. If we prove not, I can't think of anything standing in the way that can't be destroyed. *(Pause)*
Can you?

MISS ALICE *(Rather sadly)*

No. Nothing.

CURTAIN

ACT TWO

SCENE ONE

(The library—as of Act One, Scene Two. No one on stage. Evening. MISS ALICE *hurtles through the archway, half running, half backing, with the* LAWYER *after her. It is not a chase; she has just broken from him, and her hurtling is the result of sudden freeing)*

MISS ALICE
(Just before and as she is entering; her tone is neither hysterical nor frightened; she is furious and has been mildly hurt)
KEEP . . . GO! GET YOUR . . . LET GO OF ME! *(She is in the room)* KEEP OFF! KEEP OFF ME!

LAWYER
(Excited, ruffled, but trying to maintain decorum)
Don't be hysterical, now.

MISS ALICE
(Still moving away from him, as he comes on)
KEEP . . . AWAY. JUST STAY AWAY FROM ME.

LAWYER
I said don't be hysterical.

MISS ALICE
I'll *show* you hysteria. I'll give you *fireworks!* KEEP! Keep away.

LAWYER
(Soothing, but always moving in on her)
A simple touch, an affectionate hand on you; nothing more . . .

MISS ALICE *(Quiet loathing)*

You're degenerate.

LAWYER *(Steely)*

An affectionate hand, in the privacy of a hallway . . .

MISS ALICE *(Almost a shriek)*

THERE ARE PEOPLE!!

LAWYER

Where? There are no people.

MISS ALICE *(Between her teeth)*

There are people.

LAWYER *(Feigning surprise)*

There are no people. *(To a child)* Ahh! *(Walks toward the model, indicates it)* Unless you mean all the little people running around inside here. Is that what you mean?

MISS ALICE
(A mirthless, don't-you-know-it laugh)

Hunh-hunh-hunh-hunh.

LAWYER

Is that who you mean? All the little people in here? *(Change of tone to normal, if sarcastic)* Why don't we show them a few of your tricks, hunh?

MISS ALICE
(Moving away, clenched teeth again)

Keep . . . away . . . from . . . me.

LAWYER *(Without affection)*

To love is to possess, and since I desire to possess you, that must mean conversely that I love you, must it not. Come here.

MISS ALICE *(With great force)*

PEOPLE!

LAWYER

Your little priest? Your little Julian? He is not . . .

MISS ALICE

He is not a priest!

LAWYER

No. And he *is* not nearby—momentarily! *(Hissed)* I am sick of him here day after day, sick of the time you're taking. Will you get it done with!

MISS ALICE

No! He will be *up*.

LAWYER

Oh, for Christ's sake, he's a connoisseur; he'll be nosing around the goddam wine cellar for hours!

MISS ALICE

He will be *up*. *(Afterthought)* Butler!

LAWYER *(Advancing)*

Butler? Let him watch. *(A sneer)* Which is something I've been meaning to discuss with you for the longest time now. . . .

MISS ALICE

(Calm, quivering hatred; almost laughing with it)
I have a loathing for you that I can't describe.

LAWYER

You were never one with words. *(Suddenly brutal)* NOW, COME HERE.

MISS ALICE *(Shrugs)*

All right. I won't react, I promise you.

LAWYER

(Beginning to fondle her)

Won't react . . . indeed.

(During this next, MISS ALICE is backed up against something, and the LAWYER is calmly at her, kissing her neck, fondling her. She is calm, and at first he seems amused)

MISS ALICE

What causes this loathing I have for you? It's the *way* you have, I suppose; the clinical way; methodical, slow . . .

LAWYER

. . . thorough . . .

MISS ALICE

. . . uninvolved . . .

LAWYER

. . . oh, very involved . . .

MISS ALICE

. . . impersonality in the most personal things . . .

LAWYER

. . . your passivity is exciting . . .

MISS ALICE

. . . passive only to some people . . . *(He nips her)* ow.

LAWYER

A little passion; good.

MISS ALICE
(As he continues fondling her; perhaps by the end
he has her dress off her shoulders)
With so much . . . many things to loathe, I must choose
carefully, to impress you most with it.

LAWYER
Um-humh.

MISS ALICE
Is it the hair? Is it the hair on your back I loathe most?
Where the fat lies, on your shoulderblades, the hair on your
back . . . black, ugly? . . .

LAWYER
But too short to get a hold on, eh?

MISS ALICE
Is it that—the back hair? It could be; it would be enough.
Is it your . . . what is the polite word for it . . . your sex?

LAWYER *(Mocking)*
Careful now, with a man's pride.

MISS ALICE
Ugly; that too—ugly.

LAWYER *(Unruffled)*
Better than most, if you care for a *man* . . .

MISS ALICE
. . . ugly coarse uncut ragged . . . PUSH!

LAWYER
Push . . . yes . . .

MISS ALICE

. . . selfish, hurtful, ALWAYS! OVER AND OVER!

LAWYER

You like it; it feels good.

MISS ALICE
(Very calm and analytical)

But is that what I loathe most? It could be; that would be
enough, too.

LAWYER

. . . oh, what a list . . .

MISS ALICE

But I think it is most the feel of your skin . . . *(Hard)* that
you can't sweat. *(He stiffens some)* That your body is as im-
personal as your . . . self—dry, uncaring, rubbery . . . dead.
Ah . . . there . . . that is what I loathe about you most:
you're dead. Moving pushing selfish dry dead. *(Brief pause)*
Does that hurt? Does something finally, beautifully hurt?
(Self-mocking laugh) Have I finally gotten . . . into you?

LAWYER
(A little away from her now)

Insensitive, still, aren't you, after all this time. Does it hurt?
Does something finally hurt?

MISS ALICE

. . . deep, gouging hurt?

LAWYER

Everything! Everything in the day and night, eating, resting,
walking, rutting, everything! Everything *hurts.*

MISS ALICE

Awwwwww.

LAWYER

Inside the . . . sensibility, everything hurts. Deeply.

MISS ALICE *(Ridiculing)*

And is that why I loathe you?

LAWYER *(A quiet, rueful laugh)*

Probably. *(Quickly back to himself)* But you, little playmate, you're what I want now. GIVE!

MISS ALICE

If Julian comes in here . . .

LAWYER *(Shoves her)*

Are you playing it straight, hunh? Or do you like your work a little bit, hunh? *(Again)* Do you enjoy spreading your legs for the clergy? *(Again)* Hunh?

MISS ALICE

STOP! . . . YOU!

LAWYER

Is that our private donation to the Church? Our own grant? YES? *(Begins to hurt her arm)* Are we planning to turn into a charitable, educational foundation?

MISS ALICE *(In pain)*

My arm!

(BUTLER enters, unnoticed; watches)

LAWYER *(Hard and very serious)*

Don't you dare mess this thing up. You behave the way I've told you; you PLAY-ACT. You do your part; STRAIGHT.

BUTLER *(Calmly)*

Brother Julian . . .

MISS ALICE

Butler! Help me!

BUTLER
(As the LAWYER *releases her)*
. . . has now examined the wine cellar, with awe and much
murmuring, and will be with us presently. He's peeing. So I
suggest—unless you're doing this for his benefit—uh, you
stop.

MISS ALICE
(As she and the LAWYER *pull themselves together)*
He hurt me, Butler.

BUTLER
(Calmly, as if reminding her)
Often. *(To the* LAWYER, *with mock friendliness)* Up to your
old tricks, eh?

LAWYER *(Dusting himself off)*
She is . . . not behaving.

BUTLER *(Very noncommittal)*
Ah me.

MISS ALICE
(Under her breath, to the LAWYER*)*
Savage! *(Realizes)* Both of you!

.

LAWYER *(Laughs)*
The maiden in the shark pond.

MISS ALICE
He thinks I'm sleeping with Julian. *(To* LAWYER*)* You poor
jealous . . .

B U T L E R

Are you?

MISS ALICE *(Indignant)*

No! *(Almost sad about it)* No, I am not.

L A W Y E R

She is!

MISS ALICE

I said I am not!

B U T L E R

Are you going to?

MISS ALICE

(After a pause; to LAWYER*)*

Am I going to? Am I going to . . . spread my legs for the
clergy? Enjoy my work a little? Isn't that what you'd have me
do? To not mess it up? To play my part straight? Isn't that
what you'll HAVE ME DO?

L A W Y E R

You don't need urging! . . .

B U T L E R

Now, children . . .

MISS ALICE

When the time comes? Won't you have me at him? Like it
or not? Well . . . I will like it!

(A little hard breathing from MISS ALICE *and the*
LAWYER*)*

B U T L E R

Something *should* be done about the wine cellar. I've noticed
it—as a passerby would—but Brother Julian pointed out the

extent of it to me: bottles have burst, are bursting, corks rotting . . . something to do with the temperature or the dampness. It's a shame, you know.

MISS ALICE *(Surprisingly shrill)*

Well, fix it!

BUTLER *(Ignoring her tone)*

Some great years, popping, dribbling away, going to vinegar under our feet. There is a Mouton Rothschild—one I'm especially fond of—that's . . .

LAWYER *(Pacifying)*

Do. Do . . . fix it.

BUTLER *(Shakes his head)*

Going. All of it. Great shame.

LAWYER

Yes, yes.

BUTLER *(Brightly)*

Nice thing about having Julian here so much . . . he's helpful. Wines, plants . . . do you know, he told me some astonishing things about ferns. We were in the solarium . . .

MISS ALICE *(Quiet pleading)*

Please . . . stop.

BUTLER

Oh. Well, it's nice having him about.

LAWYER *(Sour)*

Oh, we'll be a foursome very soon.

MISS ALICE *(Brightly)*

Yes.

LAWYER *(With a mirthless smile)*

Warning.

BUTLER *(Cheerful again)*

It *would* be a great deal more sensible than . . . puttering
out here every day. We could put him over the chapel! Now,
that's a splendid idea. He likes the chapel, he said, not reso-
nant, too small or something, wrong angles, but he likes
it . . .

MISS ALICE

When he moves here . . .

LAWYER

He will move here when I say—and as I say.

MISS ALICE *(Fake smile)*

We shall see.

LAWYER *(Still offhand)*

We shall not see.

JULIAN *(Offstage)*

Halloo!

BUTLER

In . . . in here.

MISS ALICE
(Sotto voce to the LAWYER*)*

You say we shall not see? *Shall* we?

LAWYER *(As above)*

Warning.

*(*JULIAN *enters)*
JULIAN

Ah! There you all are.

LAWYER

We had wondered where *you* were.

MISS ALICE *(Reminding a child)*

You usually find us here after dinner.

JULIAN

Yes, and a superb dinner.

LAWYER

. . . and then Butler reminded us that you were in the cellar.

JULIAN *(Sincere, but prepared)*

Miss Alice, your . . . home possesses two things that, were I
a designer of houses—for the very wealthy, of course—I would
put in all my designs.

MISS ALICE *(Smiling)*

And what are they?

LAWYER

(To MISS ALICE, *mildly mocking* JULIAN*)*

Can't you guess?

MISS ALICE *(Charmingly)*

Of course I can guess, but I want Julian to have the pleasure
of saying it.

JULIAN

A chapel and a wine cellar.

MISS ALICE

(Agreeing, but is she making light fun?)

Yes.

LAWYER

We hear, though, that the wine cellar is a wreck. And aren't there cobwebs in the chapel, too?

JULIAN
(Light but standing up to him)
One or two spiders have been busy around the altar, and the
organ is . . . in need of use . . .

LAWYER *(Very funny to him)*

HUNH!

JULIAN *(Choosing to ignore it)*
. . . but it *is* a chapel, a good one. The wine cellar, however . . . *(Shakes his head)* . . . great, great shame.

BUTLER
Exactly my words.

MISS ALICE
Well, we must have it tended to—and especially since you
are our guest so frequently these days, and enjoy good wines.

JULIAN
I would call someone in, a specialist, if I were you.

LAWYER *(Patronizing)*
Why? Can't you take care of it? Your domain?

JULIAN *(Quietly)*
The chapel, more, I should think.

BUTLER
Where does the Church get its wine . . . for Communion
and the like?

JULIAN
Oh, it is grown, *made* . . . grown, the grapes, harvested,
pressed . . . by, by monks.

LAWYER *(False heartiness)*
A regular profit-making setup, the Church.

JULIAN *(Quietly, as usual)*
Self-sustaining . . . in some areas.

LAWYER
But not in others, eh? Sometimes the old beggar bell comes
out, doesn't it? Priest as leper.

MISS ALICE
(Mildly to the LAWYER)
It *is* true: you are not fit for God's sight.

BUTLER
(To the LAWYER; *cheerfully interested)*
Is that *so!* I wasn't sure.

LAWYER
(To MISS ALICE, *feigning curiosity and surprise)*
Who whispered it to you?

MISS ALICE
(Indicating JULIAN. *Semi-serious)*
My confessor.

LAWYER *(A sneer; to* JULIAN)
Did you? And so *you* object, as well? To my mention of the
Church as solicitor.

JULIAN
In England I believe *you* would be referred to as solicitor.

LAWYER
No, I would not. And we are not in England . . . are we?

BUTLER
This *place was* . . . in England.

MISS ALICE
(As if suddenly remembering)
Yes, it was! Every stone, marked and shipped.

JULIAN
Oh; I had thought it was a replica.

LAWYER
Oh no; that would have been too simple. Though it *is* a
replica . . . in its way.

JULIAN
Of?

LAWYER
(Pointing to the model)
Of that.
            (JULIAN laughs a little; the LAWYER shrugs)
Ah well.

JULIAN *(To MISS ALICE)*
Did your . . . did your father have it . . . put up? *(A parenthesis)* It suddenly occurred to me that I know nothing of
your family, though I . . . I don't mean to pry. . . .

MISS ALICE *(A private laugh)*
No, we must not . . . well, should we say that? That my
father put it up? No. Let us not say that.

BUTLER
*(To JULIAN, pointing first to the model, then to the
room)*
Do you mean the model . . . or the replica?

JULIAN

I mean the . . . I mean . . . what we are in.

BUTLER

Ah-ha. And which is that?

JULIAN

That we are in?

BUTLER

Yes.

LAWYER *(To* JULIAN*)*

You are clearly not a Jesuit. *(Turning)* Butler, you've put him in a clumsy trap.

BUTLER *(Shrugging)*

I'm only a servant.

LAWYER
(To JULIAN, *too sweetly)*

You needn't accept his alternative . . . that since we are clearly not in a model we must be in a replica.

BUTLER *(Vaguely annoyed)*

Why must he not accept that?

MISS ALICE

Yes. Why not?

LAWYER

I said he did not *need* to accept the alternative. I did not say it was not valid.

JULIAN *(Cheerfully)*

I will not accept it; the problem is only semantic.

BUTLER *(Perhaps too consoling)*
Well, yes; that's what I would have thought.

LAWYER
Not necessarily, though. Depends, doesn't it, on your concept
of reality, on the limit of possibilities. . . .

MISS ALICE *(Genuinely put off)*
Oh, Lord!

LAWYER
There are no limits to possibi . . . *(Suddenly embarrassed)*
I'm . . . I'm sorry.

MISS ALICE
(To JULIAN, *but at the* LAWYER)
He starts in, he *will*; give him the most sophomoric conun-
drum, and he'll bore you to death.

LAWYER *(Violently)*
I! Will! Not!

JULIAN *(To break the silence)*
Well . . . perhaps I'm at fault here.

MISS ALICE *(Quietly, kindly)*
How could you be? . . . Dear Julian.

LAWYER
(To MISS ALICE; *burning)*
I thought I had educated you; I thought I had drilled you
sufficiently in matters of consequence; *(Growing louder)* I
thought I had made it clear to you the way you were to
behave.

JULIAN
Perhaps I should leave now; I think that . . .

LAWYER

DON'T INTERRUPT ME!
 (*Glares at* JULIAN, *who moves off to the model*)

MISS ALICE
(*To the* LAWYER; *calmly*)
You forget your place.

LAWYER
(*Clearly trying to get hold of himself*)
I . . . you . . . are quite right . . . Miss Alice, and abstractions *are* upsetting.

MISS ALICE
(*To the* LAWYER; *patiently*)
Perhaps you'll go home now.

BUTLER (*Cheerfully*)
Shall I have your car brought around?

LAWYER
(*Trying to be private in public*)
I . . . I thought that with so much to attend to, I might . . . spend the night. Of course, if you'd rather I didn't . . .
 (*Leaves it unfinished.* MISS ALICE *smiles enigmatically*)

BUTLER
(*Pretending to think the remark was for him*)
I don't *mind* whether you do or not.

JULIAN
(*Peering at the model, rather amazed*)
Can it . . . can it be?

LAWYER
In the heat of . . . I, I forgot myself.

MISS ALICE *(Patronizingly sweet)*

Yes.

LAWYER *(Matter-of-fact)*

You will forgive me.

MISS ALICE *(Toying)*

Oh?

BUTLER

Shall I have his car brought around?

LAWYER *(Sudden softening)*

Let me stay.

JULIAN
(Shy attempt at getting attention)

Please . . .

MISS ALICE
(Malicious pleasure in it)

I don't know . . .

JULIAN *(More urgently)*

Please!

LAWYER *(Bitter)*

As you wish, of course.
    (Swings his hand back as if to strike her; she flinches)

JULIAN

PLEASE!

BUTLER
(Patiently amused curiosity)

What *is* it, for heaven's sake?

JULIAN *(Pointing to the model)*
The model is . . . on fire; it's on fire!

BUTLER
(Urgent dropping of butlerish attitudes)
Where!

LAWYER
Good Christ!

MISS ALICE
Quick!
(The LAWYER *and* BUTLER *rush to the model)*

BUTLER
W*here,* for Christ's sake!

JULIAN *(Jostled)*
In the . . . over the . . .

LAWYER
Find it!

BUTLER
(Peering into various windows with great agitation)
It's . . . it's the . . . where the hell is it! . . . It's the . . .
chapel! The chapel's burning!

MISS ALICE
Hurry!

BUTLER
Come on! Let's get to it! *(Begins to run out of the room)* Are
you coming? Julian!

JULIAN
(Confused, but following)
But I . . . but . . . yes, of course.
(JULIAN and BUTLER run out)

MISS ALICE
(To the LAWYER as he hangs back)
We're burning down! Hurry!

LAWYER
*(Comes up to her, grabs her by the wrist, forces her
to the ground, keeps hold)*
Burning down? Consumed? WHY NOT! Remember what I told
you. Watch . . . your . . . step!
*(He runs out after the others. MISS ALICE is left
alone; maybe we hear one or two diminishing shouts
from the others, offstage. Finally, silence. MISS ALICE
doesn't rise from the floor, but gradually assumes a
more natural position on it)*

MISS ALICE
*(She alternates between a kind of incantation-prayer
and a natural tone)*
(Prayer)
Let the fire be put out. Let the chapel be saved; let the fire
not spread; let us not be consumed.
(Natural)
He hurt me. My wrist hurts. Who was the boy when I was
little hurt my wrist? I don't remember.
(Prayer)
Let the fire not spread; let them be quick.
(Natural)
YOU PIG!
(Softly, almost a whine)
You hurt my wrist.
(Imitates the LAWYER's tone)
Watch . . . your . . . step.

(Prayer)

Oh God, I have watched my step. I have . . . trod . . . so
carefully.

(Natural and weary)

Let it all come down—let the whole place . . . go.

*(She must now, when using a natural tone, almost
give the suggestion of talking to someone in the
model. Natural)*

I don't mean that. I don't remember his name . . . or his
face; merely the hurt . . . and that continues, the hurt the
same, the name and the face changing, but it doesn't matter.
Let them save it.

(Prayer)

Let them save it. Don't . . . destroy. Let them save the
resonance.

(Natural)

Increase it. Julian says there is no resonance, that it's not
right.

(Prayer)

Let the resonance increase.

(Natural; a little-girl tone)

I have tried very hard to be careful, to obey, to withhold
my . . . nature? I have tried so hard to be good, but I'm
. . . such a stranger . . . here.

(Prayer)

I have tried to obey what I have not understood, understanding that I must obey. Don't destroy! I have tried! TRIED.

(Natural)

Is that the way about hurt? That *it* does not change . . . but
merely its agents?

(JULIAN appears, unseen by MISS ALICE)

(Natural, still)

I will hold on.

(Sweetly, apologetically)

I will try to hold on.

(Prayer)

I will try to hold on!

(Natural)

Please, please . . . if you *do* . . . be generous and gentle with me, or . . . just gentle.

JULIAN *(Softly, a little sadly)*

I don't understand anything. The chapel was in flames.

MISS ALICE

Yes.

JULIAN

. . . and yet . . . I saw the fire here in the model . . . and yet . . . the real chapel was in flames. We put it out. And now the fire here is out as well.

MISS ALICE
(Preceded by a brief, hysterical laugh)

. . . yes.

JULIAN
(Underneath the wonder, some fear)

I don't understand.

MISS ALICE
(She is shivering a little)

It's very hard. Is the chapel saved?

JULIAN
(His attention on the model)

Hm? Oh, yes . . . partially, mostly. The . . . the boards, floorboards, around the altar were . . . gave way, were burned through. The altar . . . sank, some, angled down into the burned-through floor. Marble.

MISS ALICE *(Almost a whisper)*

But the fire is out.

JULIAN

Yes. Out. The spiders, burned to a crisp, I should say, curled-up, burned balls. *(Asking the same question)* I . . . I don't understand.

MISS ALICE
(Vaguely to the model)

It is all well. We are not . . . consumed.

JULIAN

Miss Alice? Why, why did it happen that way—in both dimensions?

MISS ALICE
(Her arms out to him)

Help me.
    (JULIAN goes to her, lifts her by the arms; they stand, at arm's length, holding hands, facing each other)

JULIAN

Will you . . . tell me anything?

MISS ALICE
(A helpless laugh, though sad)

I don't know anything.

JULIAN

But you were . . . *(Stops)*

MISS ALICE *(Pleading)*

I don't *know* anything.

JULIAN *(Gently, to placate)*

Very well.

MISS ALICE
(Coming closer to him)

Come stay.

JULIAN

Miss Alice?

MISS ALICE

Come stay here. It will . . . be easier. For you.

JULIAN (*Concern, not anger*)

Did he hurt you?

MISS ALICE

Easier than going back and forth. And for me, too.

JULIAN

Did he?

MISS ALICE
(*After a pause and a sad smile*)

Some. You're shivering, Julian.

JULIAN

No, Miss Alice, it is *you* . . . you are shivering.

MISS ALICE

The Cardinal will agree to it.

JULIAN
(*Looking toward the model*)

Yes, I . . . suppose so.

MISS ALICE

Are you frightened, Julian?

JULIAN

Why, no, I . . . I *am* shivering, am I not?

MISS ALICE

Yes.

JULIAN

But I am not . . . yes, I suppose I am . . . frightened.

MISS ALICE

Of what, Julian?

JULIAN
(Looks toward the model again)
But there is . . . *(Back)* . . . of what.

MISS ALICE

Yes.

JULIAN *(Knowing there is)*
Is there anything to be frightened of, Miss Alice?

MISS ALICE *(After a long pause)*

Always.

CURTAIN

SCENE TWO

(The library—as of Act One, Scene Two. The BUTLER *is on stage. The* LAWYER *enters immediately, angry, impatient)*

LAWYER

Well, where are they today?

BUTLER *(Calm, uninvolved)*

Hm? Who?

LAWYER

WHERE IS SHE! Where is she off to now?

BUTLER

Miss Alice? Well, I don't really know. *(Thinks about it)* You look around?

LAWYER

They're not here.

BUTLER

You don't think they've eloped, do you?

LAWYER

Do you know!

BUTLER

They're moving together nicely; the fire in the chapel helped, I thought, though maybe it was intended to . . . brought them closer.

LAWYER

Where are they!

BUTLER

They spend so much time together now; everything on schedule.

LAWYER

Where have they gone!

BUTLER

I don't *know*; really. Out walking? In the gardens? Driving
somewhere? Picnicking, maybe? Cold chicken, cheese, a Mon-
trachet under an elm? I don't *know* where they are.

LAWYER

Don't you watch them?

BUTLER

Keep one eye peeled? Can't she take care of herself? She
knows her business. (*Pause; then, quietly meaningful*) Doesn't
she. (*No answer*) Doesn't she.

LAWYER

You should watch them. We don't want . . . error. She
is . . .

BUTLER

Human? Yes, and clever, too . . . isn't she. *Good* at it, wrap-
ping around fingers, enticing. I recall.

LAWYER

Too human; not playing it straight.

BUTLER

Enjoying her work a little? They're not sleeping together yet.

LAWYER

NO! NOT YET!

BUTLER *(A quiet warning)*

Well, it won't bother you when they do . . . will it.

LAWYER *(Matter-of-factly)*

I, too: human.

BUTLER

Human, but dedicated.

LAWYER *(Quiet, sick loathing)*

He doesn't deserve her.

BUTLER *(Kindly)*

Well, he'll not have her long.

LAWYER *(Weary)*

No; not long.

BUTLER

On . . . and on . . . we go.

LAWYER *(Sad)*

Yes.

BUTLER *(Too offhand, maybe)*

I've noticed, you've let your feelings loose lately; too much: possessiveness, jealousy.

LAWYER

I'm *sorry*.

BUTLER

You used to be so good.

LAWYER

I'm SORRY!

BUTLER

It's all right; just watch it.

LAWYER

Attrition: the toll time takes.

BUTLER

I watch you carefully—you, too—and it's the oddest thing:
you're a cruel person, straight through; it's not cover; you're
hard and cold, saved by dedication; just that.

LAWYER *(Soft sarcasm)*

Thank you.

BUTLER

You're welcome, but what's happened is you're acting like
the man you wish you were.

LAWYER

Yes?

BUTLER

Feeling things you can't feel. Why don't you mourn for
what you are? There's lament enough there.

LAWYER *(A sad discovery)*

I've never liked you.

BUTLER *(A little sad, too)*

I don't mind. We get along. The three of us.

LAWYER

She's *using* Julian! To humiliate me.

BUTLER *(Nodding)*

Of course. Humiliate; not hurt. Well, let her do her job the
way she wants; she'll lead him, bring him around to it.

LAWYER

But she *cares* for him.

BUTLER

Of course; human, a woman. Cares, but it won't get in the way. Let her use what she can. It will be done. Don't you think it's time you went to see His Holiness again?

LAWYER

Eminence, not Holiness. You think it's time I went again? Yes; well, it *is* time. You come, too.

BUTLER (*Mildly taunting*)

But shouldn't I stay here . . . to watch? To fill you in on the goings on? To let you be the last to know?

LAWYER

YOU COME! To back me up, when I want emphasis.

BUTLER

In the sense that my father used the word? Wants emphasis: lacks emphasis?

LAWYER

No. The touch of the proletarian: your simplicity, guileless-ness . . .

BUTLER

Aw . . .

LAWYER

His Eminence is a pompous ass.

BUTLER

Stupid? I doubt *that*.

LAWYER

Not stupid; an ass.

BUTLER

Cardinals aren't stupid; takes brains to get there; no jokes in
the Church.

LAWYER

Pompous!

BUTLER

Well, in front of you, maybe. Maybe has to wear a face;
you're not easy. What will you tell him?

LAWYER

What will I tell him? Tell me.

BUTLER

All right. You play Cardinal, I'll play you.

LAWYER
(Goes into it eagerly; with a laugh)
Ah, two of you. We are doubly honored. Will you not sit?

BUTLER

Really? Like that?

LAWYER

And how is our Brother Julian faring . . . in the world of
the moneyed and the powerful?

BUTLER

No. Really?

LAWYER

Really! And can we be of service to you, further service?

BUTLER

Maybe.

LAWYER

Maybe? Ah?

BUTLER

Yes, your Brother Julian is going to be taken from you.

LAWYER

Our Brother Julian? Taken? From us?

BUTLER

Come on, Your Eminence.

LAWYER

This is a . . . preposterous . . . We . . . we don't understand you.

BUTLER

Isn't the grant enough? Isn't a hundred million a year for twenty years enough? For one man? He's not even a priest.

LAWYER *(As the* CARDINAL*)*

A man's soul, Sir! *(Himself)* Not his soul, mustn't say that to him.

BUTLER *(Musing)*

Shall we be dishonest? Well, then, I suppose you'll have to tell him more. Tell him the whole thing.

LAWYER *(Himself)*

I will like that. It will blanch his goddam robes . . . turn 'em white.

BUTLER *(Chuckles)*

Nice when you can enjoy your work, isn't it? Tell him that

Julian is leaving him. That Julian has found what he's after.
(*Walks to the model, indicates it.*) And I suppose you'd better
tell him about . . . this, too.

LAWYER

The wonders of the world?

BUTLER

I think he'd better know . . . about this.

LAWYER

Shatter.

BUTLER

And, you know what I think would be a lovely touch?

LAWYER
(*A quiet smile that is also a grimace*)

Tell me.

BUTLER

How eager you are. I think it would be a lovely touch were
the Cardinal to marry them, to perform the wedding, to
marry Julian to . . .

LAWYER

Alice.

BUTLER

Miss Alice.

LAWYER

Alice!

BUTLER

Well, all right; one through the other. But have him marry
them.

LAWYER *(Smiles a little)*

It would be nice.

BUTLER

I thought so.

LAWYER

But *shall* we tell him the whole thing? The Cardinal? What
is happening?

BUTLER

How much can he take?

LAWYER

He is a man of God, however much he simplifies, however
much he worships the symbol and not the substance.

BUTLER

Like everyone.

LAWYER

Like most.

BUTLER

Julian can't stand that; he told me so: men make God in their
own image, he said. Those six years I told you about.

LAWYER

Yes. When he went into an asylum. YES.

BUTLER

It was—because he could not stand it, wasn't it? The use
men put God to.

LAWYER

It's perfect; wonderful.

BUTLER

Could not reconcile.

LAWYER

No.

BUTLER

God as older brother, scout leader, couldn't take that.

LAWYER

And still not reconciled.

BUTLER

Has pardoned men, I think. Is walking on the edge of an abyss, but is balancing. Can be pushed . . . over, back to the asylums.

LAWYER

Or over . . . to the Truth (*Addressing* JULIAN, *as if he were there; some thunder in the voice*) God, Julian? Yes? God? *Whose* God? Have you pardoned men their blasphemy, Julian? Have you forgiven them?

BUTLER

(*Quiet echoing answers; being* JULIAN)

No, I have not, have not really; have *let* them, but cannot accept.

LAWYER

Have not forgiven. No, Julian. Could you ever?

BUTLER (*Ibid.*)

It is their comfort; my agony.

LAWYER

Soft God? The servant? Gingerbread God with the raisin eyes?

BUTLER *(Ibid.)*

I cannot accept it.

LAWYER

Then don't accept it, Julian.

BUTLER

But there is *some*thing. There is a *true* God.

LAWYER

There is an abstraction, Julian, but it cannot be understood.
You cannot worship it.

BUTLER *(Ibid.)*

There is more.

LAWYER

There is Alice, Julian. That can be understood. Only the
mouse in the model. Just that.

BUTLER *(Ibid.)*

There must be more.

LAWYER

The mouse. Believe it. Don't personify the abstraction,
Julian, limit it, demean it. Only the mouse, the toy. And
that does not exist . . . but is all that can be worshiped.
. . . Cut off from it, Julian, ease yourself, ease off. No
trouble now; accept it.

BUTLER
(Talking to JULIAN *now)*

Accept it, Julian; ease off. Worship it . . .

LAWYER

Accept it.

BUTLER
(After a pause; normal again)
Poor, poor Julian.

LAWYER *(Normal, too)*
He can make it.

BUTLER
I hope he can.

LAWYER
If not? *(Shrugs) Out* with him.

BUTLER *(Pause)*
You cannot tell the Cardinal . . . that.

LAWYER *(Weary)*
The benefits to the Church.

BUTLER
Not simply that.

LAWYER
And a man's soul. If it be saved . . . what matter how?

BUTLER
Then we'd best go to him.

LAWYER
Yes.

BUTLER
Leave Julian to Miss Alice; he is in good hands.

LAWYER *(Quiet, sick rage rising)*
But his hands . . . on her.

BUTLER *(Soothing)*

Temporary . . . temporal. You'll have her back.

LAWYER *(Rises)*

All right.

BUTLER

Let's go.

LAWYER

(Walks to the model, addresses it; quietly, but force-fully; no sarcasm)

Rest easy; you'll have him . . . Hum; purr; breathe; rest. You will have your Julian. Wait for him. He will be yours.

CURTAIN

SCENE THREE

(MISS ALICE'S *sitting room, as of Act One, Scene Three.* JULIAN *is on stage, near the fireplace, carries a riding crop; the door to the bedroom is ajar*)

JULIAN
(*After a moment; over his shoulder*)
It was fun, Miss Alice; it was fun.

MISS ALICE
(*From behind the door*)
What, Julian?

JULIAN (*Turns*)
It was . . . I enjoyed it; very much.

MISS ALICE
(*Her head appearing from behind the door*)
Enjoyed what?

JULIAN
Riding; it was . . . exhilarating.

MISS ALICE
I would never have thought you rode. You were good. (*Disappears*)

JULIAN
(*A small, self-deprecating laugh*)
Oh. Yes. When I was young—a child—I knew a family who . . . kept horses, as a pastime, not as a business. They were moneyed—well, had *some*. It was one of their sons who was

my playmate . . . and we would ride.

MISS ALICE
(Still behind the door)
Yes.

JULIAN
You remember, you know how seriously children talk, the cabalas we have . . . had. My friend and I would take two hunters, and we would go off for hours, and talk ourselves into quite a state—mutually mesmerizing, almost an hysteria. We would forget the time, and bring the animals back quite lathered. *(Laughs)* We would be scolded—no: cursed *out*— by one groom or another; usually by a great dark Welshman —a young fellow who always scowled and had—I remember it clearly, for I found it remarkable—the hairiest hands I have ever seen, with hair—and this is what I found most remark-able—tufts of coarse black hair on his thumbs. *(Looks at his own thumbs)* Not down, or a few hairs, which many of us have, but tufts. This Welshman.

MISS ALICE
(Head appearing again)
D. H. Lawrence.

JULIAN
Pardon?

MISS ALICE
(Appearing, wearing a black negligee with great sleeves)
"Love on the Farm." Don't you know it?
(Circles him as she recites it; mock-stalks him)
"I hear his hand on the latch, and rise from my chair
Watching the door open . . .
He flings the rabbit soft on the table board
And comes toward me: he! the uplifted sword

Of his hand against my bosom! . . .
. . . With his hand he turns my face to him
And caresses me with his fingers that still smell grim
Of rabbit's fur! . . .
And down his mouth comes on my mouth! and down
His bright dark eyes over me . . .
. . . his lips meet mine, and a flood
Of sweet fire sweeps across me, so I drown
Against him, die and find death good!"
                    (Cocks her head, smiles)
No?

JULIAN *(Embarrassed)*
That was . . . not quite my reaction.

MISS ALICE
(A great, crystal laugh)
No! Silly Julian! No. *(Conspiratorial)* That was a verse I knew
at school, that I memorized. "And down his mouth comes on
my mouth." Oh! That would excite us so . . . at school;
things like that. *(Normal tone; a shrug, a smile)* Early eroti-
cism; mental sex play.

JULIAN *(Still embarrassed)*
Yes.

MISS ALICE
I've embarrassed you!

JULIAN
No! No!

MISS ALICE
Poor Julian; I have. And you were telling me about horseback
riding.

JULIAN
No, I was telling you about the groom, as far as that goes.
And I suppose . . . yes, I suppose . . . those thumbs were

. . . erotic for *me*—at that time, if you think about it; mental sex play. Unconscious.

MISS ALICE
(Sweetly, to divert him)
It *was* fun riding. *Today.*

JULIAN
Yes!

MISS ALICE
I am fond of hair—man's body hair, except that on the back. *(Very offhand)* Are you hairy, Julian?

JULIAN
I . . . my chest is rather nice, but my arms are . . . surprisingly hairless.

MISS ALICE
And you have no back hair.

JULIAN
Well . . . do you really wish to know?

MISS ALICE *(With a laugh)*
Yes!

JULIAN *(Nods in acquiescence)*
I have no . . . back hair, in the usual sense—of the shoulders . . .
(MISS ALICE nods)
. . . but there is hair, at the small of the back . . . rising.

MISS ALICE
Yes, yes, well, *that* is nice. *(Laughs, points to the crop)* You're carrying the crop. Are you still in the saddle?

JULIAN
(Laughing; shyly brandishing the crop)
Are you one of Mr. Lawrence's ladies? Do you like the smell
of saddle soap, and shall I take my crop to you?

MISS ALICE
(Briefest pause; testing)
Would you?

JULIAN *(Halfhearted laugh)*
MISS ALICE!

MISS ALICE
Nobody does things naturally any more—so few people have
the grace. A man takes a whip to you—a loving whip, you
understand—and you *know*, deep and sadly, that it's imitation—literary, seen. *(Intentionally too much)* No one has the
natural graces any more.

JULIAN
(Putting the crop down; quietly)
I have . . . not whipped . . .

MISS ALICE
But surely you have.

JULIAN *(An apology)*
I do not recall.

MISS ALICE *(Expansive)*
Oh, my Julian! How many layers! Yes?

JULIAN
We . . . simplify our life . . . as we grow older.

MISS ALICE *(Teasing him)*
But from understanding and acceptance; not from . . .

emptying ourselves.

JULIAN

There are many ways.

MISS ALICE *(Showing her outfit)*

Do you like this?

JULIAN

It is most . . . becoming.

MISS ALICE *(Giggles)*

We're dressed quite alike.

JULIAN *(He, too)*

But the effect is not the same.

MISS ALICE

No. It *is* easier for you living here . . . isn't it?

JULIAN

It's . . . more than a person could want—or *should* want,
which is something we must discuss.

MISS ALICE
(Sensing a coming disappointment)

Oh . . .

JULIAN

Really.

MISS ALICE *(Not pleasantly)*

What do we do wrong?

JULIAN

One of the sins is gluttony . . .

MISS ALICE

Are you getting a belly?

JULIAN
(Smiles, but won't be put off)

. . . and it has many faces—or many bellies, if you wish. It's a commonplace that we can have too much of things, and I have too much . . . of comfort, of surroundings, of ease, of kindness . . . of happiness. I am filled to bursting.

MISS ALICE *(Hard)*

I think perhaps you misunderstand why you're here. You're *not* here to . . . to indulge yourself, to . . .

JULIAN *(Tight-lipped)*

I'm aware of that.

MISS ALICE

. . . to . . . to ease in. You're here in service to your *Church.*

JULIAN

I've not lost sight of my function.

MISS ALICE

I wonder!

JULIAN *(Really quite angry)*

And *I* wonder! What's being *done* to me. Am I . . . am I being temp—tested in some fashion?

MISS ALICE *(Jumping on it)*

Tempted?

JULIAN

Tested in some fashion?

MISS ALICE

TEMPTED?

JULIAN

BOTH! Tested! What! My . . . my sincerity, my . . . my
other cheek? You have allowed that . . . that *man,* your
. . . your lover, to . . . ridicule me. You have permitted it.

MISS ALICE

I? Permit?

JULIAN

You have allowed him to abuse me, my position, his, the
Church; you have tolerated it, and *smiled.*

MISS ALICE

Tolerate!

JULIAN

And smiled. WHY AM I BEING TESTED! . . . And why am I
being tempted? By luxury, by ease, by . . . content . . . by
things I do not care to discuss.

MISS ALICE *(Unsympathetic)*
You're answerable to your own temptations.

JULIAN

Yes?

MISS ALICE
(Singsong and patronizing)
Or God is.
*(*JULIAN *snorts)*
No? God is not? Is not answerable?

JULIAN
Knows. But is not answerable. I.

MISS ALICE *(Softening some)*

Then *be* answerable.

JULIAN

To my temptations, I am. *(To himself more than to her)* It would be so easy to . . . fall in, to . . . accept these surroundings. Oh, life would speed by!

MISS ALICE

With all the ridicule?

JULIAN

That aside.

MISS ALICE

You *have* a friend here . . . as they put it.

JULIAN *(Smiles)*

Butler. Yes; he's nice.

MISS ALICE *(A little laugh)*

I meant me.

JULIAN

Well, of *course*. . . .

MISS ALICE

Or, do you think of me otherwise? Do *I* tempt you?

JULIAN

You, Miss Alice?

MISS ALICE

Or, is it merely the fact of temptation that upsets you so?

JULIAN

I have longed . . . to be of great service. When I was young

—and very prideful—I was filled with a self-importance that was . . . well disguised. Serve. That was the active word: I would serve! *(Clenches his fist)* I would serve, and damn any-one or anything that stood in my way. I would shout my humility from the roof and break whatever rules impeded my headlong rush toward obedience. I suspect that had I joined the Trappist order, where silence is the law, I would have chattered about it endlessly. I was impatient with God's agents, and with God, too, I see it now. A . . . novice porter, ripping suitcases from patrons' hands, cursing those who pre-ferred to carry some small parcel for their own. And I was blind to my pride, and intolerant of any who did not see me as the humblest of men.

                    MISS ALICE *(A little malice)*
You phrase it so; I suspect you've said it before.

                    JULIAN
Doubtless I have. Articulate men often carry set paragraphs.

                    MISS ALICE
Pride still.

                    JULIAN
Some.

                    MISS ALICE
And how did your ambition sit?

                    JULIAN
Ambition? Was it?
        (MISS ALICE *displays a knee casually;* JULIAN *jumps)*
What are you doing!

                    MISS ALICE *(Vague flirting)*
I'm . . . sorry.

JULIAN

Well. Ambition, yes, I suppose—ambition to be nothing, to
be least. Most obedient, humblest. How did it sit? For some,
patiently, but not well. For me? Even less well. But I . . .
learned.

MISS ALICE

To . . . subside. Is that the simplification you mentioned
before? Of your life. To subside . . . and vanish; to leave
no memory.

JULIAN

No; I wish to leave a . . . memory—of work, of things done.
I've told you; I wish to be of great service, to move great
events; but when it's all time for crediting, I'd like someone
to say no more than "Ah, wasn't there someone involved in
this, who brought it all about? A priest? Ah-*ha*, a *lay* brother
—was that it." (*Smiles*) Like that. The memory of someone
who helped.

MISS ALICE
(*Pauses, then laughs*)

You're lying!

JULIAN

I?

(*Then they both laugh, like conspiratorial children*)

MISS ALICE

Every monster was a man first, Julian; every dictator was a
colonel who vowed to retire once the revolution was done; it's
so easy to postpone elections, little brother.

JULIAN

The history of the Church . . .

MISS ALICE

The history of the Church shows half its saints were martyrs, martyred either for the Church, or by it. The chronology is jammed with death-seekers and hysterics: the bloodbath to immortality, Julian. Joan was only one of the suicides.

JULIAN
(Quivering with intensity)
I WISH TO SERVE AND . . . BE FORGOTTEN.

MISS ALICE
(Comes over, strokes his cheek)
Perhaps you will, Julian.
(He takes her hand, kisses it, puts it back on his cheek)
Yes?

JULIAN *(Guiltily)*
I wish to be of service. *(A little giggle)* I *do.*

MISS ALICE
And be forgotten.

JULIAN
Yes.

MISS ALICE *(Stroking his head)*
Not even remembered a little? By some? As a gentle man, gentle Julian . . .

JULIAN
Per . . . perhaps.

MISS ALICE
. . . my little lay brother and expert on wines; my little horseback rider and crop switcher . . .

JULIAN *(As she ruffles his hair)*

Don't . . . do that.

MISS ALICE *(Ruffles harder)*

My little whipper, and RAPIST?

JULIAN *(Rising, moving away)*

DON'T!

MISS ALICE *(Pouting, advancing)*

Julian . . .

JULIAN

No, now; no.

MISS ALICE *(Still pouting)*

Julian, come kiss me.

JULIAN

Please!

MISS ALICE *(Singsong)*

Come kiss.

JULIAN *(A plea)*

Miss Alice . . . Just . . . let me do my service, and let
me go.

MISS ALICE
(Abruptly to business; not curt, though)

But you're *doing* great service. Not many people have been
put in the position you've been graced by—not many. Who
knows—had some lesser man than you come, some bishop,
all dried and salted, clacketing phrases from memory, or . . .
one of those insinuating super-salesmen your Church uses,
had one of them come . . . who knows? Perhaps the whole
deal would have gone out the window.

JULIAN

Surely, Miss Alice, you haven't been playing games with . . .
so monumental a matter.

MISS ALICE

The rich are said to be quixotic, the very wealthy cruel, over-
bearing; who is to say—might not vast wealth, the insulation
of it, make one quite mad? Games? Oh, no, my little Julian,
there are no games played here; this is for keeps, and in dead
earnest. There *are* cruelties, for the insulation breeds a strange
kind of voyeurism; and there is impatience, too, over the need
to accomplish what should not be explained; and, at the end
of it, a madness of sorts . . . but a triumph.

JULIAN *(Hands apart)*

Use me, then . . . for the triumph.

MISS ALICE
(Moving on him again)

You are *being* used, my little Julian. *I* am being used . . . my
little Julian. You want to be . . . employed, do you not?
Sacrificed, even?

JULIAN

I have . . . there are no secrets from you, Miss Alice . . .
I have . . . dreamed of sacrifice.

MISS ALICE
(She touches his neck)

Tell me.

JULIAN

You mustn't do . . . it is not wise . . .

MISS ALICE

Tell me.

(She will circle him, touch him occasionally, kiss the back of his neck once during the next speech)

JULIAN

Still my pride . . . a vestige of it.
(He becomes quite by himself during this; unaware of her)
Oh, when I was still a child, and read of the Romans, how they used the saints as playthings—enraged children gutting their teddy bears, dashing the head of their doll against the bedpost, I could . . . I could entrance myself, and see the gladiator on me, his trident fork against my neck, and hear, even hear, as much as feel, the prongs as they entered me; the . . . the beast's saliva dripping from the yellow teeth, the slack sides of the mouth, the . . . sweet, warm breath of the lion; great paws on my spread arms . . . even the rough leather of the pads; and to the point of . . . as the great mouth opened, the breath no longer warm but hot, the fangs on my jaw and forehead, positioned . . . IN. And as the fangs sank in, the great tongue on my cheek and eye, the splitting of the bone, and the *blood* . . . just before the great sound, the coming dark and the silence. I could . . . experience it all. And was . . . engulfed. *(A brief laugh, but not breaking the trance)* Oh, martyrdom. To be that. To be able . . . to be that.

MISS ALICE

(Softly, into his ear; he does not hear it)
Marry me, Julian.

JULIAN

The . . . death of the saints . . . was always the beginning of their lives. To go bloodstained and worthy . . . upward. I could feel the blood on my robes as I went; the smell of the blood, as intense as paint . . . and warm . . . and painless.

MISS ALICE

Marry me.

JULIAN

"Here. I have come. You see my robes? They're red, are they not? Warm? And are not the folds caught together . . . as the blood coagulates? The . . . fingers of my left hand—of both!—are . . . are hard to move apart, as the blood holds finger to finger. And there is a wound in me, the warm dark flow . . . runs down my belly . . . to . . . bathing my groin. You see? I have come . . . bloodstained and worthy."

MISS ALICE

Marry me.

JULIAN *(Still self-tranced)*

Bathed . . . my groin. And as the thumbs of the gladiator pressed . . . against . . . my neck, I . . . as the lion's belly pressed on my chest, I . . . as the . . . I . . . or as the woman sank . . . on the mossy hillock by the roses, and the roar is the crunching growl is the moan is the sweat-breathing is the . . .

MISS ALICE

(Behind him, her arms around his neck, on his chest)

. . . sweat-breathing on the mossy hillock and the white mist in the perfumes . . .

JULIAN

. . . fumes . . . lying . . . on the moss hill in the white filmy gladiator's belly pressing on the chest fanged and the soft hard tongue and the *blood* . . . ENTERS . . . *(Lurches from the chair)* . . . STOP! . . . THAT!

MISS ALICE

(Coming at him slowly)

Come to Alice, Julian, in your sacrifice . . .

JULIAN
(Moving away, but helpless)
Stay . . . away . . . stay.

MISS ALICE
. . . give yourself to her, Julian . . .

JULIAN
. . . a . . . away . . .

MISS ALICE *(Sweetly singsong)*
Come marry Alice, she wants you so; she says she wants you
so, come give yourself to Alice; oh, Alice needs you and your
sacrifice . . .

JULIAN
. . . no . . . no . . .

MISS ALICE
. . . Alice says she wants you, come to Alice, Alice tells me
so, she wants you, come to Alice . . .

JULIAN
. . . no . . . sacrifice . . .

MISS ALICE
Alice tells me so, instructs me, come to her.
*(MISS ALICE has her back to the audience, JULIAN fac-
ing her, but at a distance; she takes her gown and,
spreading her arms slowly, opens the gown wide; it is
the unfurling of great wings)*

JULIAN
(Shaking, staring at her body)
. . . and . . . sacrifice . . . on the altar of . . .

MISS ALICE
Come . . . come . . .

JULIAN

. . . the . . . Lord . . . God . . . in . . . Heaven . . .

MISS ALICE

Come . . .

(JULIAN *utters a sort of dying cry and moves, his arms in front of him, to* MISS ALICE; *when he reaches her, she enfolds him in her great wings*)

MISS ALICE *(Soothing)*

You will be hers; you will sacrifice yourself to her . . .

JULIAN *(Muffled)*

Oh my God in heaven . . .

MISS ALICE

(Her head going back, calling out)

Alice! . . . Alice? . . .

JULIAN

(Slowly kneeling within the great wings)

. . . in . . . my . . . sacrifice . . .

MISS ALICE *(Still calling out)*

He will be yours! He will be yours! AAAAALLLLLIIIIIICCCCCCEEEEE!

CURTAIN

ACT THREE

(*The library, as of Act One, Scene Two. No one on stage. After a moment or so,* BUTLER *enters, carrying what looks to be a pile of gray sheets. They are clearly quite heavy. He sets them down on a table, straightens his shoulders from the effort, looks at various chairs, turns to counting the pile.* JULIAN *enters, at more than a casual pace, dressed in a suit*)

JULIAN

Butler!

BUTLER
(*Deliberate pause; then*)
. . . four . . . five . . . six . . . (*Pretending suddenly to see* JULIAN) Oh! Hello there.

JULIAN
Where . . . I . . . I feel quite *lost.*

BUTLER (*No comment*)
Why?

JULIAN (*Agitation underneath*)
Well, uh . . . I will confess I haven't participated in . . . been married before, but . . . I can't imagine it's usual for everyone to disap*pear.*

BUTLER
Has everyone?

JULIAN
Yes! (*Quieter*) Yes, I . . . per—perhaps His Eminence is

occupied, or has *business*—that's it!—has business with . . .
but—but why *she* should . . . There I was . . . one moment married, flooded with white, and . . . then . . . the
next, alone. Quite alone, in the . . . echoes.

BUTLER

There is an echo, sometimes, all through it, down every long
hall, up in the huge beams . . .

JULIAN

But to be left alone!

BUTLER

Aren't you used to that?

JULIAN

Suddenly!

BUTLER *(Sad smile)*

Like a little boy? When the closet door swings shut after
him? Locking him in the dark?

JULIAN

Hm? Yes . . . yes, like that. *(Shudders a little)* Terrifying.

BUTLER

And it's always remote, an attic closet, where one should not
have been, where no one can hear, and is not likely to come
. . . for a very long time.

JULIAN *(Asking him to stop)*

Yes!

BUTLER
(To the sheets again counting them)

We learn so early . . . are *told*, where not to go, the things
we should not do. And there's often a reason.

JULIAN

And *she* vanished as well.

BUTLER

Who?

JULIAN

My . . . my wife.

BUTLER

And who is that?

JULIAN
(As if BUTLER *had forgotten everything)*
Miss Alice!

BUTLER

Ah. Really?

JULIAN

Butler, you saw the wedding!

BUTLER *(Puzzles it a moment)*
Quite so; I did. We . . . Well. Perhaps Miss Alice is changing.

JULIAN

She *must* be; of course. But . . . for everyone to . . . vanish, as if I'd turned my back for a *moment*, and an hour elapsed, or a . . . dimension had . . .

BUTLER *(Passing it over)*
Yes, a dimension—well, that happens.

JULIAN *(Still preoccupied)*
Yes, she must be . . . upstairs. What . . . what are you doing?

BUTLER

What?

JULIAN

What are those?

BUTLER

These? *(Looks at them)* Uh . . . sheets, or covers, more accurately.

JULIAN
(Still quite nervous, staying away)
What are they for?

BUTLER

To . . . cover.

JULIAN *(Ibid.)*

Cover *what!*

BUTLER

Oh . . . nothing; no matter. Housework, that's all. One of
my labors.

JULIAN

I . . . I would have thought you'd have champagne . . .
ready, that you'd be busy with the party. . . .

BUTLER

One does *many* things. You'll have your champagne, sir, never
fear.

JULIAN

I'm sorry; I . . . I was so upset.

BUTLER

Yes.

JULIAN *(Attempting a joke)*
After all, I've not been married before.

BUTLER
No.

JULIAN
And the procedures are a little . . . well, you know.

BUTLER
Yes.

JULIAN
. . . *still* . . .

BUTLER
Yes.

JULIAN
It all *does* seem odd.

BUTLER
Marriage is a confusing business.

JULIAN
Have . . . have you been . . . married?
(BUTLER *gives a noncommittal laugh as answer*)
I . . . I don't know if marriage is, but certainly the circum-
stances surrounding this *wedding* are rather . . .

BUTLER *(A fairly chilling smile)*
Special people, special problems.

JULIAN *(Hurt)*
Oh. Well . . . yes.

BUTLER *(Disdainful curiosity)*
Do you . . . *feel* married?

JULIAN (*Withdrawn*)
Not having been, I cannot say. (*Pause*) Can I?

BUTLER
(*Takes one of the sheets, opens it with a cracking
sound, holds it in front of him, a hand on each
shoulder*)
No. (*Puts it to one side*) I suppose not.

JULIAN
No. I wonder if . . . I wonder if you could go upstairs, perhaps, and see if Miss Alice . . . my *wife* . . . is . . .

BUTLER
No. (*Then, rather stern*) I have much too much work to do.
(*Cheerful*) I'll get you some champagne, though.

JULIAN (*Rather removed*)
No, I'll . . . wait for the others, if they haven't all . . . dis-
appeared.

BUTLER (*Noncommittal*)
To leave you alone with your bride, on your wedding night?
No; not yet.

JULIAN
(*For something to say, as much as anything, yet hopeful of an answer, or an explanation*)
Miss Alice . . . chose not to invite . . . friends . . . to the
ceremony.

BUTLER (*Chuckle*)
Ah, no. Alice . . . *Miss* Alice does not have friends; ad-
mirers, yes. Worshipers . . . but not buddies.

JULIAN (*Puzzled*)
I asked her why she had not, and she replied . . .

BUTLER *(Improvising)*
. . . it is you, Julian, who are being married . . . ?

JULIAN
(Too self-absorbed to be surprised)
Yes; something like that.

BUTLER
Your wife is . . . something of a recluse.

JULIAN *(Hopeful)*
But so outgoing!

BUTLER
Yes? Well, then; you will indeed have fun. *(Mock instructions)* Uncover the chandeliers in the ballroom! Lay on some footmen! Unplug the fountains! Trim the maze!

JULIAN *(More or less to himself)*
She *must* have friends . . . *(Unsure)* must she not?

BUTLER *(Stage whisper)*
I don't know; no one has ever asked her.

JULIAN *(Laughing nervously)*
Oh, indeed!
  *(MISS ALICE comes hurriedly into the room; she has
  on a suit. She sees only BUTLER first)*

MISS ALICE
Butler! Have you seen . . . ? *(Sees JULIAN)* Oh, I'm . . .
sorry. *(She begins to leave)*

JULIAN
There you are. No, wait; wait!
  (But MISS ALICE has left the room. In need of help)
I find everything today puzzling.

BUTLER *(About to give advice)*

Look . . . *(Thinks better of it)*

JULIAN

Yes?

BUTLER *(Shrugs)*

Nothing. The wages of a wedding day.

JULIAN

Are you my friend?

BUTLER

(Takes a while to think about the answer)

I *am*; yes; but you'll probably think not.

JULIAN

Is something being kept from me?

BUTLER *(After a pause)*

You loathe sham, do you not?

JULIAN

Yes.

BUTLER

As do we all . . . most of us. You are dedicated to the reality
of things, rather than their appearance, are you not?

JULIAN

Deeply.

BUTLER

As are . . . some of us.

JULIAN

It was why I retreated . . . withdrew . . . to the asylum.

BUTLER

Yes, yes. And you are devout.

JULIAN

You know that.

BUTLER

When you're locked in the attic, Julian, in the attic closet, in the dark, do you care who comes?

JULIAN

No. But . . .

BUTLER *(Starts to leave)*

Let me get the champagne.

JULIAN

Please!

BUTLER

So that we all can toast.
        (*As* BUTLER *leaves, the* CARDINAL *enters*)
Ah! Here comes the Church.

JULIAN

(*Going to the* CARDINAL, *kneeling before him, kissing his ring, holding the ring hand afterward, staying kneeling*)
Your Eminence.

CARDINAL

Julian. Our dear Julian.

BUTLER

Have you caught the bride?

CARDINAL

No. No. Not seen her since the . . . since we married her.

JULIAN

It was good of you. I suspect she will be here soon. Butler,
would you . . . go see? If she will come here? His Eminence
would . . . Now do be good and go.

(BUTLER *exits*)

He has been a great help. At times when my service has . . .
perplexed me, till I grew despondent, and wondered if perhaps you'd not been mistaken in putting such a burden . . .

CARDINAL
(Not wanting to get into it)
Yes, yes, Julian. We have *resolved* it.

JULIAN

But then I judge it is God's doing, this . . . wrenching of my
life from one light to another . . .

CARDINAL

. . . Julian . . .

JULIAN

. . . though not losing God's light, joining it with . . . my
new. *(He is like a bubbling little boy)* I can't tell you, the . . .
radiance, humming, and the witchcraft, I think it must be,
the ecstasy of this light, as *God's* exactly; the transport the
same, the lifting, the . . . the sense of service, and the EX-
PANSION . . .

CARDINAL

. . . Julian . . .

JULIAN

. . . the blessed wonder of service with a renewing, not an
ending joy—that joy I thought possible only through martyrdom, now, now the sunlight is no longer the hope for glare

and choking in the dust and plummeting, but with cool and
green and yellow dappled . . . perfumes . . .

CARDINAL *(Sharply)*

Julian!

JULIAN *(Little-boy smile)*

Sir.

CARDINAL
(Evading JULIAN's *eyes)*
We sign the papers today, Julian. It's all arranged, the grant
is accomplished; through your marriage . . . your service.

JULIAN *(Puzzlement)*

Father?

CARDINAL
(Barely keeping pleasure in his voice)
And isn't it wonderful: that you have . . . found yourself
such great service and such . . . exceeding happiness, too;
that God's way has brought such gifts to his servant, and to
his servant's servant as well.

JULIAN *(Puzzled)*
Thank you . . . Your Eminence.

CARDINAL *(Sadly)*
It is your wedding day, Julian!

JULIAN
(Smiles, throws off his mood)
Yes, it is! It's my wedding day. And a day of glory to God,
that His Church has been blessed with great wealth, for the
suffering of the world, conversion and the pronouncement of
His Glory.

CARDINAL
(*Embarrassed; perfunctory*)

Praise God.

JULIAN

That God has seen fit to let me be His instrument in this undertaking, that God . . .

CARDINAL

Julian. (*Pause*) As you have accepted what has happened . . . removed, so far removed from . . . any thought . . . accept what . . . *will* happen, *may* happen, with the same humility and . . .

JULIAN (*Happily*)

It is my service.

CARDINAL (*Nods*)

Accept what may come . . . as God's will.

JULIAN

Don't . . . don't frighten me. Bless me, Father.

CARDINAL (*Embarrassed*)

Julian, please . . .

JULIAN
(*On his knees before the* CARDINAL)

Bless me?

CARDINAL
(*Reluctantly; appropriate gestures*)

In the name of the Father and of the Son and the Holy Ghost . . .

JULIAN

. . . Amen . . .

CARDINAL

. . . Amen. You *have* . . . confessed, Julian?

JULIAN
(Blushing, but childishly pleased)

I . . . I have, Father; I have . . . confessed, and finally, to
sins more real than imagined, but . . . but they are not sins,
are they, in God's name, done in God's name, Father?

CARDINAL

May the presence of our Lord, Jesus Christ be with you always . . .

JULIAN

. . . to . . . to shield my eyes from too much light, that I
may be always worthy . . .

CARDINAL

. . . to light your way for you in the darkness . . .

JULIAN

. . . dark, darkness, Father? . . .

CARDINAL

. . . that you may be worthy of whatever sacrifice, unto death
itself . . .

JULIAN

. . . in all this light! . . .

CARDINAL

. . . is asked of you; that you may accept what you do not
understand . . .

JULIAN *(A mild argument)*

But, Father . . .

CARDINAL

. . . and that the Lord may have mercy on your soul . . . as, indeed, may He have on us all . . . all our souls.

JULIAN

. . . A . . . Amen?

CARDINAL *(Nodding)*

Amen.

LAWYER *(Entering)*

Well, well. Your Eminence. Julian. Well, you are indeed a fortunate man, today. What more cheering sight can there be than Frank Fearnought, clean-living, healthy farm lad, come from the heartland of the country, from the asylums— you see, I know—in search of fame, and true love—never fortune, of course.

JULIAN

. . . Please . . .

LAWYER

And see what has happened to brave and handsome Frank: he has found what he sought . . . true . . . love; *and* fortune—to his surprise, for wealth had never crossed his pure mind; and fame? . . . Oooooh, there will be a private fame, perhaps.

CARDINAL

V*ery* pretty.

LAWYER

And we are dressed in city ways, too, are we not? No longer the simple gown of the farm lad, the hems trailing in the dung; no; now we are in city clothes . . . banker's clothes.

JULIAN

These are proper clothes.

LAWYER

As you will discover, poor priestlet, poor former priestlet. Dressed differently for the sacrifice, eh?

JULIAN

I . . . think I'll . . . look for Miss . . . for my wife.

LAWYER

Do.

CARDINAL

Oh, yes, Julian; please.

JULIAN
(Kneels, kisses the ring again)

Your Eminence. *(To the* LAWYER, *mildly)* We are both far too old . . . are we not . . . for all that?
*(*JULIAN *exits)*

CARDINAL *(After* JULIAN *leaves)*

Is cruelty a lesson you learned at your mother's knee? One of the songs you were taught?

LAWYER

One learns by growing, as they say. I have fine instructors behind me . . . yourself amongst them. *(A dismissing gesture)* We have no time. *(Raises his briefcase, then throws it on a table)* All here. *(Great cheerfulness)* All here! The grant: all your money. *(Normal tone again)* I must say, your Church lawyers are picky men.

CARDINAL

Thorough.

LAWYER

Picky. Humorless on small matters, great wits on the major ones; ribald over the whole proposition.

CARDINAL *(Mumbling)*

. . . hardly a subject for ribaldry . . .

LAWYER

Oh, quite a dowry, greatest marriage settlement in history, *mother* church indeed . . . things like that.

CARDINAL *(Unhappily)*

Well, it's all over now . . .

LAWYER

Almost.

CARDINAL

Yes.

LAWYER

Cheer up; the price was high enough.

CARDINAL

Then it is . . . really true? About . . . *this? (Points at the model)*

LAWYER

I haven't time to lie to you.

CARDINAL

Really . . . true.

LAWYER
(Moving to the model)

Really. Can't you accept the wonders of the world? Why not of this one, as well as the other?

CARDINAL

We should be . . . getting on.

LAWYER

Yes. (*Points to a place in the model*) Since the wedding was . . . here . . . and we are (*Indicates the room they are in*) here . . . we have come quite a . . . dimension, have we not?

(*The* LAWYER *moves away from the model to a table, as the* CARDINAL *stays at the model*)

CARDINAL (*Abstracted*)

Yes. A distance.

(*Turns, sees the* LAWYER *open a drawer, take out a pistol and check its cartridges*)

What . . . what are you doing? (*Moves toward the* LAWYER, *slowly*)

LAWYER

House pistol.

CARDINAL

But what are you doing?

LAWYER

(*Looking it over carefully*)

I've never shot one of these things . . . pistols. (*Then, to answer*) I'm looking at it . . . to be sure the cartridges are there, to see that it is oiled, or whatever is done to it . . . to see how it functions.

CARDINAL

But . . .

LAWYER (*Calmly*)

You know we may have to shoot him; you know that may be necessary.

CARDINAL (*Sadly and softly*)

Dear God, no.

LAWYER *(Looking at the gun)*
I suppose all you do is . . . pull. *(Looks at the* CARDINAL*)* If
the great machinery threatens . . . to come to a halt . . .
the great axis on which all turns . . . if it needs oil . . . well,
we lubricate it, do we not? And if blood is the only oil handy
. . . what is a little blood?

CARDINAL *(False bravura)*
But that will not be necessary. *(Great empty quiet loss)* Dear
God, let that not be necessary.

LAWYER
Better off dead, perhaps. You know? Eh?

CARDINAL
The making of a martyr? A saint?

LAWYER
Well, let's make that saint when we come to him.

CARDINAL
Dear God, let that not be necessary.

LAWYER
Why not? Give me *any* person . . . a martyr, if you wish
. . . a saint . . . He'll take what he gets for . . . what he
wishes it to be. AH, it is what I have always wanted, he'll say,
looking terror and betrayal straight in the eye. Why not:
face the inevitable and call it what you have always wanted.
How to come out on top, going under.
*(*JULIAN *enters)*

LAWYER
Ah! There you are. Still not with Miss Alice!

JULIAN
I seem not to be with anyone.

LAWYER *(Smile)*

Isn't that odd?

JULIAN
(Turning away, more to himself)
I would have thought it so.

CARDINAL
(Hearty, but ill at ease)
One would have thought to have it all now—corks popping,
glasses splintering in the fireplace . . .

LAWYER
When Christ told Peter—so legends tell—that he would
found his church upon that rock, He must have had in mind
an island in a sea of wine. How firm a foundation in the
vintage years . . .
(We hear voices from without; they do, too)

MISS ALICE *(Offstage)*
I don't *want* to go in there . . .

BUTLER *(Offstage)*
You *have* to come in, now . . .

MISS ALICE *(Offstage)*
I won't go *in* there. . . .

BUTLER *(Offstage)*
Come along now; don't be a child. . . .

MISS ALICE *(Offstage)*
I . . . won't . . . go. . . .
*(BUTLER appears; two champagne bottles in one
hand, pulling MISS ALICE with the other)*

BUTLER

Come along!

MISS ALICE
(As she enters; sotto voce)

I don't want to . . .
(As she sees the others see her, she stops talking, smiles, tries to save the entrance)

BUTLER

Lurking in the gallery, talking to the ancestral wall, but I found her.

MISS ALICE

Don't be silly; I was . . . *(Shrugs)*

BUTLER *(Shrugs, too)*

Suit yourself. Champagne, everybody!

JULIAN

Ah! Good. *(Moving toward* MISS ALICE*)* Are you all right?

MISS ALICE
(Moves away from him; rather impatiently)

Yes.

CARDINAL

But you've changed your clothes, and your wedding gown was . . .

MISS ALICE

. . . two hundred years old . . .

LAWYER

. . . fragile.

CARDINAL

Ah!

*(Something of a silence falls. The other characters
are away from* JULIAN; *unless otherwise specified,
they will keep a distance, surrounding him, but more
than at arm's length. They will observe him, rather
clinically, and while this shift of attitude must be
subtle, it must also be evident.* JULIAN *will grow to
knowledge of it, will aid us, though we will be aware
of it before he is)*

JULIAN *(To break the silence)*

Well, shall we have the champagne?

BUTLER

Stay there! *(Pause)* I'll bring it.

CARDINAL

Once, when we were in France, we toured the champagne
country . . .

LAWYER *(No interest)*

Really.

CARDINAL

Saw the . . . mechanics, so to speak, of how it was done. . . .

LAWYER

Peasants? Treading?

CARDINAL *(Laughs)*

No, no. That is for woodcuts.
(The cork pops)
Ah!

BUTLER

Nobody move! I'll bring it to you all.

(Starts pouring into glasses already placed to the side)

MISS ALICE *(To the* LAWYER*)*

The ceremony.

(He does not reply)

The ceremony!

LAWYER *(Overly sweet smile)*

Yes. *(To them all)* The ceremony.

CARDINAL

Another? Must we officiate?

LAWYER

No need.

JULIAN *(A little apprehensive)*

What . . . ceremony is this?

BUTLER *(His back to them)*

There's never as much in a champagne bottle as I expect there to be; I never learn. Or, perhaps the glasses are larger than they seem.

LAWYER *(Ironic)*

When the lights go on all over the world . . . the true world. The ceremony of Alice.

JULIAN *(To* MISS ALICE*)*

What is this about?

(She nods toward the LAWYER*)*

LAWYER

Butler? Are you poured?

BUTLER
(Finishing; squeezing the bottle)
Yeeeeesssss . . .

LAWYER
Pass.

BUTLER
(Starts passing the tray of glasses)
Miss Alice.

MISS ALICE *(Strained)*
Thank you.

BUTLER
(Starts toward JULIAN, *changes his mind, goes to the*
CARDINAL)
Your Eminence?

CARDINAL
Ahhh.

BUTLER
(Starts toward JULIAN *again, changes his mind goes*
to the LAWYER)
Sweetheart?

LAWYER
Thank you.

BUTLER
(Finally goes to JULIAN, *holds the tray at arm's*
length; speaks, not unkindly)
Our Brother Julian.

JULIAN *(Shy friendliness)*
Thank you, Butler.

LAWYER
And now . . .

BUTLER
(Moving back to the table with the tray)
Hold on; I haven't got mine yet. It's over here.

JULIAN
Yes! Butler must drink with us. *(To* MISS ALICE*)* Don't you
think so?

MISS ALICE *(Curiously weary)*
Why not? He's family.

LAWYER
(Moving toward the model)
Yes; what a large family you have.
    (The LAWYER *would naturally have to pass near*
    JULIAN; *pauses, detours)*

JULIAN
I'm sorry; am . . . am I in your way?

LAWYER
(Continues to the model)
Large family, years of adding. The ceremony, children. The
ceremony of Alice.
    (The others have turned, are facing the model. The
    LAWYER *raises his glass)*
To Julian and his bride.

CARDINAL
Hear, hear.

JULIAN *(Blushing)*
Oh, my goodness.

LAWYER
To Julian and his bride; to Alice's wisdom, wealth and whatever.

BUTLER (Quietly, seriously)

To Alice.

MISS ALICE

To Alice.

> *(Brief pause; only* JULIAN *turns his head, is about to
> speak, but)*

LAWYER

To their marriage. To their binding together, acceptance and
worship . . . received; accepted.

BUTLER

To Alice.

LAWYER

To the marriage vow between them, which has brought joy
to them both, and great benefit to the Church.

CARDINAL

Amen.

MISS ALICE

To Alice.

> *(Again only* JULIAN *responds to this; a half turn of
> the head)*

LAWYER

To their house.

BUTLER, MISS ALICE and CARDINAL
(Not quite together)

To their house.

JULIAN (After them)

To their house.

LAWYER

To the chapel wherein they were bound in wedlock.
(A light goes on in a room in the model. JULIAN
makes sounds of amazement; the others are silent)
To their quarters.
(Light goes on upstairs in the model)
To the private rooms where marriage lives.

BUTLER

To Alice.

MISS ALICE

To Alice.
(To which JULIAN does not respond this time)

LAWYER

And to this room . . .
(Another light goes on in the model)
in which they are met, in which we are met . . . to celebrate
their coming together.

BUTLER

Amen.

LAWYER

A union whose spiritual values shall be uppermost . . .

MISS ALICE

That's enough. . . .

LAWYER

. . . whose carnal side shall . . .

MISS ALICE

That's enough!

JULIAN

May . . . May I?

(It is important that he stay facing the model, not
MISS ALICE. BUTLER, *who is behind him, may look*
at him; the CARDINAL *will look to the floor)*

May I . . . propose. To the wonders . . . which may befall
a man . . . least where he is looking, least that he would
have thought; to the clear plan of that which we call chance,
to what we see as accident till our humility returns to us
when we are faced with the mysteries. To all that which we
really want, until our guile and pride . . .

CARDINAL
(Still looking at the floor)

. . . Julian . . .

JULIAN

. . . betray us? *(Looks at the* CARDINAL; *pauses, goes on, smil-*
ing sweetly) My gratitude . . . my wonder . . . and my love.

LAWYER *(Pause)*

Amen?

JULIAN

Amen.

LAWYER *(Abruptly turning)*

Then, if we're packed, let us go.

BUTLER *(Not moving)*

Dust covers.

JULIAN *(Still smiling)*

Go?

CARDINAL *(To delay)*

Well. *This* champagne glass seems smaller than one would
have guessed; it has emptied itself . . . on one toast!

LAWYER

I recall. Suddenly I recall it. When we were children. *(Quite fascinated with what he is saying)* When we were children and we would gather in the dark, two of us . . . any two . . . on a swing, side porch, or by the ocean, sitting backed against a boulder, and we would explore . . . those most private parts, of one another, any two of us . . . *(Shrugs)* boy, girl, how—when we did it—we would talk of other things . . . of our schoolwork, or where we would travel in the summer. How, as our shaking hands passed under skirts or undid buttons, sliding, how we would, both of us, talk of other things, whispering, our voices shaking as our just barely moving hands. *(Laughs, points to the* CARDINAL*)* Like you! Chattering there on the model! Your mind on us and what is happening. Oh, the subterfuges.

MISS ALICE

I am packed.

JULIAN *(Still off by himself)*

Packed? . . . Miss Alice?

MISS ALICE
(To the LAWYER; *cold)*

May we leave soon?

JULIAN

Miss . . . Alice?

MISS ALICE

May we?

LAWYER *(Pause)*

Fairly.

JULIAN *(Sharp)*

Miss Alice!

MISS ALICE
(Turns toward him; flat tone; a recitation)
I'm very happy for you, Julian, you've done well.

JULIAN
(Backing away from everyone a little)
What is . . . going on . . . here? *(To* MISS ALICE*)* Tell me!

MISS ALICE
(As if she is not interested)
I am packed. We are going.

JULIAN *(Sudden understanding)*
Ah! *(Points to himself)* We are going. But where? You . . .
didn't tell me we . . . we were . . .

MISS ALICE
(To the LAWYER, *moving away)*
Tell him.

JULIAN
. . . going somewhere. . . .

MISS ALICE *(Quite furious)*
Tell him!

LAWYER
(About to make a speech)
Brother Julian . . .

JULIAN *(Strained)*
I am no longer Brother.

LAWYER *(Oily)*
Oh, are we not all brothers?

JULIAN
(To MISS ALICE; *with a halfhearted gesture)*
Come stand by me.

MISS ALICE
(Surprisingly little-girl fright)
No!

LAWYER
Now. Julian.

CARDINAL
Order yourself, Julian.

JULIAN *(To the* CARDINAL*)*
Sir?

LAWYER
(Sarcasm is gone; all is gone, save fact)
Dear Julian; we all serve, do we not? Each of us his own
priesthood; publicly, some, others . . . within only; but we
all do—what's-his-name's special trumpet, or clear lonely
bell. Predestination, fate, the will of God, accident . . .
All swirled up in it, no matter what the name. And being
man, we have invented choice, and have, indeed, gone further, and have catalogued the underpinnings of choice. But
we do not know. Anything. End prologue.

MISS ALICE
Tell him.

LAWYER
No matter. We are leaving you now, Julian; agents, every
one of us—going. We are leaving you . . . to your accom-
plishment: your marriage, your wife, your . . . special priesthood.

JULIAN
(Apprehension and great suspicion)
I . . . don't know what you're talking about.

LAWYER *(Unperturbed)*
What is so amazing is the . . . coming together . . . of dis-
parates . . . left-fielding, out of the most unlikely. Who
would have thought, Julian? Who would have thought? You
have brought us to the end of our service here. We go on;
you stay.

BUTLER
May I begin to cover?

MISS ALICE
Not yet. *(Kindly)* Do you understand, Julian?

JULIAN *(Barely in control)*
Of course not!

MISS ALICE
Julian, I have tried to be . . . *her*. No; I have tried to be . . .
what I thought she might, what might make you happy, what
you might use, as a . . . what?

BUTLER
Play God; go on.

MISS ALICE
We must . . . represent, draw pictures, reduce or enlarge to
. . . to what we can understand.

JULIAN *(Sad, mild)*
But I have fought against it . . . all my life. When they said,
"Bring the wonders down to me, closer; I cannot see them,

touch; nor can I believe." I have fought against it . . . all my life.

BUTLER *(To* MISS ALICE; *softly)*

You see? No good.

MISS ALICE *(Shrugs)*

I have done what I can with it.

JULIAN

All my life. In and out of . . . confinement, fought against the symbol.

MISS ALICE

Then you should be happy now.

CARDINAL

Julian, it has been your desire always to serve; your sense of mission . . .

LAWYER

We are surrogates; *our* task is done now.

MISS ALICE

Stay with her.

JULIAN
(Horror behind it; disbelieving)

Stay . . . with . . . her?

MISS ALICE

Stay with her. Accept it.

LAWYER *(At the model)*

Her rooms are lighted. It is warm, there is enough.

MISS ALICE

Be content with it. Stay with her.

JULIAN

(Refusing to accept what he is hearing)

Miss Alice . . . I have married *you*.

MISS ALICE *(Kind, still)*

No, Julian; you have married *her* . . . through me.

JULIAN

(Pointing to the model)

There is nothing there! We are *here!* There is no one *there!*

LAWYER

She is there . . . we believe.

JULIAN *(To MISS ALICE)*

I have *been* with *you!*

MISS ALICE

(Not explaining; sort of dreamy)

You have felt her warmth through me, touched her lips through my lips, held hands, through mine, my breasts, hers, lain on her bed, through mine, wrapped yourself in her wings, your hands on the small of her back, your mouth on her hair, the voice in your ear, hers not mine, all hers; her. You are hers.

CARDINAL

Accept.

BUTLER

Accept.

LAWYER

Accept.

JULIAN

THERE IS NO ONE THERE!

MISS ALICE

She is there.

JULIAN
(Rushes to the model, shouts at it)
THERE IS NOTHING THERE! *(Turns to them all)* THERE IS NOTH-
ING THERE!

CARDINAL *(Softly)*

Accept it, Julian.

JULIAN *(All the power he has)*

ACCEPT IT!

LAWYER *(Quietly)*
All legal, all accomplished, all satisfied, that which we believe.

JULIAN

ACCEPT!

BUTLER
. . . that which is done, and may not be revoked.

CARDINAL *(With some difficulty)*
. . . yes.

JULIAN

WHAT AM I TO ACCEPT!

LAWYER

An act of faith.

JULIAN *(Slow, incredulous)*
An . . . act . . . of . . . faith!

LAWYER
(Snaps his fingers at the CARDINAL)
Buddy?

CARDINAL
Uh . . . yes, Julian, an . . . act of faith, indeed. It is . . .
believed.

LAWYER
(Deadly serious, but with a small smile)
Yes, it is . . . believed. It is what we believe, therefore what
we know. Is that not right? Faith is knowledge?

CARDINAL
An act of faith, Julian, however we must . . .

JULIAN (Horror)
FAITH!?

CARDINAL
. . . in God's will . . .

JULIAN
GOD'S! WILL!

CARDINAL
(As if his ears are hurting, sort of mumbling)
Yes, Julian, you see, we must accept, and . . . be glad, yes,
be glad . . . our ecstasy.

JULIAN
(Backing off a little, shaking his head)
I have not come this distance . . .

CARDINAL
(Moving toward him a little)
Julian . . .

JULIAN

Stay back! I have not come this long way . . . have not—in
all sweet obedience—walked in these . . . (*Realizes he is differently dressed*) those robes . . . to be MOCKED.

LAWYER

Accept it, Julian.

JULIAN

I have not come this long *way!*

BUTLER

Yes; oh, yes.

JULIAN

I HAVE NOT!

MISS ALICE (*Kindly*)

Julian . . . dear Julian; accept.

JULIAN
(*Turns toward her, supplicating*)

I have not worn and given up for . . . for mockery; I have
not stretched out the path of my life before me, to walk on
straight, to be . . .

MISS ALICE

Accept.

JULIAN

I have not fought the nightmares—and the waking demons,
yes—and the years of despair, those, too . . . I have not accepted *half*, for *nothing*.

CARDINAL

For everything.

MISS ALICE
Dear Julian; accept. Allow us all to rest.

JULIAN
(A child's terror of being alone)
NO!

MISS ALICE (Still kind)
You must.

BUTLER
No choice.

JULIAN
I have . . . have . . . given up everything to gain everything, for the sake of my faith and my peace; I have allowed
and followed, and sworn and cherished, but I have not, have
not . . .

MISS ALICE
Be with her. Please.

JULIAN
For hallucination? I HAVE DONE WITH HALLUCINATION.

MISS ALICE
Then have done with forgery, Julian; accept what's real. I am
the . . . illusion.

JULIAN (Retreating)
No . . . no no no, oh no.

LAWYER (Quietly)
All legal, all accomplished, all satisfied, that which we believe.

MISS ALICE

All done.

JULIAN *(Quite frightened)*

I . . . choose . . . *not.*

CARDINAL

There is no choice here, Julian. . . .

LAWYER

No choice at all.

MISS ALICE *(Hands apart)*

All done.
(JULIAN *begins backing toward the model; the* LAW-
YER *begins crossing to the desk wherein he has put
the gun)*

BUTLER *(Quietly)*

I *must* cover now; the cars are waiting.

JULIAN

No . . . no . . . I WILL NOT ACCEPT THIS.

LAWYER
(Snaps for the CARDINAL *again)*

Buddy . . .

CARDINAL

We . . . *(Harder tone)* I *order* you.

LAWYER *(Smile)*

There. Now will you accept?

JULIAN

I . . . cannot be so mistaken, to have . . . I cannot have so

misunderstood my life; I cannot have . . . was I sane *then*?
Those *years*? My time in the *asylum*? WAS THAT WHEN I WAS
RATIONAL? THEN?

CARDINAL

Julian . . .

LAWYER
(Taking the gun from the drawer, checking it; to the
CARDINAL*)*
Don't you teach your people anything? Do you let them im-
provise? *Make* their Gods? *Make* them as they *see* them?

JULIAN *(Rage in the terror)*
I HAVE ACCEPTED GOD.

LAWYER
(Turns to JULIAN, *gun in hand)*
Then accept his works. Resign yourself to the mysteries . . .

MISS ALICE
. . . to greater wisdom.

LAWYER
Take it! Accept what you're given.

MISS ALICE
Your priesthood, Julian—full, at last. Stay with her. Accept
your service.

JULIAN
I . . . cannot . . . accept . . . this.

LAWYER *(Aims)*
Very well, then.

JULIAN

I have not come this . . . given up so much for . . .

BUTLER

Accept it, Julian.

MISS ALICE

Stay with her.

JULIAN

No, no, I will . . . I will go *back!* I will . . . go *back* to it.
(Starts backing toward the stairs) To . . . to . . . I will go
back to the asylum.

LAWYER

Last chance.

MISS ALICE

Accept it, Julian.

JULIAN

To . . . my asylum. MY! ASYLUM! My . . . my refuge . . .
in the world, from all the demons waking, my . . . REFUGE!

LAWYER

Very well then.
(Shoots. Then silence. JULIAN *does not cry out, but
clutches his belly, stumbles forward a few steps, sinks
to the floor in front of the model)*

MISS ALICE
(Softly, with compassion)
Oh, Julian. *(To the* LAWYER; *calm)* He would have stayed.

LAWYER
(To MISS ALICE, *shrugging)*

It was an accident.

JULIAN

Fa . . . ther?

MISS ALICE

Poor Julian. *(To the* LAWYER*)* You did not have to do that;
I could have made him stay.

LAWYER

Perhaps. But what does it matter . . . one man . . . in the
face of so much.

JULIAN

Fa . . . ther?

BUTLER *(Going to* JULIAN*)*

Let me look.

MISS ALICE
(Starting to go to him)

Oh, poor JULIAN . . .

LAWYER *(Stopping her)*

Stay where you are.
(BUTLER *goes to* JULIAN *while the others keep their
places.* BUTLER *bends over him, maybe pulling his
head back)*

BUTLER

Do you want a doctor for him?

LAWYER *(After a tiny pause)*

Why?

BUTLER *(Straightening up)*

Because . . .

LAWYER

Yes?

BUTLER *(Quite matter-of-fact)*
Because he will bleed to death without attention?

JULIAN *(To the* CARDINAL*)*
Help . . . me?
(In answer, the CARDINAL *looks back to the* LAWYER,
asking a question with his silence)

LAWYER *(After a pause)*
No doctor.

BUTLER *(Moving away)*
No doctor.

MISS ALICE
(To the LAWYER; *great sadness)*
No?

LAWYER *(Some compassion)*
No.

JULIAN
Father!

CARDINAL *(Anguished)*
Please, Julian.

JULIAN
(Anger through the pain)
In the sight of God? You dare?

LAWYER
Or in the sight of man. He dares. *(Moves to the table, putting*

the gun away, taking up the briefcase)

JULIAN *(Again)*

You dare!?

(BUTLER goes to cover something)

LAWYER
(Taking the briefcase to the CARDINAL)
There it is, all of it. All legal now, the total grant: two billion,
kid, twenty years of grace for no work at all; no labor . . .
at least not yours. *(Holds the briefcase out)* There . . . take
it.

CARDINAL
We do not . . . fetch and carry. And have not acquiesced
. . . *(Indicates briefcase)* For *this.*

JULIAN *(Weak again)*

Father?

LAWYER

Not God's errand boy?

CARDINAL

God's; not yours.

LAWYER

Who are the Gods?

JULIAN *(Pain)*

God in heaven!

MISS ALICE

Poor Julian!
(Goes to him; they create something of a Pietà)
Rest back; lean on me.

LAWYER
(Withdrawing his offer of the briefcase)
Perhaps your *new* secretary can pick it up. You *will* go on,
won't you—red gown and amethyst, until the pelvic cancer
comes, or the coronary blacks it out, all of it? The good with
it, and the evil? *(Indicates* JULIAN*)* Even this? In the final
mercy?

> *(The* CARDINAL *looks straight ahead of him for a mo-
> ment, hesitates, then walks out, looking neither left
> nor right)*

BUTLER
*(Calling after him, halfhearted and intentionally too
late)*
Any of the cars will do . . . *(Trailing off)* . . . as they're all
hired.

JULIAN
Who . . . who left? Who!

MISS ALICE *(Comforting him)*
You're shivering, Julian . . . *so.*

JULIAN *(Almost a laugh)*
Am I?

LAWYER
(Still looking after the departed CARDINAL*)*
Once, when I was at school—our departed reminds me—
once, when I was at school, I was writing poetry—well, no,
poems, which were published in the literary magazine. And
each issue a teacher from the English Department would
criticize the work in the school newspaper a week or two
hence.

MISS ALICE *(To* JULIAN*)*
A blanket?

JULIAN

No. Hold close.

LAWYER

And one teacher, who was a wag and was, as well, a former student, wrote of one of my poems—a sonnet, as I recall—that it had all the grace of a walking crow.

MISS ALICE *(Ibid.)*

I don't want to hurt.

JULIAN

Closer . . . please. Warmth.

LAWYER

I was green in those years, and, besides, I could not recall how crows walked.

MISS ALICE *(Ibid.)*

How like a little boy you are.

JULIAN

I'm lonely.

LAWYER

Could not recall that I had ever *seen* a crow . . . walking.

MISS ALICE

Is being afraid always the same—no matter the circumstances, the age?

JULIAN

It is the attic room, always; the closet. Hold close.

LAWYER

(Fully aware of the counterpoint by now, aiding it)

And so I went to see him—the wag—about the walking crow

. . . the poem, actually.

BUTLER
(Putting a cover on something)

Crows don't walk much . . .

JULIAN

. . . and it is very dark; always. And no one will come . . . for the longest time.

MISS ALICE

Yes.

LAWYER

Yes; that is what he said—sitting with his back against all the books, "Crows don't walk much . . . if they can help it . . . if they can fly."

JULIAN

No. No one will come.

BUTLER (Snapping open a cover)

I could have told you that; surprised you didn't know it. Crows walk around a lot only when they're sick.

LAWYER

"Santayanian finesse."

JULIAN

No one will come . . . for the longest time; if ever.

MISS ALICE (Agreeing)

No.

LAWYER

That was the particular thing: "Santayanian finesse." He said that had . . . all the grace of a walking crow.

BUTLER
(*Rubbing something for dust*)
Bright man.

LAWYER (*To* BUTLER)
I don't know; he stayed on some years after I left—after our
walking bird and I left—then went on to some other school.
. . . (*To* MISS ALICE, *immediately*) Are you ready to go?

MISS ALICE
(*Looking up; sad irony*)
Am I ready to go on with it, do you mean? To move to the
city now before the train trip south? The private car? The
house on the ocean, the . . . same mysteries, the evasions,
the perfect plotting? The removed residence, the Rolls twice
weekly into the shopping strip . . . all of it?

LAWYER
Yes. All of it.

MISS ALICE
(*Looks to* JULIAN, *considers a moment*)
Are you warm now?

JULIAN
Yes . . . and cold.

MISS ALICE
(*Looks up to the* LAWYER, *smiles faintly*)
No.

LAWYER
Then get up and come along.

MISS ALICE (*To the* LAWYER)
And all the rest of it?

LAWYER

Yes.

MISS ALICE

The years of it . . . to go on? For how long?

LAWYER

Until we are replaced.

MISS ALICE
(With a tiny, tinkling laugh)

Oh God.

LAWYER

Or until everything is desert *(Shrugs)* . . . on the chance that *it* runs out before *we* do.

BUTLER
(Examining the phrenological head)

I have never even examined phrenology.

LAWYER

But more likely till we are replaced.

JULIAN
(With a sort of quiet wonder)

I am cold at the core . . . where it burns most.

MISS ALICE *(Sad truth)*

Yes. *(Then to the* LAWYER*)* Yes.

LAWYER *(Almost affectionately)*

So, come now; gather yourself.

MISS ALICE *(Restrained pleading)*

But, he is still . . . ill . . .

J U L I A N
(To MISS ALICE, *probably, but not* at *her)*
You wish to go away now?

M I S S A L I C E *(To the* LAWYER*)*
You see how he takes to me? You see how it *is* natural? Poor
Julian.

L A W Y E R
Let's go.

M I S S A L I C E *(To* JULIAN*)*
I *must* go away from you now; it is not that I wish to. *(To*
BUTLER*)* Butler, I have left my wig, it is upstairs . . .

B U T L E R *(Rather testy)*
I'm sorry, I'm covering, I'm busy.

L A W Y E R *(Turning to go)*
Let me; it's such a pretty wig, becomes you so. And there are
one or two other things I'd like to check.

M I S S A L I C E *(Sad smile)*
The pillowcases? Put your ear against them? To eavesdrop?
Or the sheets? To see if they're still writhing?
(The LAWYER *almost says something, thinks better
of it, exits)*
Poor Julian.

B U T L E R
Then we all are to be together.

M I S S A L I C E *(Small laugh)*
Oh God, you heard him: forever.

BUTLER

I like it where it's warm.

MISS ALICE

I dreaded once, when I was in my teens, that I would grow
old, look back, over the precipice, and discover that I had
not lived my life. (*Short abrupt laugh*) Oh Lord!

JULIAN
(*Now a semi-coma, almost sweet*)
How long wilt thou forget me, O Lord? Forever?

BUTLER

We live *some*thing.

MISS ALICE

Yes.

JULIAN

How long wilt thou hide thy face from me?

BUTLER (*To* JULIAN)

Psalm Thirteen.

MISS ALICE (*To* JULIAN)

Yes?

JULIAN

Yes.

BUTLER

How long shall my enemy be exalted over me?

JULIAN

Yes.

MISS ALICE

Not long.

BUTLER *(Looking at a cover)*

Consider and hear me, O Lord, my God.

JULIAN

What does it mean if the pain . . . ebbs?

BUTLER *(Considered; kindly)*

It means the agony is less.

MISS ALICE

Yes.

JULIAN *(Rueful laugh)*

Consciousness, then, is pain. *(Looks up at* MISS ALICE*)* All disappointments, all treacheries. *(Ironic laugh)* Oh, God.

BUTLER

Why are we taking separate cars, then?

MISS ALICE

Well, I might ride rubbing hips on either side with a different lover, bouncing along, but . . . Alice, Miss Alice would not. *(Pause)* Would I? I would not do that. She.

BUTLER

I love you . . . not her. Or . . . quite differently.

MISS ALICE

Shhhh . . .

BUTLER

For ages, *I* look at the sheets, listen to the pillowcases, when they're brought down, sidle into the laundry room . . .

MISS ALICE

Don't.

(JULIAN *makes a sound of great pain*)

Oh! . . . Oh! . . .

JULIAN

(*Commenting on the pain*)

Dear . . . God . . . in . . . heaven . . .

MISS ALICE

Calm; be calm now.

BUTLER (*Wistful*)

But you pass through everyone, everything . . . touching just
briefly, lightly, passing.

MISS ALICE

My poor Julian. (*To the model*) Receive him? Take him in?

JULIAN (*A little boy, scared*)

Who are you talking to?

MISS ALICE (*Breathing it*)

Alice . . .

JULIAN

Alice? Ah.

BUTLER

Will we be coming back . . . when the weather changes?

MISS ALICE (*Triste*)

Probably.

JULIAN

(*Confirming the previous exchange*)

Alice?

MISS ALICE

Yes.

JULIAN

Ah.

BUTLER
(Understanding what he has been told)

Ah.

(The LAWYER *enters with* MISS ALICE'S *wig)*

LAWYER

Bed stripped, mothballs lying on it like hailstones; no sound, movement, nothing.
(Puts the wig on the phrenological head)
Do you want company, Julian? Do you want a friend? *(To* MISS ALICE*)* Looks nice there. Leave it; we'll get you another. Are you ready to go?

MISS ALICE *(Weary)*

You want me to go now?

LAWYER *(Correcting her)*

Come.

MISS ALICE

Yes. *(Begins to disengage herself)* Butler, come help me; we can't leave Julian just . . .

BUTLER

Yes. *(Moves to help her)*

JULIAN
(As they take him by the arm)

Don't do that!

MISS ALICE

Julian, we must move you . . .

JULIAN

Don't.

LAWYER *(Without emotion)*

Leave him where he is.

JULIAN

Leave me . . . be.
(*He slides along the floor, backing up against the*
model)
Leave me . . . where I am.

LAWYER

Good pose: leave him there.

BUTLER
(*Getting a chair cushion*)

Cushion.

JULIAN

All . . . hurts.

BUTLER
(*Putting the cushion behind him*)

Easy . . .

JULIAN

ALL HURTS!!

MISS ALICE *(Coming to him)*

Oh, my poor Julian . . .

JULIAN
(*Surprisingly strong, angry*)

LEAVE ME!
(MISS ALICE *considers a moment, turns, leaves*)

LAWYER
(*Walks over to* JULIAN, *regards him; almost casually*)

Goodbye.

JULIAN
(*Softly, but a malediction*)

Instrument!

LAWYER
(*Turns on his heel, walks out, saying as he goes*)

Butler?

(*Exits*)

BUTLER
(*As* LAWYER *goes; abstracted*)

Yes . . . dear.

JULIAN
(*Half laughed, pained incredulity*)

Good . . . bye!

BUTLER *(Looks about the room)*

All in order, I think.

JULIAN *(Wistful)*

Help me?

BUTLER

My work done.

JULIAN

No?

> (BUTLER *regards* JULIAN *for a moment, then walks over, bends, kisses* JULIAN *on the forehead, not a quick kiss*)

BUTLER

Goodbye, dear Julian.
> (*As* BUTLER *exits, he closes the doors behind him*)

JULIAN
(Alone, for a moment, then, whispered)

Goodbye, dear Julian. *(Pause)* Exit . . . all. *(Softly)* Help me . . . come back, help me. *(Pause)* HELP ME! *(Pause)* No . . . no help. Kiss. A kiss goodbye, from . . . whom? . . . Oh. From, from one . . . an . . . arms: around me; warming. COME BACK AND HELP ME. *(Pause)* If only to stay *with* me, while it . . . *if* . . . while it happens. For . . . you, you would not have left me if it . . . were not . . . would you? No. *(Calling to them)* I HAVE NEVER DREAMED OF IT. NEVER . . . IMAGINED . . . *(To himself again)* what it would be like. *(As if they were near the door)* I died once, when I was little . . . almost, running, fell past jagged iron, noticed . . . only when I . . . tried to get up, that my leg, left, was torn . . . the whole thigh *and* calf . . . down. Such . . . *searing* . . . pain? Sweet smell of blood, screaming at the sight of it, so *far* . . . away from the house, and in the field, all hot . . . and yellow, white in the sun. COME BACK TO ME. Sunday, and my parents off . . . somewhere, only my grandfather, and he . . . OFF: SOMEWHERE: mousing with the dog. All the way down . . . bone, flesh, meat, moving. Help me, Grandfather! "Ere I die, ere life ebbs." *(Laughs softly)* Oh, Christ. *(Little boy)* Grandfather? Mousing? Come to me: Julian bleeds, leg torn, from short pants to shoe, bone, meat open to the sun; come to him. *(Looks at the model, above and behind him)* Ahhhh. Will no one come? *(Looks at the ceiling)* High; high walls . . . summit. *(Eyes on his leg)* Belly . . . not leg. Come, grandfather! Not leg, belly! Doublebutton. Pinpoint, searing . . . pain? "If you . . . if you die." Are you sleeping, not mousing? Sleeping on the sunporch? Hammocking? Yes. "If I die before *you* wake, will the Lord deign *your* soul take?" Grandfather? *(Cry of pain, then)* Oh . . . GOD! "I come to thee, in agony." *(Cry to the void)* HELP . . . ME! *(Pause)* No help. Stitch it up like a wineskin! Hold the wine in. Stitch it up. *(Sweet reminiscence)* And every day, put him in the sun, quarter over, for the whole stitched leg . . . to bake, in the healing sun. Green? Yes, a little, but that's the medicine. And keep him out of the fields, chuckle, chuckle. And every day, swinging in the sun, baking; good. Aching all the while, but good. The cat comes, sniffs it, won't stay. Finally . . . stays; lies in the bend, doubling it, purring, breathing, soaking in the sun, as the leg throbs, aches, heals. "How will I know thee, O Lord, when I am in thy sight? How will I know thee?" By my *faith*. Ah, I see. *(Furious, shouting at the roof)* BY FAITH? THE FAITH I HAVE SHOWN THEE? BENT MYSELF? What may we avoid! Not birth! Growing up? Yes. Maturing? Oh, *God!* Growing old, and? . . . yes, growing old; but not the last; merely when. *(Sweet singsong)* But to live again, be born once more, sure in the sight of . . . *(Shouts again)* THERE IS NO ONE! *(Turns his head toward the closed doors, sadly)* Unless you are listening there. Unless you have left me, tiptoed off some, stood whispering, smothered giggles, and . . . silently returned, your ears pressed against, or . . . or one eye into the crack so that the air smarts it sifting through. HAVE YOU COME BACK? HAVE YOU NOT LEFT ME? *(Pause)* No. No one. Out in the night . . . nothing. Night? No; what then? IS IT NIGHT . . . OR DAY? *(Great weariness)* Or does it matter? No. How long wilt thou forget me, O Lord? Forever? How long wilt thou hide thy face from me? How long shall my enemy . . . I . . . can . . . barely . . . feel. Which is a sign. A change, at any rate. *(To the rooftops again)* I DO NOT UNDERSTAND, O LORD, MY GOD, WHAT THOU WILT HAVE OF ME! *(More conversational)* I have never dreamed of it, never imagined what it would be like. I have—oh, yes—dwelt *(Laughs at the word)* . . . dwelt . . . on the *fact* of it, the . . . principle, but I have not imagined dying. Death . . . yes. Not being, but not the act of . . . dying? ALICE!? *(Laughs softly)* Oh, Alice, why hast *thou* forsaken me? *(Leans his head back to see the model)* Hast thou? Alice? *Hast* thou forsaken me . . . with . . . all the others? *(Laughs again)* Come bring me my slippers and my pipe, and push the dog into the room. Bring me my slippers, the sacramental wine, *(Little boy)* my cookie? *(Usual again)* . . . come bring me my ease, come sit with me . . .

and watch me as I die. Alice? ALICE!? (*To himself*) There is
nothing; there is no one. (*Wheedling a little*) Come talk to
me; come sit by my right hand . . . *on* the one hand . . .
come sit with me and hold my . . . what? Then come and
talk; tell me how it goes, Alice. (*Laughs*) "Raise high the
roofbeam, for the bridegroom comes." Oh, what a priesthood
is this! Oh, what a range of duties, and such parishioners, and
such a chapel for my praise. (*Turns some, leans toward the
model, where the chapel light shines*) Oh, what a priesthood,
see my chapel, how it . . .

> (*Suddenly the light in the chapel in the model goes
> out.* JULIAN *starts, makes a sound of surprise and
> fear*)

Alice? . . . God? SOMEONE? Come to Julian as he . . . ebbs.
(*We begin to hear it now, faintly at first, slowly
growing, so faintly at first it is subliminal: the
heartbeat . . . thump* thump . . . *thump* thump
. . . *And the breathing . . . the intake taking one
thump-thump, the exhaling the next.* JULIAN *neither
senses nor hears it yet, however*)
Come, comfort him, warm him. He has not been a willful
man . . . Oh, willful in his . . . cry to serve, but gentle,
would not cause pain, but bear it, *would* bear it . . . has,
even. Not much, I suppose. One man's share is not . . . another's burden. (*Notices the wig on the phrenological head;
crawls a bit toward it; half kneels in front of it*) Thou art my
bride? Thou? For thee have I done my life? Grown to love,
entered in, bent . . . accepted? For thee? Is that the . . .
awful humor? Art thou the true arms, when the warm flesh
I touched . . . rested against, was . . . nothing? And *she*
. . . was not real? Is thy stare the true look? Unblinking,
outward, through, to some horizon? And her eyes . . . warm,
accepting, were they . . . not real? Art thou my bride? (*To
the ceiling again*) Ah God! Is that the humor? THE ABSTRACT?
. . . REAL? THE REST? . . . FALSE? (*To himself, with terrible
irony*) It is what I have wanted, have insisted on. Have nagged
. . . for. (*Looking about the room, raging*) IS THIS MY PRIEST-

HOOD, THEN? THIS WORLD? THEN COME AND SHOW THYSELF!
BRIDE? GOD?

(*Silence; we hear the heartbeats and the breathing
some*)

SHOW THYSELF! I DEMAND THEE! (JULIAN *crawls back toward
the model; faces it, back to the audience, addresses it*) SHOW
THYSELF! FOR THEE I HAVE GAMBLED . . . MY SOUL? I DEMAND
THY PRESENCE. ALICE!

(*The sounds become louder now, as, in the model,
the light fades in the bedroom, begins to move across
an upper story.* JULIAN's *reaction is a muffled cry*)

AGHHH! (*On his hands and knees he backs off a little from the
model, still staring at it*) You . . . thou . . . art . . . coming to me? (*Frightened and angry*) ABSTRACTION? . . . AB-
STRACTION! . . . (*Sad, defeated*) Art coming to me. (*A shivered
prayer, quick*) How long wilt thou forget me, O Lord? Forever? How long wilt thou hide thy face from me? . . . Consider and hear me, O Lord, my God. (*Shouted now*) CONSIDER
AND HEAR ME, O LORD, MY GOD. LIGHTEN MY EYES LEST I SLEEP
THE SLEEP OF DEATH.

(*The lights keep moving; the sounds become louder*)

BUT I HAVE TRUSTED IN THY MERCY, O LORD. HOW LONG WILT
THOU FORGET ME? (*Softly, whining*) How long wilt thou hide
thy face from me? COME, BRIDE! COME, GOD! COME!

(*The breathing and heartbeats are much, much
louder now. The lights descend a stairway in the
model.* JULIAN *turns, backs against the model, his
arms way to the side of him*)

Alice? (*Fear and trembling*) Alice? ALICE? MY GOD, WHY HAST
THOU FORSAKEN ME?

(*A great shadow, or darkening, fills the stage; it is
the shadow of a great presence filling the room. The
area on* JULIAN *and around him stays in some light,
but, for the rest, it is as if ink were moving through
paper toward a focal point. The sounds become enormous.* JULIAN *is aware of the presence in the room,
"sees" it, in the sense that his eyes, his head move to*

all areas of the room, noticing his engulfment. He
almost-whispers loudly)
The bridegroom waits for thee, my Alice . . . is thine. O
Lord, my God, I have awaited thee, have served thee in thy
. . . ALICE? *(His arms are wide, should resemble a crucifixion.*
With his hands on the model, he will raise his body some,
backed full up against it) ALICE? . . . GOD?
          (The sounds are deafening. JULIAN *smiles faintly)*
I accept thee, Alice, for thou art come to me. God, Alice
. . . I accept thy will.
          (Sounds continue. JULIAN *dies, head bows, body re-*
          laxes some, arms stay wide in the crucifixion. Sounds
          continue thusly: thrice after the death . . . thump
          thump *thump* thump *thump* thump. *Absolute si-*
          lence for two beats. The lights on JULIAN *fade slowly*
          to black. Only then, when all is black, does the cur-
          tain slowly fall)

A Delicate Balance

FOR

JOHN STEINBECK

AFFECTION AND ADMIRATION

FIRST PERFORMANCE

September 12, 1966, New York City, Martin Beck Theatre

JESSICA TANDY *as* AGNES

HUME CRONYN *as* TOBIAS

ROSEMARY MURPHY *as* CLAIRE

CARMEN MATHEWS *as* EDNA

HENDERSON FORSYTHE *as* HARRY

MARIAN SELDES *as* JULIA

Directed by ALAN SCHNEIDER

THE PLAYERS

AGNES
A handsome woman in her late 50's

TOBIAS
Her husband, a few years older

CLAIRE
Agnes' sister, several years younger

JULIA
Agnes' and Tobias' daughter, 36, angular

EDNA AND HARRY
Very much like Agnes and Tobias

THE SCENE

The living room of a large and well-appointed suburban house. Now.

ACT ONE

(In the library-livingroom. AGNES *in a chair,* TOBIAS *at a shelf, looking into cordial bottles)*

AGNES

(Speaks usually softly, with a tiny hint of a smile on her face: not sardonic, not sad . . . wistful, maybe)
What I find most astonishing—aside from that belief of mine, which never ceases to surprise me by the very fact of its surprising lack of unpleasantness, the belief that I might very easily—as they say—lose my mind one day, not that I suspect I am about to, or am even . . . nearby . . .

TOBIAS

(He speaks somewhat the same way)
There is no saner woman on earth, Agnes.
(Putters at the bottles)

AGNES

. . . for I'm not that sort; merely that it is not beyond . . . happening: some gentle loosening of the moorings sending the balloon adrift—and I think that is the only outweighing thing: adrift; the . . . becoming a stranger in . . . the world, quite . . . uninvolved, for I never see it as violent, only a drifting—what are you looking for, Tobias?

TOBIAS

We will all go mad before you. The anisette.

AGNES

(A small happy laugh)
Thank you, darling. But I could never do it—go adrift—for

what would become of you? Still, what I find most astonishing, aside, as I said, from that speculation—and I wonder,
too, sometimes, if I am the only one of you to admit to it:
not that *I* may go mad, but that each of you wonders if each
of *you* might not—why on earth do you want anisette?

TOBIAS
(Considers)
I thought it might be nice.

AGNES
(Wrinkles her nose)
Sticky. I will do cognac. It is supposed to be healthy—the
speculation, or the assumption, I suppose, that if it occurs to
you that you might be, then you are not; but I've never been
much comforted by it; it follows, to my mind, that since I
speculate I might, some day, or early evening I think more
likely—some autumn dusk—go quite mad, then I very well
might.
(Bright laugh)
Some autumn dusk: Tobias at his desk, looks up from all
those awful bills, and sees his Agnes, mad as a hatter, chew-
ing the ribbons on her dress. . . .

TOBIAS
(Pouring)
Cognac?

AGNES
Yes; Agnes Sit-by-the-fire, her mouth full of ribbons, her
mind aloft, adrift; nothing to do with the poor old thing
but put her in a bin somewhere, sell the house, move to
Tucson, say, and pine in the good sun, and live to be a hun-
dred and four.
(He gives her her cognac)
Thank you, darling.

TOBIAS
(Kisses her forehead)
Cognac is sticky, too.

AGNES
Yes, but it's nicer. Sit by me, hm?

TOBIAS
(Does so; raises his glass)
To my mad lady, ribbons dangling.

AGNES
(Smiles)
And, of course, I haven't worn the ribbon dress since Julia's
remarriage. Are you comfortable?

TOBIAS
For a little.

AGNES
What astonishes me most—aside from my theoretically
healthy fear—no, not fear, how silly of me—healthy speculation that I might some day become an embarrassment to you
. . . what I find most astonishing in this world, and with all
my years . . . is Claire.

TOBIAS
(Curious)
Claire? Why?

AGNES
That anyone—be they one's sister, or not—can be so . . .
well, I don't want to use an unkind word, 'cause we're cozy
here, aren't we?

TOBIAS
(Smiled warning)
Maybe.

AGNES

As the saying has it, the one thing sharper than a serpent's tooth is a sister's ingratitude.

TOBIAS
(Getting up, moving to a chair)
The saying does not have it that way.

AGNES

Should. Why are you moving?

TOBIAS

It's getting uncomfortable.

AGNES
(Semi-serious razzing)
Things get hot, move off, huh? Yes?

TOBIAS
(Not rising to it)
I'm not as young as either of us once was.

AGNES
(Toasting him)
I'm as young as the day I married you—though I'm certain I don't look it—because you're a very good husband . . . most of the time. But I was talking about Claire, or was beginning to.

TOBIAS
(Knowing shaking of the head)
Yes, you were.

AGNES

If I were to list the mountain of my burdens—if I had a thick pad and a month to spare—that bending my shoulders *most*, with the possible exception of Julia's trouble with marriage, would be your—it must be instinctive, I think, or *reflex*, that's more like it—your reflex defense of everything that Claire . . .

TOBIAS
(Very nice, but there is steel underneath)
Stop it, Agnes.

AGNES
(A little laugh)
Are you going to throw something at me? Your glass? My goodness, I hope not . . . that awful anisette all over everything.

TOBIAS
(Patient)
No.

AGNES
(Quietly daring him)
What then?

TOBIAS
(Looking at his hand)
I shall sit very quietly . . .

AGNES
. . . as always . . .

TOBIAS
. . . yes, and I shall will you to apologize to your sister for what I must in truth tell you I thought a most . . .

AGNES
Apologize! To her? To Claire? I have spent my adult life apologizing *for* her; I will not double my humiliation by apologizing *to* her.

TOBIAS
(*Mocking an epigram*)
One does not apologize to those for whom one must?

AGNES
(*Winking slowly*)
Neat.

TOBIAS
Succinct, but one of the rules of an aphorism . . .

AGNES
An epigram, I thought.

TOBIAS
(*Small smile*)
An epigram is usually satiric, and you . . .

AGNES
. . . and I am grimly serious. Yes?

TOBIAS
I fear so.

AGNES
To revert specifically from Claire to . . . her effect, what
would you do were I to . . . spill my marbles?

TOBIAS
(*Shrugs*)
Put you in a bin somewhere, sell the house and move to
Tucson. Pine in the hot sun and live forever.

AGNES
(*Ponders it*)
Hmmm, I bet you would.

TOBIAS
(*Friendly*)
Hurry, though.

AGNES

Oh, I'll *try*. It won't be simple paranoia, though, I know
that. I've tried so hard, to . . . well, you know how little I
vary; goodness, I can't even raise my voice except in the most
calamitous of events, and I find that both joy and sorrow
work their . . . wonders on me more . . . evenly, slowly,
with*in*, than most: a suntan rather than a scalding. There
are no mountains in my life . . . nor chasms. It is a rolling,
pleasant land . . . verdant, my darling, thank you.

TOBIAS
(*Cutting a cigar*)
We do what we can.

AGNES
(*Little laugh*)
Our motto. If we should ever go downhill, have a crest made,
join things, we must have that put in Latin—We do what
we can—on your blazers, over the mantel; maybe we could
do it on the linen, as well. . . .

TOBIAS
Do you think I should go to Claire's room?

AGNES
(*Silence: then stony, firm*)
No.

(TOBIAS *shrugs, lights his cigar*)
Either she will be down, or not.

TOBIAS
We do what we can?

AGNES
Of course.
(*Silence*)
So, it will not be simple paranoia. Schizophrenia, on the

other hand, is far more likely—even given the unlikelihood.
I believe it can be chemically induced . . .
(Smiles)
if all else should fail; if sanity, such as it is, should become
too much. There are times when I think it would be so . . .
proper, if one could take a pill—or even inject—just . . .
remove.

TOBIAS
(Fairly dry)
You should take drugs, my dear.

AGNES
Ah, but those are temporary; even addiction is a repeated
temporary . . . stilling. I am concerned with peace . . . not
mere relief. And I am not a compulsive—like . . . like some
. . . like our dear Claire, say.

TOBIAS
Be kind. Please?

AGNES
I think I should want to have it fully . . . even on the
chance I could not . . . come back. Wouldn't that be terrible, though? To have done it, induced, if naturally looked
unlikely and the hope was there?
(Wonder in her voice)
Not be able to come back? Why did you put my cognac in
the tiny glass?

TOBIAS
(Rising, going to her)
Oh . . . I'm sorry. . . .

AGNES
(Holding her glass out to him; he takes it from her)
I'm not a sipper tonight; I'm a breather: my nose buried in
the glass, all the wonder there, and very silent.

TOBIAS
(Getting her a new cognac)
I thought Claire was much better tonight. I didn't see any
need for you to give her such a going-over.

AGNES
(Weary)
Claire was *not* better tonight. Honestly, Tobias!

TOBIAS
(Clinging to his conviction)
I thought she was.

AGNES
(Putting an end to it)
Well, she was *not*.

TOBIAS
Still . . .

AGNES
(Taking her new drink)
Thank you. I have decided, all things considered, that I shall
not induce, that all the years we have put up with each other's wiles and crotchets have earned us each other's company.
And I promise you as well that I shall think good thoughts—
healthy ones, positive—to ward off madness, should it come
by . . . uninvited.

TOBIAS
(Smiles)
You mean I have no hope of Tucson?

AGNES
None.

TOBIAS
(Mock sadness)

Hélas . . .

AGNES

You have hope, only, of growing even older than you are in
the company of your steady wife, your alcoholic sister-in-law
and occasional visits . . . from our melancholy Julia.
(A little sad)
That is what you have, my dear Tobias. Will it do?

TOBIAS
(A little sad, too, but warmth)

It will do.

AGNES
(Happy)

I've never doubted that it would.
(Hears something, says sourly)
Hark.
(CLAIRE has entered)
Did I hear someone?

TOBIAS
*(Sees CLAIRE standing, uncomfortably, away from
them)*
Ah, there you are. I said to Agnes just a moment ago . . .

CLAIRE
*(To AGNES' back, a rehearsed speech, gone through
but hated)*
I must apologize, Agnes; I'm . . . very sorry.

AGNES
(Not looking at her; mock surprise)
But what are you sorry *for*, Claire?

CLAIRE

I apologize that my nature is such to bring out in you the full force of your brutality.

TOBIAS
(To placate)
Look, now, I think we can do without any of this sort of . . .

AGNES
(Rises from her chair, proceeds toward exiting)
If you come to the dinner table unsteady, *if* when you try to say good evening and weren't the autumn colors lovely today you are nothing but vowels, and *if* one smells the vodka on you from across the room—and *don't* tell me again, *either* of you! that vodka leaves nothing on the breath: if you are expecting it, if you are sadly and wearily expecting it, it *does* —*if* these conditions exist . . . *persist* . . . then the reaction of one who is burdened by her love is not brutality— though it would be excused, believe me!—not brutality at all, but the souring side of love. If I scold, it is becaues I wish I needn't. If I am sharp, it is because I am neither less nor more than human, and if I am to be accused once again of making too much of things, let me remind you that it is my manner and not the matter. I apologize for being articulate. Tobias, I'm going to call Julia, I think. Is it one or two hours difference? . . . I can never recall.

TOBIAS
(Dry)
Three.

AGNES
Ah, yes. Well, be kind to Claire, dear. She is . . . injured.
(Exits. A brief silence)

TOBIAS

Ah, well.

CLAIRE

I have never known whether to applaud or cry. Or, rather, I never know which would be the more appreciated—expected.

TOBIAS
(Rather sadly)

You are a great damn fool.

CLAIRE
(Sadly)

Yes. Why is she calling Julia?

TOBIAS

Do you want a quick brandy before she comes back?

CLAIRE
(Laughs some)

Not at all; a public one. Fill the balloon half up, and I shall sip it ladylike, and when she . . . glides back in, I shall lie on the floor and balance the glass on my forehead. That will give her occasion for another paragraph, and your ineffectual stop-it-now's.

TOBIAS
(Pouring her brandy)

You *are* a great damn fool.

CLAIRE

Is Julia having another divorce?

TOBIAS

Hell, I don't know.

CLAIRE
(*Takes the glass*)
It's only your daughter. Thank you. I should imagine—from
all that I have . . . watched, that it is come-home time.
(*Offhand*)
Why don't you kill Agnes?

TOBIAS
(*Very offhand*)
Oh, no, I couldn't do that.

CLAIRE
Better still, why don't you wait till Julia separates and comes
back here, all sullen and confused, and take a gun and blow
all our heads off? . . . Agnes first—through respect, of course,
then poor Julia, and finally—if you have the kindness for
it—me?

TOBIAS
(*Kind, triste*)
Do you really want me to shoot you?

CLAIRE
I want you to shoot Agnes first. Then I'll think about it.

TOBIAS
But it would have to be an act of passion—out of my head,
and all that. I doubt I'd stand around with the gun smoking,
Julia locked in her room screaming, wait for you to decide if
you wanted it or not.

CLAIRE
But unless you kill Agnes . . . how shall I ever know whether
I want to live?
(*Incredulous*)
An act of passion!?

TOBIAS
(Rather hurt)

Well . . . yes.

CLAIRE
(Laughs)

Oh, my; that's funny.

TOBIAS
(Same)

I'm sorry.

CLAIRE
(Friendly laugh)

Oh, my darling Tobias, I'm sorry, but I just don't see you in
the role, that's all—outraged, maddened into action, pro-
ceeding by reflex . . . Can you see yourself, though? In front
of the judge? Predictable, stolid Tobias? "It all went blank,
your honor. One moment, there I was, deep in my chair,
drinking my . . ." What is that?

TOBIAS

Anisette.

CLAIRE

"Anisette." Really? Anisette?

TOBIAS
(Slightly edgy)

I like it.

CLAIRE
(Wrinkles her nose)

Sticky. "There I was, your honor, one moment in my chair,
sipping at my anisette . . . and the next thing I knew . . .
they were all lying about, different rooms, heads blown off,
the gun still in my hand. I . . . I have no recollection of it,
sir." Can you imagine that, Tobias?

Of course, with all of you dead, your brains lying around in the rugs, there'd be no one to say it *wasn't* an act of passion.

CLAIRE

Leave me till last. A breeze might rise and stir the ashes. . . .

TOBIAS

Who's that?

CLAIRE

No one, I think. Just sounds like it should be.

TOBIAS

Why don't you go back to your . . . thing . . . to your alcoholics thing?

CLAIRE
(Half serious)
Because I don't like the people. . . .

TOBIAS

What is it called?

CLAIRE

Anonymous.

TOBIAS

Yes; that. Why don't you go back?

CLAIRE
(Suddenly rather ugly)
Why don't you mind your own hooting business?

TOBIAS
(Offended)
I'm sorry, Claire.

CLAIRE
(Kisses at him)
Because.

TOBIAS
It was better.

CLAIRE
(Holds her glass out; he hesitates)
Be a good brother-in-law; it's only the first I'm not supposed
to have.

TOBIAS
(Pouring for her)
I thought it was better.

CLAIRE
Thank you.
*(Lies on the floor, balances glass on her forehead,
puts it beside her, etc.)*
You mean Agnes thought it was better.

TOBIAS
(Kindly, calmly)
No, I thought so too. That it would be.

CLAIRE
I told you: not our type; nothing in common with them.
When you used to go to business—before you became a
squire, parading around in jodhpurs, confusing the gardener . . .

TOBIAS
(Hurt)
I've never done any such thing.

CLAIRE

Before all that . . .
(Smiles, chuckles)
sweet Tobias . . . when you used to spend all your time in
town . . . with your business friends, your indistinguishable
if not necessarily similar friends . . . what did you have in
common with them?

TOBIAS

Well, uh . . . well, everything.
(Maybe slightly on the defensive, but more . . .
vague)
Our business; we all mixed well, were friends away from the
office, too . . . clubs, our . . . an, an environment, I guess.

CLAIRE

Unh-huh. But what did you have in common with them?
Even Harry: your very best friend . . . in all the world—as
far as you know; I mean, you haven't met everybody . . .
are you switching from anisette?

TOBIAS
(Pouring himself brandy)
Doesn't go for a long time. All right?

CLAIRE

Doesn't matter to *me*. Your very best friend . . . Tell me,
dear Tobias; what do you have in common with him? Hm?

TOBIAS
(Softly)

Please, Claire . . .

CLAIRE

What do you really have in common with your **very** best

friend . . . 'cept the coincidence of having cheated on your wives in the same summer with the same woman . . . girl . . . woman? What except that? And hardly a distinction. I believe she was upended that whole July.

TOBIAS
(Rather tight-mouthed)
If you'll forgive me, Claire, common practice is hardly . . .

CLAIRE
Poor girl, poor whatever-she-was that hot and very *wet* July.

(Hard)

The distinction would have been to have not: to have been the one or two of the very, very many and oh, God, similar who did not upend the poor . . . unfamiliar thing that dry and oh, so wet July.

TOBIAS
Please! Agnes!

CLAIRE
(Quieter)
Of course, you had the wanton only once, while Harry! Good friend Harry, I have it from the horse's mouth, was on top for good and keeps twice, with a third try not so hot in the gardener's shed, with the mulch, or whatever it is, and the orange pots. . . .

TOBIAS
(Quietly)
Shut your mouth.

CLAIRE
(Stands, faces TOBIAS; softly)
All right.

(Down again)

What was her name?

TOBIAS
(A little sad)

I don't remember.

CLAIRE
(Shrugs)

No matter; she's gone.

(Brighter)

Would you give friend Harry the shirt off your back, as they say?

TOBIAS
(Relieved to be on something else)

I *suppose* I would. He *is* my best friend.

CLAIRE
(Nicely)

How sad does that make you?

TOBIAS
(Looks at her for a moment, then)

Not much; some; not much.

CLAIRE

No one to listen to Bruckner with you; no one to tell you're sick of golf; no one to admit to that—now and then—you're suddenly frightened and you don't know why?

TOBIAS
(Mild surprise)

Frightened? No.

CLAIRE
(Pause; smile)

All right. Would you like to know what happened last time I climbed the stairs to the fancy alkie club, and why I've not gone back? What I have *not* in common with those people?

TOBIAS
(Not too enthusiastic)
Sure.

CLAIRE
(Chuckle)
Poor Tobias. "Sure." Light me a cigarette?
       (TOBIAS hesitates a moment, then lights her one)
That will give me everything.
       (He hands the lighted cigarette to her; she is still on
       the floor)
I need. A smoke, a sip and a good hard surface. Thank you.
              (Laughs a bit at that)

TOBIAS
(Standing over her)
Comfy?

CLAIRE
(Raises her two arms, one with the cigarette, the
other the brandy glass; it is a casual invitation. TO-
BIAS looks at her for a moment, moves a little away)
Very. Do you remember the spring I moved out, the time I
was *really* sick with the stuff: was drinking like the famous
fish? Was a source of great embarrassment? So that you and
Agnes set me up in the apartment near the station, and Agnes
was *so* good about coming to see me?
              (TOBIAS sighs heavily)
Sorry.

TOBIAS
(Pleading a little)
When will it all . . . just go in the past . . . forget itself?

CLAIRE
When all the defeats are done, admitted. When memory
takes over and corrects fact . . . makes it tolerable. When
Agnes lies on her deathbed.

TOBIAS

Do you know that Agnes has . . . such wonderful control I haven't seen her cry in . . . for the longest time . . . no matter what?

CLAIRE

Warn me when she's coming; I'll act drunk. Pretend you're very sick, Tobias, like you were with the stomach business, but pretend you feel your insides are all green, and stink, and mixed up, and your eyes hurt and you're half deaf and your brain keeps turning off, and you've got peripheral neuritis and you can hardly walk and you hate. You hate with the same green stinking sickness you feel your bowels have turned into . . . yourself, and *everybody*. Hate, and, oh, God!! you want love, l-o-v-e, so badly—comfort and snuggling is what you really mean, of course—but you hate, and you notice—with a sort of detachment that amuses you, you think—that you're more like an animal every day . . . you snarl, and *grab* for things, and hide things and forget where you hid them like not-very-bright dogs, and you wash less, prefer to *be* washed, and once or twice you've actually soiled your bed and laid in it because you can't get up . . . pretend all that. No, you don't like that, Tobias?

TOBIAS

I don't know why you want to . . .

CLAIRE

You want to know what it's like to be an alkie, don't you, boy?

TOBIAS
(Sad)

Sure.

CLAIRE

Pretend all that. So the guy you're spending your bottles with starts you going to the old A.A. And, you sit there at the alkie

club and watch the . . . better ones—not recovered, for once
an alkie, always, and you'd better remember it, or you're gone
the first time you pass a saloon—you watch the better ones
get up and tell their stories.

TOBIAS
(Wistful, triste)
Once you drop . . . you can come back up part way . . .
but never . . . really back again. Always . . . descent.

CLAIRE
(Gently, to a child)
Well, that's life, baby.

TOBIAS
You are a great, damn fool.

CLAIRE
But, I'm not an alcoholic. I am not now and never was.

TOBIAS
(Shaking his head)
All the promise . . . all the chance . . .

CLAIRE
It would be so much simpler if I were. An alcoholic.
(She will rise and re-enact during this)
So, one night, one month, sometime, I'd had one martini—
as a Test to see if I could—which, given my . . . stunning
self-discipline, had become three, and I felt . . . rather daring and nicely detached and a little bigger than life and not
snarling yet. So I marched, more or less straight, straight up
to the front of the room, hall, and faced my peers. And I
looked them over—all of them, trying so hard, grit and guilt
and failing and trying again and loss . . . and I had a moment's—sweeping—pity and disgust, and I almost cried, but
I didn't—like sister like sister, by God—and I heard myself

say, in my little-girl voice—and there were a lot of different me's by then—"I am a alcoholic."

(*Little-girl voice*)

"My name is Claire, and I am a alcoholic."

(*Directly to* TOBIAS)

You try it.

TOBIAS
(*Rather vague, but not babytalk*)

My name is . . . My name is Claire, and I am an alcoholic.

CLAIRE

A alcoholic.

TOBIAS
(*Vaguer*)

A alcoholic.

CLAIRE

"My name is Claire, and I am a . . . alcoholic." Now, I was supposed to go on, *you* know, say how bad I was, and didn't want to be, and How It Happened, and What I Wanted To Happen, and Would They Help Me Help Myself . . . but I just stood there for a . . . ten seconds maybe, and then I curtsied; I made my little-girl curtsy, and on my little-girl feet I padded back to my chair.

TOBIAS
(*After a pause; embarrassedly*)

Did they laugh at you?

CLAIRE

Well, an agnostic in the holy of holies doesn't get much camaraderie, a little patronizing, maybe. Oh, they were taken by the *vaude*ville, don't misunderstand me. But the one lady was nice. She came up to me later and said, "You've taken the first step, dear."

TOBIAS
(Hopeful)

That was nice of her.

CLAIRE
(Amused)

She didn't say the first step toward *what*, of course. Sanity, *in*sanity, revelation, self-deception. . . .

TOBIAS
(Not much help)

Change . . . sometimes . . . no matter what . . .

CLAIRE
(Cheerful laugh)

Count on you, Tobias . . . snappy phrase every time. But it *hooked* me—the applause, the stage presence . . . that beginning; no school tot had more gold stars for never missing class. I went; oh, God, I *did*.

TOBIAS

But stopped.

CLAIRE

Until I learned . . .
    (AGNES *enters, unobserved by either* TOBIAS *or* CLAIRE)
. . . and being a slow student in my young middle-age, slowly . . . that I was not, nor had ever been . . . a alcoholic . . . or an. Either. What I did not have in common with those people. That they were alcoholics, and I was not. That I was just a drunk. That they couldn't help it; I could, and wouldn't. That they were sick, and I was merely . . . willful.

AGNES

I have talked to Julia.

TOBIAS

Ah! How is she?

AGNES
(*Walking by* CLAIRE)
My, what an odd glass to put a soft drink in. Tobias, you have a quiet sense of humor, after all.

TOBIAS

Now, Agnes . . .

CLAIRE

He has not!

AGNES
(*Rather heavy-handed*)
Well, it *can't* be brandy; Tobias is a grown-up, and knows far better than to . . .

CLAIRE
(*Harsh, waving her glass*)
A toast to you, sweet sister; I drink your—not health; persistence—in good, hard brandy, *âge inconnu*.

AGNES
(*Quiet, tight smile, ignoring* CLAIRE)
It *would* serve you right, my dear Tobias, were I to go away, drift off. You would not have a woman left about you—only Claire and Julia . . . not even people; it would serve you right.

CLAIRE
(*Great mocking*)
But I'm not an alcoholic, baby!

TOBIAS

She . . . she can drink . . . a little.

AGNES

*(There is true passion here; we see under the calm
a little)*
I WILL NOT TOLERATE IT!! I WILL NOT HAVE YOU!
(Softer, but tight-lipped)
Oh, God. I wouldn't mind for a moment if you filled your
bathtub with it, lowered yourself in it, DROWNED! I rather wish
you would. It would give me the peace of mind to know you
could do something well, thoroughly. If you want to kill yourself—then do it *right!*

TOBIAS

Please, Agnes . . .

AGNES

What I cannot stand is the selfishness! Those of you who
want to die . . . and take your whole lives doing it.

CLAIRE

(Lazy, but with loathing under it)
Your wife is a perfectionist; they are *very* difficult to live with,
these people.

TOBIAS

(To AGNES, a little pleading in it)
She isn't an alcoholic . . . she says; she can drink some.

CLAIRE

(Little-child statement, but not babytalk)
I am not a alcoholic!

AGNES

We think that's very nice. We shall all rest easier to know
that it is willful; that the vomit and the tears, the muddy

mind, the falls and the absences, the cigarettes out on the tabletops, the calls from the club to come and get you please . . . that they are all . . . willful, that it *can* be helped.
(*Scathing, but softly*)
If you are not an alcoholic, you are beyond forgiveness.

CLAIRE
(*Ibid.*)
Well, I've been that for a long time, haven't I, sweetheart?

AGNES
(*Not looking at either of them*)
If we change for the worse with drink, we are an alcoholic. It is as simple as that.

CLAIRE

And who is to say!

AGNES

I!

CLAIRE
(*A litany*)
If we are to live here, on Tobias' charity, then we are subject to the will of his wife. If we were asked, at our father's dying . . .

AGNES
(*Final*)
Those are the ground rules.

CLAIRE
(*A sad smile*)

Tobias?

(*Pause*)

Nothing?

(Pause)

Are those the ground rules? Nothing? Too . . . settled? Too
. . . dried up? Gone?

(Nicely)

All right.

(Back to AGNES*)*

Very well, then, Agnes, you win. I shall be an alcoholic.

(The smile too sweet)

What are you going to do about it?

AGNES

(Regards CLAIRE *for a moment, then decides she—*
CLAIRE*—is not in the room with them.* AGNES *will
ignore* CLAIRE's *coming comments until otherwise
indicated.* TOBIAS *will do this, too, but uncomfortably, embarrassedly)*

Tobias, you will be unhappy to know it, I suppose, or of
mixed emotions, certainly, but Julia is coming home.

CLAIRE

(A brief laugh)

Naturally.

TOBIAS

Yes?

AGNES

She is leaving Douglas, which is no surprise to *me*.

TOBIAS

But, wasn't Julia happy? You didn't tell me anything
about . . .

AGNES

If Julia were happy, she would not be coming home. *I* don't
want her here, God knows. I mean she's welcome, of
course . . .

CLAIRE

Right on schedule, once every three years. . . .

AGNES

(Closes her eyes for a moment, to keep ignoring
CLAIRE*)*

. . . it *is* her home, we are her parents, the *two* of us, and we
have our obligations to her, and I have reached an age, Tobias,
when I wish we were always alone, you and I, without . . .
hangers-on . . . or anyone.

CLAIRE

(Cheerful but firm)

Well, I'm not going.

AGNES

. . . but if she and Doug are through—and I'm not suggest-
ing *she* is in the right—then her place is properly here, as for
some it is not.

CLAIRE

One, two, three, four, down they go.

TOBIAS

Well, I'd like to talk to Doug.

AGNES

(As if the opposite answer were expected from her)
I wish you would! If you had talked to Tom, or Charlie, yes!
even Charlie, or . . . uh . . .

CLAIRE

Phil?

AGNES

(No recognition of CLAIRE *helping her)*
. . . Phil, it might have done some good. If you've decided
to assert yourself, finally, too late, I imagine . . .

CLAIRE

Damned if you do, damned if you don't.

AGNES

. . . Julia might, at the very least, come to think her father cares, and that might be consolation—if not help.

TOBIAS

I'll . . . I'll talk to Doug.

CLAIRE

Why don't you invite him *here?* And while you're at it, bring the others along.

AGNES
(Some reproach)
And you might talk to Julia, too. You don't, very much.

TOBIAS

Yes.

CLAIRE
(A mocking sing-song)
Philip loved to gamble.
Charlie loved the boys,
Tom went after women,
Douglas . . .

AGNES
(Turning on CLAIRE*)*
Will you stop that?

CLAIRE

Ooh, I *am* here, after all. I exist!

AGNES

Why don't you go off on a vacation, Claire, now that Julia's coming home again? Why don't you go to Kentucky, or Tennessee, and visit the distilleries? Or why don't you lock yourself in your room, or find yourself a bar with an apartment in the back. . . .

CLAIRE

Or! Agnes; why don't you die?
(AGNES *and* CLAIRE *lock eyes, stay still*)

TOBIAS
(Not rising from his chair, talks more or less to himself)
If I saw some point to it, I might—if I saw some reason, chance. If I thought I might . . . break through to her, and say, "Julia . . . ," but then what would I say? "Julia . . ." Then, nothing.

AGNES
(Breaking eye contact with CLAIRE, *says, not looking at either)*
If we do not love someone . . . never have loved them . . .

TOBIAS
(Soft correction)
No; there can be silence, even having.

AGNES
(More curious than anything)
Do you really want me dead, Claire?

CLAIRE
Wish, yes. Want? I don't know; probably, though I might regret it if I had it.

AGNES
Remember the serpent's tooth, Tobias.

TOBIAS
(Recollection)

The cat that I had.

AGNES

Hm?

TOBIAS

The cat that I had . . . when I was—well, a year or so before I *met* you. She was very old; I'd had her since I was a
kid; she must have been fifteen, or more. An alley cat. She
didn't like people very much, I think; when people came
. . . she'd . . . pick up and walk away. She liked *me*; or,
rather, when I was alone with her I could see she was content; she'd sit on my lap. I don't know if she was happy, but
she was content.

AGNES

Yes.

TOBIAS

And how the thing happened I don't really know. She . . .
one day she . . . well, one day I realized she no longer liked
me. No, that's not right; one day I realized she must have
stopped liking me some time before. One evening I was alone,
home, and I was suddenly aware of her absence, not just that
she wasn't in the room with me, but that she hadn't been, in
rooms with me, watching me shave . . . just *about* . . . for
. . . and I couldn't place *how* long. She hadn't gone *away*,
you understand; well, she *had*, but she hadn't run off. I knew
she was *around*; I remembered I had caught sight of her—
from time to time—under a chair, moving out of a room, but
it was only when I realized something had happened that I
could give any pattern to things that had . . . that I'd noticed. She didn't like me any more. It was that simple.

CLAIRE

Well, she was old.

TOBIAS

No, it wasn't that. She didn't like me any more. I tried to force myself on her.

AGNES

Whatever do you mean?

TOBIAS

I'd close her in a room with me; I'd pick her up, and I'd *make* her sit in my lap; I'd make her stay there when she didn't want to. But it didn't work; she'd abide it, but she'd get down when she could, go away.

CLAIRE

Maybe she was ill.

TOBIAS

No, she wasn't; I had her to the vet. She didn't like me any more. One night—I was *fixed* on it now—I had her in the room with me, and on my lap for the . . . the what, the fifth time the same evening, and she lay there, with her back to me, and she wouldn't purr, and I *knew*: I knew she was just waiting till she could get down, and I said, "Damn you, you like me; God damn it, you stop this! I haven't *done* anything to you." And I shook her; I had my hands around her shoulders, and I shook her . . . and she bit me; hard; and she hissed at me. And so I hit her. With my open hand, I hit her, smack, right across the head. I . . . I *hated* her!

AGNES

Did you hurt her badly?

TOBIAS

Yes; well, not badly; she . . . I must have hurt her ear some; she shook her head a lot for a day or so. And . . . you see, there was no *reason*. She and I had lived together and been, well, you know, friends, and . . . there was no *reason*. And I hated her for that. I hated her, well, I suppose because I was

being accused of something, of . . . failing. But, I hadn't
been cruel, by design; if I'd been neglectful, well, my life was
. . . I resented it. I resented having a . . . being judged. Being *betrayed.*

CLAIRE

What did you do?

TOBIAS

I had *lived* with her; I had done . . . *everything.* And . . .
and if there was a, any responsibility I'd failed in . . . well
. . . there was nothing I could *do.* And, and I was being accused.

CLAIRE

Yes; what did you do?

TOBIAS
(Defiance and self-loathing)

I had her killed.

AGNES
(Kindly correcting)

You had her put to sleep. She was old. You had her put to
sleep.

TOBIAS
(Correcting)

I had her killed. I took her to the vet and he took her . . .
he took her into the back and
(Louder)
he gave her an injection and killed her! I had her *killed!*

AGNES
(After a pause)

Well, what else could you have done? There was nothing to
be done; there was no . . . meeting between you.

TOBIAS

I might have tried longer. I might have gone on, as long as cats live, the same way. I might have worn a hair shirt, locked myself in the house with her, done penance. For *something*. For *what*. God knows.

CLAIRE

You probably did the right *thing*. Distasteful alternatives; the less . . . ugly choice.

TOBIAS

Was it?

(A silence from them all)

AGNES

(Noticing the window)

Was that a car in the drive?

TOBIAS

"If we do not love someone . . . never have loved someone . . ."

CLAIRE

(An abrupt, brief laugh)

Oh, stop it! "Love" is not the problem. You love Agnes and Agnes loves Julia and Julia loves me and I love you. We all love each other; yes we do. We love each other.

TOBIAS

Yes?

CLAIRE

(Something of a sneer)

Yes; to the depths of our self-pity and our greed. What else but love?

TOBIAS

Error?

CLAIRE
(Laughs)
Quite possibly: love and error.
(There is a knock at the door; AGNES *answers it)*

AGNES
Edna? Harry? What a surprise! Tobias, it's Harry and Edna.
Come in. Why don't you take off your . . .
*(*HARRY *and* EDNA *enter. They seem somewhat ill at*
ease, strained for such close friends)

TOBIAS
Edna!

EDNA
Hello, Tobias.

HARRY
(Rubbing his hands; attempt at being bluff)
Well, now!

TOBIAS
Harry!

CLAIRE
(Too much surprise)
Edna!
(Imitates HARRY'S *gruff voice)*
Hello, there, Harry!

EDNA
Hello, dear Claire!
(A little timid)
Hello, Agnes.

HARRY
(Somewhat distant)
Evening . . . Claire.

AGNES
(Jumping in, just as a tiny silence commences)
Sit *down*. We were just having a cordial. . . .
(Curiously loud)
Have you been . . . out? Uh, to the club?

HARRY
(Is he ignoring AGNES' *question?)*
I like this room.

AGNES
To the club?

CLAIRE
(Exaggerated, but not unkind)
How's the old Harry?

HARRY
(Self-pity entering)
Pretty well, Claire, not as good as I'd like, but . . .

EDNA
Harry's been having his shortness of breath again.

HARRY
(Generally)
I can't breathe sometimes . . . for just a bit.

TOBIAS
(Joining them all)
Well, two sets of tennis, you know.

EDNA
(As if she can't remember something)
What have you done to the room, Agnes?

AGNES
(Looks around with a little apprehension, then relief)
Oh, the summer *things* are off.

EDNA

Of course.

AGNES
(Persisting in it, a strained smile)
Have you been to the club?

HARRY
(To TOBIAS*)*
I was talking to Edna, 'bout having our books done in leather;
bound.

TOBIAS

Oh? Yes?
(Brief silence)

CLAIRE
The question—'less I'm going deaf from all the alcohol—was
(Southern accent)
"Have you-all been to the club?"

AGNES
(Nervous, apologetic covering)
I wondered!

HARRY
(Hesitant)
Why . . . no, no.

EDNA
(Ibid.)
Why, why, no, Agnes. . . .

AGNES

I wondered, for I thought perhaps you'd dropped by here on
your way from there.

HARRY

. . . no, no . . .

AGNES

. . . or perhaps that we were having a party, and I'd lost a
day. . . .

HARRY

No, we were . . . just sitting home.

EDNA
(Some condolence)

Agnes.

HARRY
(Looking at his hands)

Just . . . sitting home.

AGNES
(Cheerful, but lack of anything better to say)

Well.

TOBIAS

Glad you're here! Party or not!

HARRY
(Relieved)

Good to see you, Tobias!

EDNA
(All smiles)

How is Julia?!

CLAIRE

Wrong question.
(*Lifts her glass*)
May I have some brandy, Tobias?

AGNES
(*A savage look to* CLAIRE, *back to* EDNA)
She's coming home . . . I'm afraid.

EDNA
(*Disappointment*)
Oh . . . not again!

TOBIAS
(*Getting* CLAIRE's *glass, attempted levity*)
Just can't keep that one married, I guess.

EDNA

Oh, Agnes, what a shame!

HARRY
(*More embarrassed than sorry*)
Gee, that's too bad.
(*Silence*)

CLAIRE

Why *did* you come?

AGNES

Please! Claire!
(*Back, reassuring*)
We're *glad* you're here; we're glad you came to surprise us!

TOBIAS
(*Quickly*)
Yes!
(HARRY *and* EDNA *exchanges glances*)

HARRY
(Quite sad and curious about it)
We were . . . sitting home . . . just sitting home. . . .

EDNA
Yes . . .

AGNES
(Mildly reproving)
We're *glad* to *see* you.

CLAIRE
(Eyes narrowing)
What happened, Harry?

AGNES
(Sharp)
Claire! Please!

TOBIAS
(Wincing a little, shaking his head)
Claire . . .

EDNA
(Reassuring him)
It's all right, Tobias.

AGNES
I don't see why people have to be questioned when they've
come for a friendly . . .

CLAIRE
(Small victory)
Harry wants to tell you, Sis.

EDNA
Harry?

HARRY

We . . . well, we were sitting home . . .

TOBIAS

Can I get you a drink, Harry?

HARRY
(Shakes his head)
. . . I . . . we thought about going to the club, but . . .
it's, it's so crowded on a Friday night . . .

EDNA
(Small voice, helpful, quiet)
. . . with the canasta party, and getting ready for the dance
tomorrow . . .

HARRY

. . . we didn't want to do that, and I've . . . been tired,
and we didn't want to do that . . .

EDNA

. . . Harry's been tired this whole week.

HARRY

. . . so we had dinner home, and thought we'd stay . . .

EDNA

. . . rest.

AGNES

Of course.

CLAIRE

Shhhhh.

AGNES
(Rather vicious)
I WILL NOT SHHHH!

HARRY

Please?

(Waits a moment)

TOBIAS
(Kind)

Go on, Harry.

HARRY

So we were sitting, and Edna was doing that—that panel
she works on . . .

EDNA
(Wistful, some loss)

. . . my needlepoint . . .

HARRY

. . . and I was reading my French; I've got it pretty good
now—not the accent, but the . . . the words.
(A brief silence)

CLAIRE
(Quietly)

And then?

HARRY
*(Looks over to her, a little dreamlike, as if he didn't
know where he was)*
Hmm?

CLAIRE
(Nicely)

And then?

HARRY
(Looks at EDNA*)*
I . . . I don't know quite what happened then; we . . . we
were . . . it was all very quiet, and we were all alone . . .

(EDNA *begins to weep, quietly;* AGNES *notices, the
others do not;* AGNES *does nothing*)
. . . and then . . . nothing happened, but . . .
(EDNA *is crying more openly now*)
. . . nothing at all happened, but . . .

EDNA
(*Open weeping; loud*)
WE GOT . . . FRIGHTENED.
(*Open sobbing; no one moves*)

HARRY
(*Quiet wonder, confusion*)
We got scared.

EDNA
(*Through her sobbing*)
WE WERE . . . FRIGHTENED.

HARRY
There was nothing . . . but we were very scared.
(AGNES *comforts* EDNA, *who is in free sobbing an-
guish.* CLAIRE *lies slowly back on the floor*)

EDNA
We . . . were . . . terrified.

HARRY
We were scared.
(*Silence;* AGNES *comforting* EDNA. HARRY *stock still.
Quite innocent, almost childlike*)
It was like being lost: very young again, with the dark, and
lost. There was no . . . thing . . . to be . . . frightened of,
but . . .

EDNA
(Tears; quiet hysteria)
WE WERE FRIGHTENED . . . AND THERE WAS NOTHING.
(Silence in the room)

HARRY
(Matter-of-fact, but a hint of daring under it)
We couldn't stay there, and so we came here. You're our very
best friends.

EDNA
(Crying softly now)
In the whole world.

AGNES
(Comforting, arms around her)
Now, now, Edna.

HARRY
(Apologizing some)
We couldn't go anywhere else, so we came here.

AGNES
(A deep breath, control)
Well, we'll . . . you did the right thing . . . of course.

TOBIAS
Sure.

EDNA
Can I go to bed now? Please?

AGNES
(Pause; then, not quite understanding)
Bed?

HARRY

We can't go back there.

EDNA

Please?

AGNES
(Distant)

Bed?

EDNA

I'm so . . . tired.

HARRY

You're our best friends in the world. Tobias?

TOBIAS
(A little bewilderment; rote)

Of course we are, Harry.

EDNA
(On her feet, moving)

Please?

(Cries a little again)

AGNES
(A million things going through her head, seeping
through management)

Of . . . of course you can. There's . . . there's Julia's room,
and . . .

(Arm around EDNA)

Come with me, dear.

(Reaches doorway; turns to TOBIAS; a question that
has no answer)

Tobias?

HARRY
(Rises, begins to follow EDNA, *rather automaton-like)*
Edna?

TOBIAS
(Confused)

Harry?

HARRY
(Shaking his head)
There was no one else we could go to.
(Exits after AGNES *and* EDNA. CLAIRE *sits up, watches*
TOBIAS, *as he stands for a moment, looking at the*
floor: silence)

CLAIRE
(A small, sad chuckle)
I was wondering when it would begin . . . when it would
start.

TOBIAS
(Hearing her only after a moment)
Start?
(Louder)
START?
(Pause)
WHAT?!

CLAIRE
(Raises her glass to him)
Don't you know yet?
(Small chuckle)
You will.

CURTAIN

ACT TWO

SCENE ONE

(Same set; before dinner, next evening. JULIA *and* AGNES
alone. AGNES *sitting,* JULIA *on her feet, pacing, maybe)*

JULIA
(Anger and self-pity; too loud)
Do you think I like it? Do you?

AGNES
(No pleading)

Julia! Please!

JULIA
DO YOU!? Do you think I enjoy it?

AGNES

Julia!

JULIA
Do you think it gives me some kind of . . . martyr's pleasure? Do you?

AGNES

Will you be still?

JULIA
WELL!?

AGNES
THERE IS A HOUSE FULL OF PEOPLE!

JULIA
Yes! What *about* that! I come home: my room is full of
Harry and Edna. I have no place to put my things. . . .

AGNES
(Placating)
They'll go to Tobias' room, he'll sleep with me. . . .

JULIA
(Muttered)
That'll be different.

AGNES
What did you say, young lady?

JULIA
I SAID, THAT WILL BE NICE.

AGNES
You did *not* say any such thing. You said . . .

JULIA
What are they *doing* here? Don't they have a house any
more? Has the market gone bust without my knowing it? I
may have been out of touch, but . . .

AGNES
Just . . . let it be.

JULIA
(Between her teeth; controlled hysteria)
Why are they here?

AGNES
(Weary; head back; calm)
They're . . . frightened. Haven't you heard of it?

JULIA
(Incredulous)
They're . . . what!?

AGNES
(Keeping her voice down)
They're frightened. Now, will you let it be!

JULIA
(Offended)
What are they frightened of? Harry and *Edna?* Frightened?

AGNES
I don't . . . I don't know yet.

JULIA
Well, haven't you *talked* to them about it? I mean, for God's
sake. . . .

AGNES
(Trying to stay calm)
No. I haven't.

JULIA
What have they done: stayed up in their room all day—*my*
room!—not come down? Locked in?

AGNES
Yes.

JULIA
Yes what?

AGNES
Yes, they have stayed up in their room all day.

JULIA
My room.

AGNES
Your room. Now, let it be.

JULIA
(Almost goes on in the same tone; doesn't; very nice,
now)
No, I . . .

AGNES

Please?

JULIA
I'm sorry, Mother, sorry for screeching.

AGNES
I am too old—as I remember—to remember what it is like to
be a daughter, if my poor parents, in their separate heavens,
will forgive me, but I am sure it is simpler than being a
mother.

JULIA
(Slight edge)
I said I was sorry.

AGNES
(All of this more for her own bemusement and
amusement than anything else)
I don't recall if I ever asked my poor mother that. I do wish
sometimes that I had been born a man.

JULIA
(Shakes her head; very matter-of-fact)
Not so hot.

AGNES
Their concerns are so simple: money and death—making
ends meet until they meet the end.
(Great self-mockery and exaggeration)
If they *knew* what it was like . . . to be a wife; a mother; a

lover; a homemaker; a nurse; a hostess, an agitator, a pacifier, a truth-teller, a deceiver . . .

JULIA
(Saws away at an invisible violin; sings)
Da-da-dee; da-da-da.

AGNES
(Laughs softly)
There is a book out, I believe, a new one by one of the thirty million psychiatrists practicing in this land of ours, a book which opines that the sexes are reversing, or coming to resemble each other too much, at any rate. It is a book to be read and disbelieved, for it disturbs our sense of well-being. If the book is right, and I suspect it is, then I would be no better off as a man . . . would I?

JULIA
(Sober, though tongue-in-cheek agreement; shaking of head)
No. Not at all.

AGNES
(Exaggerated fret)
Oh! There is nowhere to rest the weary head . . . or whatever.
(Hand out; loving, though a little grand)
How are you, my darling?

JULIA
(A little abrupt)
What?

AGNES
(Hand still out; somewhat strained)
How are you, my darling?

JULIA
(Gathering energy)
How is your darling? Well, I was trying to tell you before you
shut me up with Harry and Edna hiding upstairs, and . . .

AGNES

ALL RIGHT!

(Pause)

JULIA
(Strained control)
I will try to tell you, Mother—once again—before you've
turned into a man. . . .

AGNES
I shall try to hear you out, but if I feel my voice changing, in
the middle of your . . . rant, you will have to forgive my
male prerogative, if I become uncomfortable, look at my
watch, or jiggle the change in my pocket . . .
(Sees JULIA *marching toward the archway as* TOBIAS
enters)
. . . where do you think you're going?

JULIA
(Head down, muttered)
. . . you go straight to hell. . . .

TOBIAS
(Attempt at cheer)
Now, now, what's going on here?

JULIA
(Right in front of him; force)
Will you shut her up?

TOBIAS
(Overwhelmed)
Will I . . . what?

AGNES
(Marching toward the archway herself)
Well, there you are, Julia; your father may safely leave the
room now, I think.
(Kisses TOBIAS *on the cheek)*
Hello, my darling.
(Back to JULIA*)*
Your mother has arrived. Talk to *him!*
(To TOBIAS*)*
Your daughter is in need of consolation or a great cuffing
around the ears. I don't know which to recommend.

TOBIAS
(Confused)
Have . . . have Harry and Edna . . . ?

AGNES
(Exiting)
No, they have not.
(Gone)

TOBIAS
(After her, vaguely)
Well, I thought maybe . . .
(To JULIA, *rather timid)*
What was that . . . all about?

JULIA
As they say: I haven't the faintest.

TOBIAS
(Willing to let it go)
Oh.

JULIA
(Rather brittle)
Evening papers?

TOBIAS

Oh, yes; want them?

JULIA

Anything happy?

TOBIAS
(Hopefully)

My daughter's home.

JULIA
(Not giving in)

Any other joys?

TOBIAS

Sorry.

(Sighs)

No; small wars, large anxieties, our dear Republicans as dull
as ever, a teen-age marijuana nest not far from here. . . .

(Some wonder)

I've never had marijuana . . . in my entire life.

JULIA

Want some?

TOBIAS

Wasn't fashionable.

JULIA

What the hell do Harry and Edna want?

TOBIAS
(Scratches his head)

Just let it be.

JULIA

Didn't you try to talk to them today? I mean . . .

TOBIAS
(Not embarrassed, but not comfortable either)
Well, no; they weren't down when I went off to the club,
and . . .

JULIA

Good old golf?

TOBIAS
(Surprisingly nasty)
Don't ride me, Julia, I warn you.

JULIA
(Nervously nicer)
I've never had any marijuana, either. Aren't I a good old girl?

TOBIAS
(Thinking of something else)
Either that or slow.

JULIA
(Exploding; but anger, not hysteria)
Great Christ! What the hell did I come home to? **And why?**
Both of you? Snotty, mean . . .

TOBIAS

LOOK!
(Silence; softer, but no nonsense)
There are some . . . times, when it all gathers up . . . too
much.

JULIA
(Nervously)

Sure, sure.

TOBIAS
(Not put off)
Some *times* when it's going to be Agnes and Tobias, and not
just Mother and Dad. Right? Some *times* when the allow-

ances aren't going to be made. What are you doing, biting off
your fingernails now?

JULIA
(Not *giving in*)

It broke off.

TOBIAS

There are some *times* when it's all . . . too much. I don't
know what the hell Harry and Edna are doing sitting up in
that bedroom! Claire is drinking, she and Agnes are at each
other like a couple of . . . of . . .

JULIA
(Softly)

Sisters?

TOBIAS

What? The goddamn government's at me over some deduc-
tions, and you!

JULIA
(Head high, defiant)

And me? Yes?

TOBIAS

This isn't the first time, you know. This isn't the first time
you've come back with one of your goddamned marriages on
the rocks. Four! Count 'em!

JULIA
(Rage)

I know how many marriages I've gotten myself into, you . . .

TOBIAS

Four! You expect to come back here, nestle in to being fifteen
and misunderstood each time!? You are thirty-six years old,
for God's sake! . . .

JULIA

And you are one hundred! Easily!

TOBIAS

Thirty-six! Each time! Dragging your . . . your—I was going
to say pride—your marriage with you like some Raggedy Ann
doll, by the foot. You, you fill this house with your whining. . . .

JULIA
(Rage)

I DON'T ASK TO COME BACK HERE!!

TOBIAS

YOU BELONG HERE!
*(Heavy breathing from both of them, finally a little
rueful giggle; TOBIAS speaks rather nonchalantly now)*
Well. Now that I've taken out on my only daughter the . . .
disgust of my declining years, I'll mix a very good and very
strong martini. Join me?

JULIA
(Rather wistful)

When I was a very little girl—well, when I was a little girl:
after I'd gotten over my two-year burn at suddenly having a
brother, may his soul rest, when I was still a little girl, I
thought you were a marvel—saint, sage, daddy, everything.
And then, as the years turned and I reached my . . . somewhat angular adolescence . . .

TOBIAS
(At the sideboard; unconcerned)

Five to one? Or more?

JULIA

And then, as the years turned—poor old man—you sank to
cipher, and you've stayed there, I'm afraid—very nice but

ineffectual, essential, but not-really-thought-of, gray . . . non-eminence.

TOBIAS
(Mixing, hardly listening)

Unh-hunh . . .

JULIA

And now you've changed again, sea monster, ram! Nasty, violent, absolutely human man! Yes, as you make it, five to one, or better.

TOBIAS

I made it about seven, I think.

JULIA

Your transformations amaze me. How can I have changed so much? Or *is* it really you?
> *(He hands her a drink)*

Thank you.

TOBIAS
(As they both settle)

I told Agnes that I'd speak to Doug . . . if you think that would do any good. By golly, Dad, that's a good martini!

JULIA

Do you really want to talk to Doug? You won't get anywhere: the compulsives you can get somewhere with—or the illusion of getting—the gamblers, the fags, the lechers . . .

TOBIAS

. . . of this world . . .

JULIA

. . . yes, you can have the illusion 'cause they're after something, the jackpot, somehow: break the bank, find the boy, climb the babe . . . something.

TOBIAS

You do pick 'em.

JULIA
(Pregnant)

Do I?

TOBIAS

Hm?

JULIA

Do I pick 'em? I thought it was fifteen hundred and six, or so, where daughter went with whatever man her parents thought would hold the fief together best, or something. "Love will come after."

TOBIAS
(Grudging)

Well, you may have been pushed on Charlie. . . .

JULIA

Poor Charlie.

TOBIAS
(Temper rising a little)

Well, for Christ's sake, if you miss him so much . . .

JULIA

I do not miss him! Well, yes, I do, but not that way. Because he seemed so like what Teddy would have been.

TOBIAS
(Quiet anger and sorrow)

Your brother would not have grown up to be a fag.

JULIA
(Bitter smile)

Who is to say?

TOBIAS
(*Hard look*)

I!

(*Pause.* CLAIRE *in the archway*)

CLAIRE

Do I breathe gin?
(JULIA *sees her, runs to her, arms out, both of them,*
they envelop each other)
Darling!

JULIA

Oh, my sweet Claire!

CLAIRE

Julia Julia.

JULIA
(*Semi-mock condemnation*)
I must say the welcome-home committee was pretty skimpy,
you and Daddy gone. . . .

CLAIRE

Oh, now.
(*To* TOBIAS)
I said, do I breathe gin?

TOBIAS
(*Not rising*)

You do.

CLAIRE
(*Appraising* JULIA)
Well, you don't look too bad for a quadruple amputee, I
must say. Are you going to make me a whatever, Tobias?
(*To* JULIA)
Besides, my darling, it's getting to be rather a habit, isn't it?

JULIA
(False smile)

Yes, I suppose so.

CLAIRE
(Sees TOBIAS *is not moving)*
Then I shall make my own.

TOBIAS
(Getting up; wearily)
Sit down, Claire, I'll do it.

CLAIRE
I wouldn't want to tax you, now.
(Generally)
Well, I had an adventure today. Went into town, thought I'd shake 'em up a little, so I tried to find me a topless bathing suit.

JULIA
(Giggling)

You didn't!

TOBIAS
(At the sideboard, disapproving)
Really, Claire.

CLAIRE
Yes, I did. I went into what's-their-names', and I went straight up to the swim-wear, as they call it, department and I got me an eighteen-nineties schoolteacher type, who wondered what she could do for me.
(JULIA giggles)
and I felt like telling her, "Not much, sweetheart" . . .

TOBIAS
Are you sure you wouldn't rather have a . . .

CLAIRE

Very. But I said, "Hello, there, I'm in the market for a topless swimsuit."

JULIA

You know! They *are* wearing them on the coast. I've . . .

CLAIRE

Hush. Hurry up there, Toby. "A what, Miss?" she said, which I didn't know whether to take as a compliment or not. "A topless swimsuit," I said. "I don't know what you mean," she said after a beat. "Oh, certainly you do," I said, "no top, stops at the waist, latest thing, lots of freedom." "Oh, yes," she said, looking at me like she was seeing the local madam for the first time, "those." Then a real sniff. "I'm afraid we don't carry . . . those."

JULIA

I could have brought you one! . . .
                    (Afterthought)
If I'd known I was coming home.

CLAIRE

"Well, in that case," I told her, "do you have any separates?" "Those we carry," she said, "those we do." And she started going under the counter, and I said, "I'll just buy the bottoms of one of those."

JULIA

No! You didn't!

CLAIRE

Yes, I did. She came up from under the counter, adjusted her spectacles and said, "What did you say?"

TOBIAS

Shall I bring it, or will you come for it?

CLAIRE

You bring. I said, "I said, 'I'll buy the bottom of one of those.'" She thought for a minute, and then she said, with ice in her voice, "And what will we do with the tops?" "Well," I said, "why don't you save 'em? Maybe bottomless swimsuits'll be in *next* year."

(JULIA *laughs openly*)

Then the poor sweet thing gave me a look I couldn't tell was either a D minus, or she was going to send me home with a letter to my mother, and she said, sort of far away, "I think you need the manager." And off she walked.

TOBIAS

(*Handing* CLAIRE *her martini; mildly amused throughout*)

What were you doing buying a bathing suit in October, anyway?

JULIA

Oh, Dad!

CLAIRE

No, now; it's a man's question.

(*Sips*)

Wow, what a good martini.

TOBIAS

(*Still standing over her, rather severe*)

Truth will get you nowhere. Why?

CLAIRE

Why? Well . . .

(*Thinks*)

. . . maybe I'll go on a trip somewhere.

TOBIAS

That would please Agnes.

CLAIRE
(Nods)

As few things would. What I meant was, maybe Toby'll walk
in one day, trailing travel folders, rip his tie off, annonuce he's
fed up to there with the north, the east, the suburbs, the
regulated great gray life, dwindling before him—poor Toby
—and has bought him an island off Paraguay . . .

TOBIAS

. . . which has no seacoast . . .

CLAIRE

. . . yes, *way* off—has bought him this island, and is taking
us all to *that,* to hack through the whatever, build us an
enormous lean-to, all of us. Take us away, to where it is always good and happy.
(Watches TOBIAS, *who looks at his drink, frowning
a little)*

JULIA
(She, too)

Would you, Dad?

TOBIAS
*(Looks up, sees them both looking at him, frowns
more)*

It's . . . it's too late, or something.
(Small silence)

CLAIRE
(To lighten it)

Or, maybe I simply wanted a topless bathing suit.
(Pause)

No? Well, then . . . maybe it's more complicated yet. I
mean, Claire couldn't find herself a man if she tried, and
here comes Julia, home from the wars. . . .

TOBIAS
(*Quiet contradiction*)
You could find a man.

CLAIRE
(*Some bitterness*)
Indeed, I have found several, briefly, and none my own.

TOBIAS
(*To* JULIA; *terribly offhand*)
Julia, don't you think Auntie Claire could find herself a man?

JULIA
(*Didactic*)
I *don't* like the subject.

CLAIRE
. . . and here comes Julia, home from the wars, four purple
hearts . . .

JULIA
Why don't you just have another drink and stop it, Claire?

CLAIRE
(*Looks at her empty glass, shrugs*)
All right.

JULIA
(*Rather defensive*)
I have *left* Doug. We are not *divorced*.

CLAIRE
Yet! Are you cooking a second batch, Tobias?
(*Back to* JULIA)
But you've come back home, haven't you? And didn't you—
with the others?

JULIA
(Her back up)
Where else am I supposed to go?

CLAIRE
It's a great big world, baby. There are hotels, new cities.
Home is the quickest road to Reno I know of.

JULIA
(Condescending)
You've had a lot of experience in these matters, Claire.

CLAIRE
Sidelines! Good seats, right on the fifty-yard line, objective
observer.
(Texas accent, or near it)
I swar! Ef I din't love muh sister so, Ah'd say she got yuh
hitched fur the pleasure uh gettin' yuh back.

JULIA	TOBIAS
ALL RIGHT!	THAT WILL DO NOW!

CLAIRE
(In the silence that follows)
Sorry. Very . . . very sorry.
(AGNES appears through the archway)

AGNES
(What she may have overheard she gives no indica-
tion of)
"They" tell me in the kitchen . . . "they" tell me we are
about to dine. In a bit. Are we having a cocktail? I think one
might be nice.
(Puts her arm around JULIA as she passes her)
It's one of those days when everything's underneath. But, we
are all together . . . which is something.

JULIA

Quite a few of us.

TOBIAS

Any word from . . .
(Points to the ceiling)
. . . up there?

AGNES

No. I dropped upstairs—well, *that* doesn't make very much
sense, does it?—I *happened* upstairs, and I knocked at Harry
and Edna's *Julia's* room, door, and after a moment I heard
Harry say, "It's all right; we're all right." I didn't have the
. . . well, I felt such an odd mixture of . . . embarrassment
and irritation, and . . . apprehension, I suppose, and . . .
fatigue . . . I didn't persevere.

TOBIAS

Well, haven't they been *out?* I mean, haven't they eaten or
anything?

AGNES

Will you make me a . . . thing, a martini, please? I am told
—*"they"* tell me that while we were all out, at our various
whatever-they-may-be's, Edna descended, asked them to make
sandwiches, which were brought to the closed door and
handed in.

TOBIAS

Well, God, I mean . . .

AGNES
(Rather a recitation)
There is no point in pressing it, they are our very dear
friends, they will tell us in good time.

CLAIRE
(Looking through her glass)
I had a glimmer of it last night; thought I knew.

AGNES
(So gracious)
That which we see in the bottom of our glass is most often
dregs.

CLAIRE
(Peers into her glass, over-curious)
Really? Truly so?

TOBIAS
(Holding a glass out to AGNES*)*
Did you say you wanted?

AGNES
(Her eyes still on CLAIRE*)*
Yes, I did, thank you.

CLAIRE
I have been trying, without very much success, to find out
why Miss Julie here is come home.

AGNES
I would imagine Julia is home because she wishes to be, and
it is where she belongs if she wants.

TOBIAS
That's logistics, isn't it?

AGNES
You too?

JULIA
He's against everything!

AGNES
Your father?

JULIA

Doug!

AGNES

You needn't make a circus of it; tell me later, when . . .

JULIA

War, marriage, money, children . . .

AGNES

You needn't!

JULIA

You! Daddy! Government! Claire—if he'd met her . . . everything!

CLAIRE

Well, I doubt he'd dislike *me*; I'm against everything too.

AGNES
(To JULIA)

You're tired; we'll talk about it after . . .

JULIA
(Sick disgust)

I've talked about it! I just talked about it!

AGNES
(Quiet boring in)

I'm sure there's more.

JULIA

There is no more.

AGNES
(Clenched teeth)

There is a great deal more, and I'll hear it from you later,

when we're alone. You have not come to us in your fourth
debacle . . .

JULIA

HE IS OPPOSED! AND THAT IS ALL! TO EVERYTHING!

AGNES
(After a small silence)
Perhaps after dinner.

JULIA

NO! NOT PERHAPS AFTER DINNER!

TOBIAS

ALL OF YOU! BE STILL!
(Silence)

CLAIRE
(Flat; to TOBIAS*)*
Are we having our dividend, or are we not?
(Silence; then, a gentle mocking apology)
"All happy families are alike."
*(*HARRY *and* EDNA *appear in the archway, coats on or
over arms)*

HARRY
(A little embarrassed)
Well.

CLAIRE
(Exaggerated bonhomie)
Well, look who's here!

TOBIAS
(Embarrassed)
Harry, just in time for a martini. . . .

HARRY

No, no, we're . . . Julia, there you are!

EDNA
(Affectionate commiseration)

Oh, Julia.

JULIA
(Bravely, nicely)

Hello there.

AGNES
(On her feet)

There's just time for a drink before dinner, if my husband
will hurry some . . .

HARRY

No, we're . . . going home now.

AGNES
(Relief peeking through the surprise)

Oh? Yes?

EDNA

Yes.

(Pause)

AGNES

Well.

(Pause)

If we were any help at all, we . . .

HARRY

To . . . uh, to get our things.

(Silence)

Our clothes, and things.

EDNA

Yes.

HARRY

We'll be back in . . . well, after dinner, so don't . . .

EDNA

An hour or two. It'll take us a while.
(Silence)

HARRY

We'll let ourselves . . . don't bother.
*(They start out, tentatively, see that the others are
merely staring at them. Exit. Silence)*

JULIA
(Controlled, but near tears)
I want my room back! I want my room!

AGNES
(Composed, chilly, standing in the archway)
I believe that dinner is served. . . .

TOBIAS
(Vacant)

Yes?

AGNES

If any of you have the stomach for it.

CURTAIN

SCENE TWO

(Same set, after dinner, the same evening. AGNES *and* TOBIAS
to one side, AGNES *standing,* TOBIAS *not;* JULIA *in another corner, not facing them)*

JULIA
(A statement, directed to neither of them)
That was, without question, the *ugliest* dinner I have ever sat
through.

AGNES
(Seemingly pleased)
What did you say?
(No answer)
Now, what can you mean? Was the ragout not to your pleas-
ure? Did the floating island sink? Watch what you say, for
your father is proud of his wines. . . .

JULIA
No! You! Sitting there! Like a combination . . . pope, and
. . . "We will not discuss it"; "Claire, be still"; "No, Tobias,
the table is not the proper place"; "Julia!" . . . nanny! Like
a nanny!

AGNES
When we are dealing with children . . .

JULIA
I must discover, sometime, who you think you are.

AGNES
(Icy)
You will learn . . . one day.

JULIA

No, more like a drill sergeant! *You* will do this, *you* will not
say that.

AGNES

"To keep in shape." Have you heard the expression? Most
people misunderstand it, assume it means alteration, when
it does not. Maintenance. When we keep something in shape,
we maintain its shape—whether we are proud of that shape,
or not, is another matter—we keep *it* from falling apart. We
do not attempt the impossible. We maintain. We hold.

JULIA

Yes? So?

AGNES
(Quietly)

I shall . . . keep this family in shape. I shall maintain it;
hold it.

JULIA
(A sneer)

But you won't attempt the impossible.

AGNES
(A smile)

I shall keep it in shape. If I am a drill sergeant . . . so be it.
Since nobody . . . *really* wants to talk about your latest . . .
marital disorder, really wants to talk *around* it, use it as an
excuse for all sorts of horrid little revenges . . . I think we
can at least keep the table . . . unlittered of *that*.

JULIA
(Sarcastic salute, not rising though)

Yes, sir.

AGNES
(Reasonable)
And, if I shout, it's merely to be heard . . . above the awful
din of your privacies and sulks . . . all of you. I am not being an ogre, am I?

TOBIAS
(Not anxious to argue)
No, no; very . . . reasonable.

AGNES
If I am a stickler on certain points
(Just as JULIA's *mouth opens to speak)*
—a martinet, as Julia would have it, would you not, sweet?,
in fact, were you not about to?—if I am a stickler on points
of manners, timing, tact—the graces, I almost blush to call
them—it is simply that I am the one member of this . . .
reasonably happy family blessed and burdened with the abil-
ity to view a situation objectively while I am in it.

JULIA
(Not really caring)
What time is it?

AGNES
(A little harder now)
The double position of seeing not only facts but their impli-
cations . . .

TOBIAS
Nearly ten.

AGNES
(Some irritation toward both of them)
. . . the longer view as well as the shorter. There *is* a balance
to be maintained, after all, though the rest of you teeter, unconcerned, or uncaring, *assuming* you're on level ground

. . . by divine right, I gather, though that is hardly so. And
if I must be the fulcrum . . .
> *(Sees neither of them is really listening, says in the*
> *same tone)*

. . . I think I shall have a divorce.
> *(Smiles to see that her words have had no effect)*

TOBIAS
> *(It sinks in)*

Have what? A *what?*

AGNES

No fear; merely testing. Everything is taken for granted and
no one listens.

TOBIAS
> *(Wrinkling his nose)*

Have a divorce?

AGNES

No, no; Julia has them for all of us. Not even separation; that
is taken care of, and in life: the gradual . . . demise of intensity, the private preoccupations, the substitutions. We become allegorical, my darling Tobias, as we grow older. The
individuality we hold so dearly sinks into crotchet; we see
ourselves repeated by those we bring into it all, either by mirror or rejection, honor or fault.
> *(To herself, really)*

I'm not a fool; I'm really not.

JULIA
> *(Leafing a magazine; clear lack of interest but not*
> *insulting)*

What's Claire up to?

AGNES
> *(Walking to* TOBIAS, *a hand on his shoulder)*

Really not at all.

TOBIAS
(Looking up; fondness)
No; really not.

AGNES
(Surprisingly unfriendly; to JULIA*)*
How would I know what she's doing?

JULIA
(She too)
Well, you are the fulcrum and all around here, the double vi-
sion, the great balancing act. . . .
(Lets it slide away)

AGNES
(A little triste; looking away)
I dare say she's in her room.

JULIA
(Little girl)
At least she has one.

AGNES
(Swinging around to face her; quite hard)
Well, why don't you run upstairs and claim your goddamn
room back! Barricade yourself in there! Push a bureau in front
of the door! Take Tobias' pistol while you're at it! Arm yourself!
(A burst from an accordion; CLAIRE *appears in the
archway, wearing it)*

CLAIRE
Barricades? Pistols? Really? So soon?

JULIA
(Giggling in spite of herself)
Oh, Claire . . .

AGNES
(Not amused)
Claire, will you take off that damned thing!

CLAIRE
"They laughed when I sat down to the accordion." Take it off? No, I will not! This is going to be a festive night—from the smell of it, and sister Claire wants to do her part—pay her way, so to speak . . . justify.

AGNES
You're not going to play that dreadful instrument in here, and . . .
(But the rest of what she wants to say is drowned out by a chord from the accordion)
Tobias?
(Calm)
Do something about that.

TOBIAS
(He, too, chuckling)
Oh, now, Agnes . . .

CLAIRE
So . . .
(Another chord)
. . . shall I wait? Shall I start now? A polka? What?

AGNES
(Icy, but to TOBIAS*)*
My sister is not *really* lazy. The things she has learned since leaving the nest!: gaucherie, ingratitude, drunkenness, and even . . . this. She has become a musician, too.

CLAIRE
(A twang in her voice)
Maw used to say: "Claire, girl" . . . she had an uncle named

Claire, so she always called me Claire-girl—

AGNES
(No patience with it)
That is not so.

CLAIRE
"Claire girl," she used to say, "when you go out into the world, get dumped outa the nest, or pushed by your sister . . .

AGNES
(Steady, but burning)
Lies.
(Eyes slits)
She kept you, allowed you . . . tolerated! Put up with your filth, your . . . "emancipated womanhood."
(To JULIA, overly sweet)
Even in her teens, your Auntie Claire had her own and very special ways, was very . . . advanced.

CLAIRE
(Laughs)
Had a ball, the same as you, 'cept I wasn't puce with socially proper remorse every time.
(To JULIA)
Your mommy got her pudenda scuffed a couple times herself 'fore she met old Toby, you know.

TOBIAS
Your what?

AGNES
(Majesty)
My pudenda.

CLAIRE
(A little grumpy)
You can come on all forgetful in your old age, if you want
to, but just remember . . .

AGNES
(Quiet anger)
I am not an old woman.
(Sudden thought; to TOBIAS)
Am I?

TOBIAS
(No help; great golly-gosh)
Well, you're my old lady . . .
(AGNES almost says something, changes her mind,
shakes her head, laughs softly)

CLAIRE
(A chord)
Well, what'll it be?

JULIA
(Glum)
Save it for Harry and Edna.

CLAIRE
Save it for Harry and Edna? Save it for them?
(Chord)

AGNES
(Nice)
Please.

CLAIRE
All right; I'll unload.
(Removes accordion)

AGNES

I dare say . . .
          (Stops)

TOBIAS

What?

AGNES

No. Nothing.

CLAIRE
(Half-smile)
We're waiting, aren't we?

TOBIAS

Hm?

CLAIRE
Waiting. The room; the doctor's office; beautiful unconcern; intensive study of the dreadful curtains; absorption in *Field and Stream*, waiting for the Bi-op-*see*.
          (Looks from one to the other)
No? Don't know what I mean?

JULIA
(Rather defiant)
What *about* Harry and Edna?

CLAIRE
(Echo; half-smile)
We don't want to talk about it.

AGNES

If they come back . . .

CLAIRE

If!?

AGNES
(Closes her eyes briefly)
If they come back . . . we will . . .
(Shrugs)

CLAIRE
You've only got two choices, Sis. You take 'em in, or you
throw 'em out.

AGNES
Ah, how simple it is from the sidelines.

TOBIAS
(Sees through the window)
We'll do neither, I'd imagine. Take in; throw out.

CLAIRE
Oh?

TOBIAS
(A feeling of nakedness)
Well, yes, they're just . . . passing through.

CLAIRE
As they have been . . . all these years.

AGNES
Well, we shall know soon enough.
(Not too much pleasure)
They're back.

TOBIAS
(Rises, goes to the window with her)
Yes?

JULIA
I think I'll go up . . .

AGNES

You stay right here!

JULIA

I want to go to my . . .

AGNES

It is their room! For the moment.

JULIA
(Not nice)

Among Doug's opinions, you might like to know, is that
when you and your ilk are blown to pieces by a Chinese
bomb, the world will be a better place.

CLAIRE

Isn't ilk a lovely word?

TOBIAS
(Disbelief)

Oh, come on now!

CLAIRE

It will certainly be a less crowded one.

AGNES
(Dry)

You choose well, Julia.

JULIA
(Retreating into uncertainty)

That's what he says.

AGNES

Have, always. Did he include *you* as ilk, as well? Will you be
with us when "the fatal mushroom" comes, as those dirty
boys put it? Are we to have the pleasure?

JULIA
(After a pause; as much a threat as a promise)
I'll be right here.

TOBIAS

Agnes!

JULIA
Would you like to know something else he says?

AGNES
(Patiently)

No, Julia.

JULIA

Dad?

TOBIAS
(Some apology in it)
Not . . . right this minute, Julia.

JULIA
(Defiance)

Claire? You?

CLAIRE
Well, come on! You *know* I'd like to hear about it—love to—
but Toby and Ag've got an invasion on their hands, and . . .

AGNES
We have no such thing.

CLAIRE
. . . and maybe you'd better save it for Harry and Edna, too.

AGNES
It does not concern Edna and Harry.

CLAIRE

Best friends.

AGNES

Tobias?

TOBIAS
(Reluctantly on his feet)
Where . . . what do you want me to do with everything?
Every . . . ?

AGNES
(Heading toward the archway)
Well for God's sake! I'll do it.
(They exit)

JULIA
(As CLAIRE *moves to the sideboard)*
What . . . what do they want? Harry and Edna.

CLAIRE
(Pouring for herself)

Hmm?

JULIA
You'll make Mother mad. Harry and Edna: what do they
want?

CLAIRE

Succor.

JULIA
(Tiny pause)

Pardon?

CLAIRE
(Brief smile)

Comfort.

(Sees JULIA *doesn't understand)*

Warmth. A special room with a night light, or the door ajar
so you can look down the hall from the bed and see that
Mommy's door is open.

JULIA
(No anger; loss)

But that's my room.   *

CLAIRE

It's . . . the *room*. Happens you were in it. You're a visitor
as much as anyone, now.

(We hear mumbled conversation from the hallway)

JULIA
(Small whine)

But I *know* that room.

CLAIRE
(Pointed, but kind)

Are you home for good now?

*(*JULIA *stares at her)*

Are you home forever, back from the world? To the sadness
and reassurance of your parents? Have you come to take my
place?

JULIA
(Quiet despair)

This is my home!

CLAIRE

This . . . ramble? Yes?

(Surprised delight)

You're laying claim to the cave! Well, I don't know how
they'll take to that. We're not a communal nation, dear;

*(*EDNA *appears in the archway, unseen)*

giving, but not sharing, outgoing, but not friendly.

EDNA

Hello.

CLAIRE
(Friendly, but not turning to look at her)

Hello!
(Back to JULIA*)*
We submerge our truths and have our sunsets on untroubled
waters. C'mon in, Edna.

EDNA

Yes.

CLAIRE
(Back to JULIA*)*
We live with our truths in the grassy bottom, and we ex-
amine aalllll the interpretations of aalllll the implications
like we had a life for nothing else, for God's sake.
(Turns to EDNA*)*
Do *you* think we can walk on the water, Edna? Or do you
think we sink?

EDNA
(Dry)

We sink.

CLAIRE
And we better develop gills. Right?

EDNA

Right.

JULIA
I didn't see you come in.

EDNA
We drove around the back. Harry is helping Agnes and
Tobias get our bags upstairs.

JULIA
(Slight schoolteacher tone)
Don't you mean Agnes and Tobias are helping Harry?

EDNA
(Tired)
If you like.
(To CLAIRE)
What were you two up to?

CLAIRE
I think Julia is home for good this time.

JULIA
(Annoyed and embarrassed)
For Christ's sake, Claire!

EDNA
(Rather as if JULIA were not in the room)
Oh? Is it come to that?

CLAIRE
I always said she would, finally.

JULIA
(Under her breath, to CLAIRE)
This is family business!

EDNA
(Looking around the room)
Yes, but I'm not sure Agnes and Tobias have seen it as clearly.
I do wish Agnes would have that chair recovered. Perhaps
now . . .

JULIA
(Exploding)
Well, why don't you call the upholsterers! Now that you're
living here!

CLAIRE
(Quiet amusement)

All in the family.

EDNA

You're not a child any more, Julia, you're nicely on your way to forty, and you've not helped . . . wedlock's image any, with your . . . shenanigans . . .

JULIA
(Full, quivering rage)

YOU ARE A GUEST IN THIS HOUSE!!

EDNA
(Lets a moment pass, continues quietly)

. . . and if you *have* decided to . . .
(Wistful)

return forever? . . . then it's a matter of some concern for quite a few peo—

JULIA

You are a *guest!*

CLAIRE
(Quietly)

As you.

EDNA

. . . for quite a few people . . . whose lives are . . . moved —if not necessarily touched—by your actions. Claire, where does Agnes have her upholstery done? Does she use . . .

JULIA

NO!

EDNA
(Strict, soft and powerful)

Manners, young lady!

CLAIRE
(Pointed)
Julia, why don't you ask Edna if she'd like something?

JULIA
(Mouth agape for a moment)
NO!
(To EDNA)
You have no rights here. . . .

EDNA
I'll have a cognac, Julia.
(JULIA stands stock still. EDNA continues; precise and
pointed)
My husband and I are your parents' best friends. We are, in
addition, your godparents.

JULIA
DOES THIS GIVE YOU RIGHTS?!

CLAIRE
(Smile)
Some.

EDNA
Some. Rights and responsibilities. Some.

CLAIRE
(Seeing HARRY in the archway)
Hello, there, Harry; c'mon in. Julia's about to fix us all some-
thing. What'll you . . .

HARRY
(Rubbing his hands together; quite at ease)
I'll do it; don't trouble yourself, Julia.

JULIA
(Rushes to the sideboard, her back to it, spreads her arms, protecting it, curiously disturbed and frightened by something)
NO! Don't you come near it! Don't you take a step!

HARRY
(Patiently, moving forward a little)
Now, Julia . . .

JULIA
NO!

EDNA
(Sitting, relaxing)
Let her do it, Harry. She wants to.

JULIA
I DON'T WANT TO!!

HARRY
(Firm)
Then I'll do it, Julia.

JULIA
(Suddenly a little girl; crying)
Mother!? MOTHER!?

EDNA
(Shaking her head; not unkindly)
Honestly.

JULIA
MOTHER!?

CLAIRE
(The way a nurse speaks to a disturbed patient)
Julia? Will you let me do it? May I get the drinks?

JULIA
(Hissed)
Stay away from it! All of you!

CLAIRE
(Rising)
Now, Julia . . .

HARRY
Oh, come on, Julie, now . . .

EDNA
Let her *go*, Harry.

JULIA
MOTHER? FATHER! HELP ME!!
(AGNES enters)

AGNES
(Pained)
Julia? You're shouting?

JULIA
Mother!

AGNES
(Quite conscious of the others)
What *is* it, dear?

JULIA
(Quite beside herself, seeing no sympathy)
THEY! THEY WANT!

EDNA
Forget it, Julia.

HARRY
(A tiny, condescending laugh)
Yes, for God's sake, forget it.

JULIA
THEY WANT!

AGNES
(Kindly, but a little patronizing)
Perhaps you *had* better go upstairs.

JULIA
(Still semi-hysterical)
Yes? Where!? What room!?

AGNES
(Patient)
Go up to my room, lie down.

JULIA
(An ugly laugh)
Your room!

EDNA
(Calm)
You may lie down in *our* room, if you prefer.

JULIA
(A trapped woman, surrounded)
Your room!
(To AGNES)
Your room? MINE!!
(Looks from one to another, sees only waiting faces)
MINE!!

HARRY
(Makes a move toward the sideboard)
God.

JULIA

Don't you go near *that!*

AGNES

Julia . . .

JULIA

I *want!*

CLAIRE
(Sad smile)

What do you want, Julia?

JULIA

I . . .

HARRY

Jesus.

JULIA

I WANT . . . WHAT IS MINE!!

AGNES
(Seemingly dispassionate; after a pause)

Well, then, my dear, you will have to decide what that is, will
you not.

JULIA
(A terrified pause; runs from the room)

Daddy? Daddy?
(A silence; HARRY *moves to the sideboard, begins to
make himself a drink)*

AGNES
(As if very little had happened)
Why, I do believe that's the first time she's called on her fa-
ther in . . . since her childhood.

CLAIRE
When she used to skin her knees?

AGNES
(A little laugh)
Yes, and she would come home bloody. I *assumed* she was
clumsy, but it crossed my mind a time or two . . . that she
was religious.

EDNA
Praying on the gravel? A penance?

AGNES
(Chuckles, but it covers something else)
Yes. Teddy had just died, I think, and it was an . . . unreal
time . . . for a number of us, for me.
(Brief sorrow clearly shown)
Poor little boy.

EDNA
Yes.

AGNES
It was an unreal time: I thought Tobias was out of love with
me—or, rather, was tired of it, when Teddy died, as if that
had been the string.

HARRY
Would you like something, Edna?

EDNA
(*Her eyes on* AGNES; *rather dreamy*)
Um-humh.

AGNES
(*Not explaining, and to none of them, really*)
Ah, the things I doubted then: that I was loved—that *I* loved, for that matter!—that Teddy had ever lived at all—my mind, you see. That Julia would be with us long. I think . . . I think I thought Tobias was unfaithful to me then. Was he, Harry?

EDNA
Oh, Agnes.

HARRY
(*Unsubtle*)
Come on, Agnes! Of course not! No!

AGNES
(*Faint amusement*)
Was he, Claire? That hot summer, with Julia's knees all bloody and Teddy dead? Did my husband . . . cheat on me?

CLAIRE
(*Looks at her steadily, toasts her; then*)
Ya got me, Sis.

AGNES
(*An amen*)
And that will have to do.

EDNA
Poor *Julia*.

AGNES
(Shrugs)
Julia is a fool. Will you make me a drink, Harry, since you're
being Tobias? A Scotch?

HARRY
(Hands EDNA *a drink)*
Sure thing. Claire?

CLAIRE
Why not.

AGNES
(An overly sweet smile)
Claire could tell us so much if she cared to, could you not,
Claire. Claire, who watches from the sidelines, has seen so
very much, has seen us all so clearly, have you not, Claire.
You were not named for nothing.

CLAIRE
(A pleasant warning)
Lay off, Sis.

AGNES
(Eyes level on EDNA *and* HARRY; *precisely and not
too nicely)*
What do you *want?*

HARRY
(After a pause and a look at EDNA)
I don't know what you mean.

EDNA
(Seemingly puzzled)
Yes.

AGNES
(Eyes narrow)
What do you *really* . . . *want?*

CLAIRE
You gonna tell her, Harry?

HARRY
I, *I* don't know what you mean, Claire. Scotch, was it, Agnes?

AGNES
I *said.*

HARRY
(Less than pleasant)
Yes, but I don't remember.

EDNA
(Her eyes narrowing, too)
Don't talk to Harry like that.

AGNES
(About to attack, thinks better of it)
I . . . I'm sorry, Edna. I forgot that you're . . . very fright-
ened people.

EDNA
DON'T YOU MAKE FUN OF US!

AGNES
My dear Edna, I am not mak—

EDNA
YES YOU ARE! YOU'RE MAKING FUN OF US.

AGNES
I assure you, Edna . . .

HARRY
(Handing AGNES *a drink; with some disgust)*
Here's your drink.

AGNES

I, I assure you.

CLAIRE
(Putting on her accordion)
I think it's time for a little music, don't you, kids! I yodel a
little, too, nowadays, if anybody . . .

AGNES
(Exasperated)
We *don't* want music, Claire!

HARRY
(Horrified and amused)
You, you *what!?* You *yodel!?*

CLAIRE
(As if it were the most natural thing in the world)
Well . . . sure.

EDNA
(Dry)

Talent will out.

HARRY
(Continuing disbelief)
You yodel!

CLAIRE
(Emphatic; babytalk)
'ES!

*(*TOBIAS *has appeared in the archway)*

HARRY

She yodels!

CLAIRE
(Bravura)
What would ya like, Harry? A chorus of "Take me to the greenhouse, lay me down . . ."?

AGNES

Claire!

TOBIAS
I . . . I wonder if, before the concert, one of you would mind telling me why, uh, my daughter is upstairs, in hysterics?

CLAIRE
Envy, baby; she don't sing, or nothin'.
(A chord)

TOBIAS

PLEASE!

TOBIAS
(To the others)
Well? Will any of you tell me?

AGNES
(Controlled)
What, what was she doing, Tobias?

TOBIAS
I told you! She's in hysterics!

AGNES
(Tight smile)
That is a condition; I inquired about an action.

EDNA
(More sincere than before)
Poor Julia.

HARRY
I don't understand that girl.

TOBIAS
(Quite miffed)
An action? Is that what you want? O.K., how about
(Demonstrates this)
pressed against a corner of the upstairs hall, arms wide, palms
back? Eyes darting? Wide?
(EDNA *shakes her head*)
How about tearing into Harry and Edna's room . . . ripping
the clothes from the closets, hangers and all on the floor? The
same for the bureaus?

AGNES
(Steady)
I see.

TOBIAS
More?

AGNES
(Steady)
All right.

TOBIAS
Or into your room next? Twisted on your bed, lots of breathing and the great wide eyes? The spread all gathered under
her, your big lace pillow in her arms—like a lover—her eyes
wide open, no tears now? Though if you come near her the
sounds start and you think she'll scream if you touch her?
(Pause)
How's that?

CLAIRE
(Pause)

Pretty good.

AGNES
(Pause)

And accurate, I imagine.

TOBIAS
(Daring her)
You're damned right! Now, why?

AGNES
(To TOBIAS *with a sad smile, ironic)*
Would it seem . . . incomplete to you, my darling, were I
to tell you Julia is upset that Har—Edna and Harry are here,
that . . .

HARRY
(Arms wide, helplessly)
I was making myself a drink, for God's sake. . . .

EDNA
I asked her to *make* me something. . . .

TOBIAS

Oh, come on!

EDNA
(Some pleasure)
She rose . . . like a silent film star, ran to the sideboard, de-
fended it, like a princess in the movies, hiding her lover in the
closet from the king.

CLAIRE
That sound incomplete to you, Toby?

TOBIAS
(Stern)
Somewhat.

AGNES
Julia *has* been through a trying time, Tobias. . . .

HARRY
(A little apologetic)
I suppose we did upset her some. . . .

EDNA
(Consoling)
Of course!

TOBIAS
(To AGNES; *a kind of wondrous bewilderment)*
Don't you think you should go tend to her?
(The others all look to AGNES)

AGNES
(Shakes her head; lightly)
No. She will be down or she will not. She will stop, or she
will . . . go on.

TOBIAS
(Spluttering)
Well, for God's sake, Agnes . . . !

AGNES
(An end to it; hard)
I haven't the time, Tobias.
(Gentler)
I haven't time for the four-hour talk, the soothing recapitula-
tion. You don't go through it, my love: the history. Nothing
is calmed by a pat on the hand, a gentle massage, or slowly,
slowly combing the hair, no: the history. Teddy's birth, and

how she felt unwanted, tricked; his death, and was she more
relieved than lost . . . ? All the schools we sent her to, and
did she fail in them through hate . . . or love? And when we
come to marriage, dear: each one of them, the fear, the happiness, the sex, the stopping, the infidelities . . .

TOBIAS
(Nodding; speaks softly)
All right, Agnes.

AGNES
(Shakes her head)
Oh, my dear Tobias . . . my life is gone through more than
hers. I see myself . . . growing old each time, see my own
life passing. No, I haven't time for it now. At midnight,
maybe . . .
(Sad smile)
when you're all in your beds . . . safely sleeping. Then I will
comfort our Julia, and lose myself once more.

CLAIRE
(To break an uncomfortable silence)
I tell ya, there are so many martyrdoms here.

EDNA
(Seeing a hangnail)
One to a person.

AGNES
(Dry)
That is the usual,

(A glance at CLAIRE*)*
though I do believe there are some with none, and others who

have known Job. The helpless are the cruelest lot of all: they shift their burdens so.

CLAIRE

If you interviewed a camel, he'd admit he loved his load.

EDNA
(Giving up on the hangnail)
I wish you two would stop having at each other.

HARRY

Hell, yes! Let's have a drink, Tobias?

TOBIAS
(From deep in thought)
Hm?

HARRY

What can I make yuh, buddy?

CLAIRE
(Rather pleased)
Why, Edna; you've actually spoken your mind.

TOBIAS
(Confused as to where he is)
What can *you* make *me*?

EDNA

I do . . . sometimes.

HARRY

Well, sure; I'm here.

EDNA
(Calm)
When an environment is not all that it might be.

TOBIAS
Oh. Yeah; Scotch.

AGNES
(Strained smile)
Is that for you to say?

CLAIRE
(A chord; then)
Here we come!

AGNES
Stop it, Claire, dear.
(To EDNA*)*
I said: Is that for you to say?

EDNA
(To AGNES; *calm, steady)*
We must be helpful when we can, my dear; that is the . . .
responsibility, the double demand of friendship . . . is it
not?

AGNES
(Slightly schoolteacherish)
But, when we are *asked*.

EDNA
(Shakes her head, smiles gently)
No. Not only.
(This heard by all)
It seemed to me, to us, that since we were living *here* . . .
(Silence, AGNES *and* TOBIAS *look from* EDNA *to* HARRY*)*

CLAIRE

That's my cue!
> (*A chord, then begins to yodel, to an ump-pah base.*
> JULIA *appears in the archway, unseen by the others;*
> *her hair is wild, her face is tear-streaked; she carries*
> TOBIAS' *pistol, but not pointed; awkwardly and facing*
> *down*)

JULIA

(Solemnly and tearfully)
Get them out of here, Daddy, getthemoutofheregetthemoutof-
heregetthemoutofheregetthemoutofheregetthemoutofhere....
> (*They all see* JULIA *and the gun simultaneously;* EDNA
> *gasps but does not panic;* HARRY *retreats a little;* TO-
> BIAS *moves slowly toward* JULIA)

AGNES

Julia!

JULIA

Get them out of here, Daddy!

TOBIAS

(Moving toward her, slowly, calmly, speaking in a
quiet voice)
All right, Julia, baby; let's have it now. . . .

JULIA

Get them out of here, Daddy. . . .

TOBIAS

(As before)
Come on now, Julia.

JULIA

(Calmly, she hands the gun to TOBIAS, *nods)*
Get them out of here, Daddy.

AGNES
(Soft intensity)
You ought to be horsewhipped, young lady.

TOBIAS
(Meant for both JULIA *and* AGNES)
All right, now . . .

JULIA
Do it, Daddy? Or give it back?

AGNES
(Turns on JULIA; *withering)*
How dare you come into this room like that! How dare you
embarrass me and your father! How dare you frighten Edna
and Harry! How dare you come into this room like that!

JULIA
(To HARRY *and* EDNA; *venom)*
Are you going?

AGNES

Julia!

TOBIAS
(Pleading)

Julia, please. . . .

JULIA
ARE YOU!?
(Silence, all eyes on HARRY *and* EDNA)

EDNA
(Finally; curiously unconcerned)
Going? No, we are not going.

HARRY

No.

JULIA
(To all)

YOU SEE!?

HARRY

Coming down here with a gun like that . . .

EDNA
(Becoming AGNES*)*

You return to your nest from your latest disaster, dispossessed, and suddenly dispossessing; screaming the house down, clawing at order . . .

JULIA

STOP HER!

EDNA

. . . willful, wicked, wretched girl . . .

JULIA

You are not my . . . YOU HAVE NO RIGHTS!

EDNA

We have rights here. *We* belong.

JULIA

MOTHER!

AGNES
(Tentative)

Julia . . .

EDNA

We belong here, do we not?

JULIA
(Triumphant distaste)
FOREVER!!

(Small silence)
HAVE YOU COME TO STAY FOREVER??
(Small silence)

EDNA
(Walks over to her, calmly slaps her)
If need be.
(To TOBIAS *and* AGNES, *calmly)*
Sorry; a godmother's duty.
*(This next calm, almost daring, addressed at, rather
than to the others)*
If we come to the point . . . *if* we are at home one evening,
and the . . . terror comes . . . descends . . . if all at once
we . . . NEED . . . we come where we are wanted, where we
know we are expected, not only where we want; we come
where the table has been laid for us in such an event . . .
where the bed is turned down . . . and warmed . . . and
has been ready should we need it. We are not . . . transients
. . . like some.

JULIA
NO!

EDNA
(To JULIA*)*
You must . . . what is the word? . . . coexist, my dear.
(To the others)
Must she not?
(Silence; calm)
Must she not. This is what you have meant by friendship
. . . is it not?

AGNES
(Pause; finally, calmly)
You have come to live with us, then.

EDNA
(After a pause; calm)

Why, yes; we have.

AGNES
(Dead calm; a sigh)

Well, then.

(Pause)

Perhaps it is time for bed, Julia? Come upstairs with me.

JULIA
(A confused child)

M-mother?

AGNES

Ah-ah; let me comb your hair, and rub your back.

    (Arm over JULIA's *shoulder, leads her out. Exiting)*
And we shall soothe . . . and solve . . . and fall to sleep.
Tobias?

(Exits with JULIA. *Silence)*

EDNA

Well, I think it's time for bed.

TOBIAS
(Vague, preoccupied)

Well, yes; yes, of course.

EDNA
(She and HARRY *have risen; a small smile)*

We know the way.

    (Pauses as she and HARRY *near the archway)*
Friendship *is* something like a marriage, is it not, Tobias? For
better and for worse?

TOBIAS
(Ibid.)

Sure.

EDNA
(Something of a demand here)
We *haven't* come to the wrong place, *have* we?

HARRY
(Pause; shy)
Have we, Toby?

TOBIAS
(Pause; gentle, sad)
No.
(Sad smile)
No; of course you haven't.

EDNA
Good night, dear Tobias. Good night, Claire.

CLAIRE
(A half smile)
Good night, you two.

HARRY
(A gentle pat at TOBIAS *as he passes)*
Good night, old man.

TOBIAS
(Watches as the two exit)
Good . . . good night, you two.
      *(*CLAIRE *and* TOBIAS *alone;* TOBIAS *still holds the
      pistol)*

CLAIRE
(After an interval)
Full house, Tobias, every bed and every cupboard.

TOBIAS
(Not moving)
Good night, Claire.

CLAIRE
(*Rising, leaving her accordion*)
Are you going to stay up, Tobias? Sort of a nightwatch, guarding? *I've done it.* The breathing, as you stand in the quiet halls, slow and heavy? And the special . . . warmth, and . . . permeation . . . of a house . . . asleep? When the house is sleeping? When the people *are* asleep?

TOBIAS
Good night, Claire.

CLAIRE
(*Near the archway*)
And the difference? The different breathing and the cold, when every bed is awake . . . all night . . . very still, eyes open, staring into the dark? Do you know that one?

TOBIAS
Good night, Claire.

CLAIRE
(*A little sad*)
Good night, Tobias.
(*Exit as the curtain falls*)

ACT THREE

(Seven-thirty the next morning; same set. TOBIAS *alone, in a chair, wearing pajamas and a robe, slippers. Awake.* AGNES *enters, wearing a dressing gown which could pass for a hostess gown. Her movements are not assertive, and her tone is gentle)*

AGNES
(Seeing him)

Ah; there you are.

TOBIAS
(Not looking at her, but at his watch; there is very little emotion in his voice)

Seven-thirty A.M., and all's well . . . I guess.

AGNES

So odd.

TOBIAS

Hm?

AGNES

There was a stranger in my room last night.

TOBIAS

Who?

AGNES

You.

TOBIAS

Ah.

AGNES

It was nice to have you there.

TOBIAS
(*Slight smile*)

Hm.

AGNES

Le temps perdu. I've never understood that; *perdu* means lost, not merely . . . past, but it was nice to have you there, though I remember, when it was a constancy, how easily I would fall asleep, pace my breathing to your breathing, and if we were touching! ah, what a splendid cocoon that was. But last night—what a shame, what sadness—you were a stranger, and I stayed awake.

TOBIAS

I'm sorry.

AGNES

Were you asleep at all?

TOBIAS

No.

AGNES

I would go half, then wake—your unfamiliar presence, sir. I *could* get used to it again.

TOBIAS

Yes?

AGNES

I think.

TOBIAS

You didn't have your talk with Julia—your all-night lulling.

AGNES

No; she wouldn't let me stay. "Look to your own house," is what she said. You stay down long?

TOBIAS

When?

AGNES

After . . . before you came to bed.

TOBIAS

Some.
(*Laughs softly, ruefully*)
I almost went into *my* room . . . by habit . . . by mistake, rather, but then I realized that your room is my room because my room is Julia's because Julia's room is . . .

AGNES

. . . yes.
(*Goes to him, strokes his temple*)
And I was awake when you left my room again.

TOBIAS
(*Gentle reproach*)
You could have said.

AGNES
(*Curious at the truth*)
I felt shy.

TOBIAS
(*Pleased surprise*)
Hm!

AGNES

Did you go to Claire?

TOBIAS

I never go to Claire.

AGNES

Did you go to Claire to talk?

TOBIAS

I never go to Claire.

AGNES

We must always envy someone we should not, be jealous of those who have so much less. You and Claire make so much sense together, talk so well.

TOBIAS

I never go to Claire at night, or talk with her alone—save publicly.

AGNES
(Small smile)
In public rooms . . . like this.

TOBIAS

Yes.

AGNES

Have *never*.

TOBIAS

Please?

AGNES

Do we dis*like* happiness? We manufacture such a portion of our own despair . . . such busy folk.

TOBIAS

We are a highly moral land: we assume we have done great wrong. We find the things.

AGNES

I shall start missing you again—when you move from my room . . . if you do. I had stopped, I believe.

TOBIAS

(*Grudging little chuckle*)

Oh, you're an honest woman.

AGNES

Well, we need *one* . . . in every house.

TOBIAS

It's very strange . . . to be downstairs, in a room where everyone has been, and is gone . . . very late, after the heat has gone—the furnace *and* the bodies: the hour or two before the sun comes up, the furnace starts again. And tonight especially: the cigarettes still in the ashtrays—odd, metallic smell. The odors of a room don't mix, late, when there's no one there, and I think the silence helps it . . . and the lack of bodies. Each . . . thing stands out in its place.

AGNES

What did you decide?

TOBIAS

And when you *do* come down . . . if you do, at three, or four, and you've left a light or two—in case someone should come in late, I suppose, but who is there left? The inn is full —it's rather . . . Godlike, if I may presume: to look at it all, reconstruct, with such . . . de*tach*ment, see your*self*, you, Julia . . . Look at it all . . . play it out again, *watch*.

AGNES

Judge?

TOBIAS

No; that's being in it. Watch. And if you have a drink or two . . .

AGNES
(Mild surprise)

Did you?

TOBIAS
(Nods)

And if you have a drink or two, very late, in the quiet, tired, the mind . . . lets loose.

AGNES

Yes?

TOBIAS

And you watch it as it reasons, all with a kind of . . . grateful delight, at the same time sadly, 'cause you know that when the daylight comes the pressures will be on, and all the insight won't be worth a damn.

AGNES

What did you decide?

TOBIAS

You can sit and watch. You can have . . . so clear a picture, see everybody moving through his own jungle . . . an insight into all the reasons, all the needs.

AGNES

Good. And what did you decide?

TOBIAS
(No complaint)

Why is the room so dirty? Can't we have better servants, some help who . . . help?

AGNES

They keep far better hours than we, that's all. They are a comment on our habits, a reminder that we are out of step—

that is why we pay them . . . so very, very much. Neither a servant nor a master be. Remember?

TOBIAS

I remember when . . .

AGNES
(Picking it right up)

. . . you were very young and lived at home, and the servants were awake whenever you were: six A.M. for your breakfast when you wanted it, or five in the morning when you came home drunk and seventeen, washing the vomit from the car, and you, telling no one; stealing just enough each month, by arrangement with the stores, to keep them in a decent wage; generations of them: the laundress, blind and always dying, and the cook, who did a better dinner drunk than sober. Those servants? Those days? When you were young, and lived at home?

TOBIAS
(Memory)

Hmmm.

AGNES
(Sweet; sad)

Well, my darling, you are not young now, and you do not live at home.

TOBIAS
(Sad question)

Where do I live?

AGNES
(An answer of sorts)

The dark sadness. Yes?

TOBIAS
(Quiet, rhetorical)
What are we going to do?

AGNES
What did you decide?

TOBIAS
(Pause; they smile)
Nothing.

AGNES
Well, you must. Your house is not in order, sir. It's full to bursting.

TOBIAS
Yes. You've got to help me here.

AGNES
No. I don't *think* so.

TOBIAS
(Some surprise)
No?

AGNES
No. I thought a little last night, too: while you were seeing everything so clearly here. I lay in the dark, and I . . . revisited—our life, the years and years. There are many things a woman does: she bears the children—if there *is* that blessing. Blessing? Yes, I suppose, even with the sadness. She runs the house, for what that's worth: makes sure there's food, and not just anything, and decent linen; looks well; assumes whatever duties are demanded—if she is in love, or loves; and plans.

TOBIAS
(Mumbled; a little embarrassed)
I know, I know. . . .

AGNES
And plans. Right to the end of it; expects to be alone one day,
abandoned by a heart attack or the cancer, *prepares* for that.
And prepares earlier, for the children to become *adult* strangers instead of growing ones, for that loss, and for the body
chemistry, the end of what the Bible tells us is our usefulness.
The reins we hold! It's a team of twenty horses, and we sit
there, and we watch the road and check the leather . . .
if our . . . man is so disposed. But there are things we do
not do.

TOBIAS
(Slightly edgy challenge)
Yes?

AGNES
Yes.
(Harder)
We don't decide the route.

TOBIAS
You're copping out . . . as they say.

AGNES
No, indeed.

TOBIAS
(Quiet anger)
Yes, you are!

AGNES
(Quiet warning)
Don't you yell at me.

TOBIAS

You're copping *out!*

AGNES
(Quiet, calm, and almost smug)
We follow. We let our . . . men decide the moral issues.

TOBIAS
(Quite angry)
Never! You've never done that in your life!

AGNES
Always, my darling. Whatever you decide . . . I'll make it
work; I'll run it for you so you'll never know there's been a
change in anything.

TOBIAS
(Almost laughing; shaking his head)
No. No.

AGNES
(To end the discussion)
So, let me know.

TOBIAS
(Still almost laughing)
I *know* I'm tired. I know I've hardly slept at all: I know I've
sat down here, and thought . . .

AGNES
And made your decisions.

TOBIAS
But I have not *judged.* I told you that.

AGNES
(Almost a stranger)
Well, when you have . . . you let me know.

TOBIAS
(Frustration and anger)

NO!

AGNES
(Cool)

You'll wake the house.

TOBIAS
(Angry)

I'll wake the house!

AGNES

This is not the time for you to lose control.

TOBIAS

I'LL LOSE CONTROL! I have *sat* here . . . in the cold, in the empty cold, I have sat here alone, and . . .
(Anger has shifted to puzzlement, complaint)
I've looked at *every*thing, *all* of it. I thought of you, and Julia, and Claire. . . .

AGNES
(Still cool)

And Edna? And Harry?

TOBIAS
(Tiny pause; then anger)

Well, of course! What do you think!

AGNES
(Tiny smile)

I don't know. I'm listening.
(JULIA appears in the archway; wears a dressing gown; subdued, sleepy)

JULIA

Good morning. I don't suppose there's . . . shall I make some coffee?

AGNES
(Chin high)

Why don't you do that, darling.

TOBIAS
(A little embarrassed)

Good morning, Julie.

JULIA
(Hating it)

I'm sorry about last night, Daddy.

TOBIAS

Oh, well, now . . .

JULIA
(Bite to it)

I mean I'm sorry for having embarrassed you.
(Starts toward the hallway)

AGNES

Coffee.

JULIA
(Pausing at the archway; to TOBIAS*)*

Aren't you sorry for embarrassing me, too?
(Waits a moment, smiles, exits. Pause)

AGNES

Well, isn't that nice that Julia's making coffee? No? If the help aren't up, isn't it nice to have a daughter who can put a pot to boil?

TOBIAS
(Under his breath, disgusted)
"Aren't you sorry for embarrassing me, too."

AGNES
You have a problem there with Julia.

TOBIAS
I? I have a problem!

AGNES
Yes.
(Gentle irony)
But at least you have your women with you—crowded 'round,
firm arm, support. *That* must be a comfort to you. *Most* ex-
plorers go alone, don't have their families with them—pitch-
ing tents, tending the fire, shooing off the . . . the antelopes
or the bears or whatever.

TOBIAS
(Wanting to talk about it)
"Aren't you sorry for embarrassing me, too."

AGNES
Are you quoting?

TOBIAS
Yes.

AGNES
Next we'll have my younger sister with us—another porter
for the dreadful trip.
(Irony)
Claire has never missed a chance to participate in watching.
She'll be here. We'll have us all.

TOBIAS

And you'll all sit down and watch me carefully; smoke your
pipes and stir the cauldron; watch.

AGNES
(Dreamy; pleased)

Yes.

TOBIAS

You, who make all the decisions, really rule the game . . .

AGNES
(So patient)

That is an *illusion* you have.

TOBIAS

You'll all sit here—too early for . . . *anything* on this . . .
stupid Sunday—all of you and . . . and *dare* me?—when it's
just as much your choice as mine?

AGNES

Each time that Julia comes, each clockwork time . . . do
you send her back? Do you tell her, "Julia, go home to your
husband, try it again"? Do you? No, you let it . . . slip. It's
your decision, sir.

TOBIAS

It is not! I . . .

AGNES

. . . and I must live with it, resign myself one marriage
more, and wait, and hope that Julia's motherhood will come
. . . one day, one marriage.
(Tiny laugh)
I am almost too old to be a grandmother as I'd hoped . . .
too young to be one. Oh, I had wanted that: the *youngest*
older woman in the block. *Julia* is almost too old to have

a child properly, *will* be if she ever does . . . if she marries again. *You* could have pushed her back . . . if you'd wanted to.

TOBIAS
(Bewildered incredulity)
It's very early yet: that must be it. I've never heard such . . .

AGNES
Or Teddy! No? No stammering here? You'll let this pass?

TOBIAS
(Quiet embarrassment)
Please.

AGNES
(Remorseless)
When Teddy died?
(Pause)
We *could* have had another son; we could have tried. But no . . . those months—or was it a year—?

TOBIAS
No more of this!

AGNES
. . . I think it was a year, when you spilled yourself on my belly, sir? "Please? Please, Tobias?" No, you wouldn't even say it out: I don't want another child, another loss. "Please? Please, Tobias?" And guiding you, *trying* to hold you in?

TOBIAS
(Tortured)
Oh, Agnes! Please!

AGNES
"Don't leave me then, like that. Not again, Tobias. Please? *I*

can take care of it: we *won't* have another child, but please
don't . . . leave me like that." Such . . . silent . . . sad,
disgusted . . . love.

TOBIAS
(Mumbled, inaudible)

I didn't want you to have to.

AGNES

Sir?

TOBIAS
(Numb)

I didn't want you to have to . . . you know.

AGNES
(Laughs in spite of herself)

Oh, that was thoughtful of you! Like a pair of adolescents in
a rented room, or in the family car. Doubtless you hated it as
much as I.

TOBIAS
(Softly)

Yes.

AGNES

But wouldn't let me help you.

TOBIAS
(Ibid.)

No.

AGNES
(Irony)

Which is why you took to your own sweet room instead.

TOBIAS
(Ibid.)

Yes.

AGNES

The theory being pat: that a half a loaf is worse than none.
That you are racked with guilt—stupidly!—and I must *suffer*
for it.

TOBIAS
(Ibid.)

Yes?

AGNES
(Quietly; sadly)
Well, it was your decision, was it not?

TOBIAS
(Ibid.)

Yes.

AGNES

And I have made the best of it. Have lived with it. Have I
not?

TOBIAS
(Pause; a plea)
What are we going to do? About everything?

AGNES
(Quietly; sadly; cruelly)
Whatever you like. Naturally.
(Silence. CLAIRE *enters, she, too, in a dressing gown)*

CLAIRE
(Judges the situation for a moment)
Morning, kids.

AGNES
(To TOBIAS, *in reference to* CLAIRE)
All I can do, my dear, is run it for you . . . and forecast.

TOBIAS
(Glum)
Good morning, Claire.

AGNES
Julia is in the kitchen making coffee, Claire.

CLAIRE
Which means, I guess, I go watch Julia grind the beans and
drip the water, hunh?
(Exiting)
I tell ya, she's a real pioneer, that girl: coffee pot in one hand,
pistol in t'other.
(Exits)

AGNES
(Small smile)
Claire is a comfort in the early hours . . . I have been told.

TOBIAS
(A dare)
Yes?

AGNES
(Pretending not to notice his tone)
That is what I have been *told.*

TOBIAS
(Blurts it out)
Shall I ask them to leave?

AGNES
(Tiny pause)
Who?

TOBIAS
(Defiant)
Harry and Edna?

AGNES
(Tiny laugh)
Oh. For a moment I thought you meant Julia and Claire.

TOBIAS
(Glum)
No. Harry and Edna. Shall I throw them out?

AGNES
(Restatement of a fact)
Harry is your very best friend in the whole . . .

TOBIAS
(Impatient)
Yes, and Edna is yours. Well?

AGNES
You'll have to live with it either way: do or don't.

TOBIAS
(Anger rising)
Yes? Well, then, why *don't* I throw Julia and Claire out instead? Or better yet, why don't I throw the whole bunch out!?

AGNES
Or get rid of me! That would be easier: rid yourself of the harridan. Then you can run your mission and take out sainthood papers.

TOBIAS
(Clenched teeth)
I think you're stating an opinion, a preference.

AGNES

But if you *do* get rid of me . . . you'll no longer have your
life the way you want it.

TOBIAS
(Puzzled)

But that's not my . . . that's not all the choice I've got, is it?

AGNES

I don't care very much what choice you've got, my darling,
but I *am* concerned with what choice you *make*.
(JULIA *and* CLAIRE *enter;* JULIA *carries a tray with
coffee pot, cups, sugar, cream;* CLAIRE *carries a tray
with four glasses of orange juice)*
Ah, here are the helpmeets, what would we do without them.

JULIA
(Brisk, efficient)

The coffee is instant, I'm afraid; I couldn't find a bean:
Those folk must lock them up before they go to bed.
(Finds no place to put her tray down)
Come on, Pop; let's clear away a little of the debris, hunh?

TOBIAS

P-Pop?

AGNES
(Begins clearing)

It's true: we cannot drink our coffee amidst a sea of last
night's glasses. Tobias, do be a help.
(TOBIAS *rises, takes glasses to the sideboard, as* AGNES
moves some to another table)

CLAIRE
(Cheerful)

And I didn't have to do a thing; thank God for pre-squeezed
orange juice.

JULIA
(Setting the tray down)
There; now that's much better, isn't it?

TOBIAS
(In a fog)
Whatever you say, Julie.
(JULIA pours, knows what people put in)

CLAIRE
Now, I'll play waiter. Sis?

AGNES
Thank you, Claire.

CLAIRE
Little Julie?

JULIA
Just put it down beside me, Claire. I'm pouring, you can see.

CLAIRE
(Looks at her a moment, does not, offers a glass to
TOBIAS*)*
Pop?

TOBIAS
(Bewildered, apprehensive)
Thank you, Claire.

CLAIRE
(Puts JULIA's glass on the mantel)
Yours is here, daughter, when you've done with playing early-morning hostess.

JULIA
(Intently pouring; does not rise to the bait)
Thank you, Claire.

CLAIRE

Now; one for little Claire.

JULIA
(Still pouring; no expression)
Why don't you have some vodka in it, Claire? To start the
Sunday off?

AGNES
(Pleased chuckle)

Julia!

TOBIAS
(Reproving)

Please, Julie!

JULIA
(Looks up at him; cold)
Did I say something wrong, Father?

CLAIRE

Vodka? Sunday? Ten to eight? Well, hell, why not!

TOBIAS
(Quietly, as she moves to the sideboard)
You don't *have* to, Claire.

JULIA
(Dropping sugar in a cup)
Let her do what she wants.

CLAIRE
(Pouring vodka into her glass)
Yes I *do*, Tobias; the rules of the guestbook—be polite. We
have our friends and guests for patterns, don't we?—known
quantities. The drunks stay drunk; the Catholics go to Mass,
the bounders bound. We can't have changes—throws the balance off.

JULIA
(Ibid.)
Besides; you like to drink.

CLAIRE
Besides, I like to drink. Just think, Tobias, what would happen if the patterns changed: you wouldn't know where you stood, and the world would be full of strangers; that would never do.

JULIA
(Not very friendly)
Bring me my orange juice, will you please.

CLAIRE
(Getting it for her)
Oooh, Julia's back for a spell, I think—settling in.

JULIA
(Handing TOBIAS *his coffee)*
Father?

TOBIAS
(Embarrassed)
Thank you, Julia.

JULIA
Mother?

AGNES
(Comfortable)
Thank you, darling.

JULIA
Yours is here, Claire; on the tray.

CLAIRE
(Considers a moment, looks at JULIA's *orange juice,*
still in one of her hands, calmly pours it on the rug)
Your juice is here, Julia, when you want it.

AGNES
(Furious)

CLAIRE!

TOBIAS
(Mild reproach)
For God's sake, Claire.

JULIA
(Looks at the mess on the rug; shrugs)
Well, why not. Nothing changes.

CLAIRE
Besides, our friends upstairs don't like the room; they'll want
some alterations.
*(*CLAIRE *sits down)*

TOBIAS
(Lurches to his feet; stands, legs apart)
Now! All of you! Sit down! Shut up. I want to talk to you.

JULIA
Did I give you sugar, Mother?

TOBIAS
BE QUIET, JULIA!

AGNES
Shhh, my darling, yes, you did.

TOBIAS
I want to talk to you.
(Silence)

CLAIRE
(Slightly mocking encouragement)
Well, go *on,* Tobias.

TOBIAS
(A plea)
You, too, Claire? Please.
*(Silence. The women stir their coffee or look at him,
or at the floor. They seem like children about to be
lectured, unwilling, and dangerous, but, for the mo-
ment, behaved)*
Now.
(Pause)
Now, something happened here last night, and I don't mean
Julia's hysterics with the gun—be quiet, Julia!—though I *do*
mean that, in part. I mean . . .
(Deep sigh)
. . . Harry and Edna . . . coming here . . .
(JULIA snorts)
Yes? Did you want to say something, Julia? No? I came down
here and I sat, all night—hours—and I did something rather
rare for this family: I *thought* about something. . . .

AGNES
(Mild)
I'm sorry, Tobias, but that's not fair.

TOBIAS
(Riding over)
I *thought.* I sat down here and I thought about all of us . . .
and everything. Now, Harry and Edna have come to us and
. . . asked for help.

JULIA
That is not *true.*

TOBIAS
Be quiet!

JULIA

That is not true! They have not *asked* for anything!

AGNES

. . . please, Julia . . .

JULIA

They have *told!* They have come in here and *ordered!*

CLAIRE
(*Toasts*)

Just like the family.

TOBIAS

Asked! If you're begging and you've got your pride . . .

JULIA

If you're begging, then you may not have your pride!

AGNES
(*Quiet contradiction*)

I don't think that's true, Julia.

CLAIRE

Julia wouldn't know. Ask me.

JULIA
(*Adamant*)

Those people have no right!

TOBIAS

No right? All these years? We've known them since . . . for
God's sake, Julia, those people are our *friends!*

JULIA
(*Hard*)

THEN TAKE THEM IN!

(Silence)

Take these . . . intruders in.

CLAIRE

(To JULIA: *hard)*

Look, baby; didn't you get the message on rights last night?
Didn't you learn about intrusion, what the score is, who belongs?

JULIA

(To TOBIAS*)*

You bring these people in here, Father, and I'm leaving!

TOBIAS

(Almost daring her)

Yes?

JULIA

I don't mean coming and going, Father; I mean as *family!*

TOBIAS

(Frustration and rage)

HARRY AND EDNA ARE OUR FRIENDS!!

JULIA

(Equal)

THEY ARE INTRUDERS!!

(Silence)

CLAIRE

(To TOBIAS, *laughing)*

Crisis sure brings out the best in us, don't it, Tobe? The family circle? Julia standing there . . . *asserting;* perpetual brat,
and maybe ready to pull a Claire. *And* poor Claire! Not much
help there either, is there? And lookit Agnes, talky Agnes,
ruler of the roost, and maître d', *and* licensed wife—silent. All

cozy, coffee, thinking of the menu for the week, *planning*.
Poor Tobe.

AGNES
(Calm, assured)

Thank you, Claire; I was merely waiting—until I'd heard,
and thought a little, listened to the rest of you. I thought
someone should sit back. Especially me: ruler of the roost,
licensed wife, midnight . . . nurse. And I've been thinking
about Harry and Edna; about disease.

TOBIAS
(After a pause)

About what?

CLAIRE
(After a swig)

About disease.

JULIA

Oh, for God's sake . . .

AGNES

About disease—or, if you like, the terror.

CLAIRE
(Chuckles softly)

Unh, hunh.

JULIA
(Furious)

TERROR!?

AGNES
(Unperturbed)

Yes: the terror. Or the plague—they're both the same. Edna
and Harry have come to us—dear friends, our very best,

though there's a judgment to be made about that, I think
—have come to us and brought the plague. Now, poor Tobias
has sat up all night and wrestled with the moral problem.

TOBIAS

(Frustration; anger)

I've not been . . . *wrestling* with some . . . abstract problem! These are *people!* Harry and Edna! These are our
friends, God damn it!

AGNES

Yes, but they've brought the plague with them, and that's
another matter. Let me tell you something about disease . . .
mortal illness; you either are immune to it . . . or you fight
it. If you are immune, you wade right in, you treat the patient
until he either lives, or dies of it. But if you are *not* immune,
you risk infection. Ten centuries ago—and even less—the
treatment was quite simple . . . burn them. Burn their
bodies, burn their houses, burn their clothes—and move to
another town, if you were enlightened. But now, with mod-
ern medicine, we merely isolate; we quarantine, we ostracize
—if we are not immune ourselves, or unless we are saints. So,
your night-long vigil, darling, your reasoning in the cold, pure
hours, has been over the patient, and not the illness. It is not
Edna and Harry who have come to us—our friends—it is a
disease.

TOBIAS

(Quiet anguish, mixed with impatience)

Oh, for God's sake, Agnes! It is our friends! What am I supposed to do? Say: "Look, you can't stay here, you two, you've
got trouble. You're friends, and all, but you come in here
clean." Well, I can't do that. No. Agnes, for God's sake, if
. . . if that's all Harry and Edna mean to us, then . . . then
what about *us?* When we talk to each other . . . what have
we meant? Anything? When we touch, when we promise, and
say . . . yes, or please . . . with our*selves?* . . . have we

meant, yes, but only if . . . if there's any condition, Agnes!
Then it's . . . all been empty.

AGNES
(*Noncommittal*)
Perhaps. But blood binds us. Blood holds us together when
we've no more . . . deep affection for ourselves than others.
I am *not* asking you to choose between your family and . . .
our friends. . . .

TOBIAS
Yes you are!

AGNES
(*Eyes closed*)
I am merely saying that there is *disease* here! And I ask you:
who in this family is immune?

CLAIRE
(*Weary statement of fact*)
I am. I've had it. I'm still alive, I think.

AGNES
Claire is the strongest of us all: the walking wounded often
are, the least susceptible; but think about the rest of us. Are
we immune to it? The plague, my darling, the terror sitting in
the room upstairs? Well, if we are, then . . . on with it! And,
if we're not . . .
(*Shrugs*)
well, why not be infected, why not die of it? We're bound to
die of something . . . soon, or in a while. Or shall we burn
them out, rid ourselves of it all . . . and wait for the next
invasion. You decide, my darling.
(*Silence.* TOBIAS *rises, walks to the window; the
others sit.* HARRY *and* EDNA *appear in the archway,
dressed for the day, but not with coats*)

EDNA
(No emotion)

Good morning.

AGNES
(Brief pause)

Ah, you're up.

CLAIRE

Good morning, Edna, Harry.
(JULIA *does not look at them;* TOBIAS *does, but says nothing)*

EDNA
(A deep breath, rather a recitation)

Harry wants to talk to Tobias. I think that they should be alone. Perhaps . . .

AGNES

Of course.
(The three seated women rise, as at a signal, begin to gather the coffee things)
Why don't we all go in the kitchen, make a proper breakfast.

HARRY

Well, now, no; you don't have to . . .

AGNES

Yes, yes, we want to leave you to your talk. Tobias?

TOBIAS
(Quiet)

Uh . . . yes.

AGNES
(To TOBIAS; *comfortingly)*

We'll be nearby.

(The women start out)
Did you sleep well, Edna? Did you sleep at all? I've never had
that bed, but I know that when . . .
(The women have exited)

HARRY
(Watching them go; laughs ruefully)
Boy, look at 'em go. They got outa *here* quick enough. You'd
think there was a . . .
(Trails off, sees TOBIAS *is ill at ease; says, gently)*
Morning, Tobias.

TOBIAS
(Grateful)
Morning, Harry.
(Both men stay standing)

HARRY
(Rubs his hands together)
You, ah . . . you know what I'd like to do? Something I've
never done in my life, except once, when I was about twenty-
four?

TOBIAS
(Not trying to guess)
No? What?

HARRY
Have a drink before breakfast? Is, is that all right?

TOBIAS
(Smiles wanly, moves slowly toward the sideboard)
Sure.

HARRY
(Shy)
Will you join me?

TOBIAS
(Very young)

I guess so, yes. There isn't any ice.

HARRY

Well, just some whiskey, then; neat.

TOBIAS

Brandy?

HARRY

No, oh, God, no.

TOBIAS

Whiskey, then.

HARRY

Yes. Thank you.

TOBIAS
(Somewhat glum)

Well, here's to youth again.

HARRY

Yes.
(Drinks)

Doesn't taste too bad in the morning, does it?

TOBIAS

No, but I had some . . . before.

HARRY

When?

TOBIAS

Earlier . . . oh, three, four, while you all were . . . asleep,
or whatever you were doing.

HARRY
(Seemingly casual)
Oh, you were . . . awake, hunh?

TOBIAS
Yes.

HARRY
I slept a *little*.
(Glum laugh)
God.

TOBIAS
What?

HARRY
You know what I did last night?

TOBIAS
No?

HARRY
I got out of bed and I . . . crawled in with Edna?

TOBIAS
Yes?

HARRY
She held me. She let me stay awhile, then I could see she wanted to, and I didn't . . . so I went back. But it was funny.

TOBIAS
(Nods)
Yeah.

HARRY
Do you . . . do you, uh, like Edna . . . Tobias?

TOBIAS
(Embarrassed)
Well, sure I *like* her, Harry.

HARRY
(Pause)
Now, Tobias, about last night, and yesterday, and our coming
here, now . . .

HARRY	TOBIAS
I was talking about it to Edna, last night, and I said, "Look, Edna, what do we think we're doing."	I sat up all night and I thought about it, Harry and I talked to Agnes this morning, before you all came down.

HARRY
I'm sorry.

TOBIAS
I said, I sat up all night and I thought about it, Harry, and I
talked to Agnes, too, before you all came down, and . . . By
God, it isn't easy, Harry . . . but we can make it . . . if you
want us to. . . . I can, I mean, I *think* I can.

HARRY
No . . . we're . . . we're going, Tobias.

TOBIAS
I don't know what help . . . I don't know *how* . . .

HARRY
I said: we're *going*.

TOBIAS
Yes, but . . . you're going?

HARRY
(Nice, shy smile)
Sure.

TOBIAS
But, but you can *try* it here . . . or we can, God, I don't
know, Harry. You can't go back there; you've got to . . .

HARRY
Got to what? Sell the house? Buy another? Move to the club?

TOBIAS
You came *here!*

HARRY
(Sad)
Do you *want* us here, Tobias?

TOBIAS
You *came* here.

HARRY
Do you *want* us here?

TOBIAS
You *came! Here!*

HARRY
(Too clearly enunciated)
Do   you   want   us   here?
(Subdued, almost apologetic)
Edna and I . . . there's . . . so much . . . over the dam,
so many . . . disappointments, evasions, I guess, lies maybe
. . . so much we remember we wanted, once . . . so little
that   we've . . . settled   for . . . we   talk,   sometimes,   but

mostly . . . no. We don't . . . "like." Oh, sure, we *like*
. . . but I've always been a little shy—gruff, you know, and
. . . shy. And Edna isn't . . . happy—I suppose that's it.
We . . . we like you and . . . and Agnes, and . . . well
Claire, and Julia, too, I guess I mean . . . I like you, and you
like me, I think, and . . . you're our best friends, but . . .
I told Edna upstairs, I said: Edna, what if they'd come to us?
And she didn't say anything. And I said: Edna, if they'd come
to us like this, and even though we don't have . . . Julia, and
all of that, I . . . Edna, I wouldn't take them in.

(*Brief silence*)

I wouldn't take them in, Edna; they don't . . . they don't
have any right. And she said: yes, I know; they wouldn't have
the right.

(*Brief silence*)

Toby, I wouldn't let *you* stay.

(*Shy, embarrassed*)

You . . . you don't *want* us, do you, Toby? You don't want
us here.

TOBIAS

(*This next is an aria. It must have in its performance
all the horror and exuberance of a man who has kept
his emotions under control too long.* TOBIAS *will be
carried to the edge of hysteria, and he will find himself laughing, sometimes, while he cries from sheer release. All in all, it is genuine and bravura at the same
time, one prolonging the other. I shall try to notate
it somewhat*)

(*Softly, and as if the word were unfamiliar*)

Want?

(*Same*)

What? Do I what?

(*Abrupt laugh; joyous*)

DO I WANT?

(*More laughter; also a sob*)

DO I WANT YOU HERE!

(Hardly able to speak from the laughter)

> You come in here, you come in
> here with your . . . wife, and
> with your . . . terror! And you
> ask me if I want you here!

(Great breathing sounds)

> YES! OF COURSE! I WANT YOU HERE!
> I HAVE BUILT THIS HOUSE! I WANT
> YOU IN IT! I WANT YOUR PLAGUE!
> YOU'VE GOT SOME TERROR WITH
> YOU? BRING IT IN!

(Pause, then, even louder)

> BRING IT IN!! YOU'VE GOT THE EN-
> TREE, BUDDY, YOU DON'T NEED A
> KEY! YOU'VE GOT THE ENTREE,
> BUDDY! FORTY YEARS!

(Soft, now; soft and fast, almost a monotone)

> You don't need to ask me, Harry,
> you don't need to ask a thing;
> you're our friends, our very best
> friends in the world, and you
> don't have to ask.

(A shout)

> WANT? ASK?

(Soft, as before)

> You come for dinner don't you
> come for cocktails see us at the
> club on Saturdays and talk and
> lie and laugh with us and pat old
> Agnes on the hand and say you
> don't know what old Toby'd do
> without her and we've known you
> all these years and we love each
> other don't we?

(Shout)

> DON'T WE?! DON'T WE LOVE EACH
> OTHER?

(Soft again, laughter and tears in it)

> Doesn't friendship grow to that? To love? Doesn't forty years amount to anything? We've cast our lot together, boy, we're friends, we've been through lots of thick OR thin together. Which is it, boy?

(Shout)

> WHICH IS IT, BOY?!
> THICK?!
> THIN?!
> WELL, WHATEVER IT IS, WE'VE BEEN THROUGH IT, BOY!

(Soft)

> And you don't have to ask. I like you, Harry, yes, I really do, I don't like Edna, but that's not half the point, I like you fine; I find my liking you has limits . . .

(Loud)

> BUT THOSE ARE MY LIMITS!
> NOT YOURS!

(Soft)

> The fact I like you well enough, but not enough . . . that best friend in the world should be something else—more—well, that's my poverty. So, bring your wife, and bring your terror, bring your plague.

(Loud)

> BRING YOUR PLAGUE!

(The four women appear in the archway, coffee cups in hand, stand, watch)

> I DON'T WANT YOU HERE!
> YOU ASKED?!

NO! I DON'T

(Loud)

BUT BY CHRIST YOU'RE GOING TO
STAY HERE!
YOU'VE GOT THE RIGHT!
THE RIGHT!
DO YOU KNOW THE WORD?
THE RIGHT!

(Soft)

You've put nearly forty years in it,
baby; so have I, and if it's nothing, I don't give a damn, you've
got the right to be here, you've
earned it

(Loud)

AND BY GOD YOU'RE GOING TO
TAKE IT!
DO YOU HEAR ME?!
YOU BRING YOUR TERROR AND YOU
COME IN HERE AND YOU LIVE
WITH US!
YOU BRING YOUR PLAGUE!
YOU STAY WITH US!
I DON'T WANT YOU HERE!
I DON'T LOVE YOU!
BUT BY GOD . . . YOU STAY!!

(Pause)

STAY!

(Softer)

Stay!

(Soft, tears)

Stay. Please? Stay?

(Pause)

Stay? Please? Stay?

(A silence in the room. HARRY, *numb, rises; the
women come into the room, slowly, stand. The
play is quiet and subdued from now until the end)*

EDNA

(Calm)

Harry, will you bring our bags down? Maybe Tobias will help you. Will you ask him?

HARRY

(Gentle)

Sure.

(Goes to TOBIAS, *who is quietly wiping tears from his face, takes him gently by the shoulder)*

Tobias? Will you help me? Get the bags upstairs?

*(*TOBIAS *nods, puts his arm around* HARRY. *The two men exit. Silence)*

EDNA

(Stirring her coffee; slightly strained, but conversational)

Poor Harry; he's not a . . . callous man, for all his bluff.

(Relaxing a little, almost a contentment)

He . . . he came to my bed last night, got in with me, I . . . let him stay, and talk. I let him think I . . . wanted to make love; he . . . it pleases him, I think—to know he would be wanted, if he . . . He said to me . . . He . . . he lay there in the dark with me—this man—and he said to me, very softly, and like a little boy, rather: "Do they love us? Do they love us, Edna?" Oh, I let a silence go by. "Well . . . as much as we love them . . . I should think."

(Pause)

The hair on his chest is very gray . . . and soft. "Would . . . would we let them stay, Edna?" Almost a whisper. Then still again.

(Kindly)

Well, I hope he told Tobias something simple, something to help. We mustn't press our luck, must we: test.

(Pause. Slight smile)

It's sad to come to the end of it, isn't it, nearly the end; so

much more of it gone by . . . than left, and still not know—
still not have learned . . . the boundaries, what we may not
do . . . not ask, for fear of looking in a mirror. We *shouldn't*
have come.

AGNES
(A bit by rote)

Now, Edna . . .

EDNA

For our own sake; our own . . . lack. It's sad to know you've
gone through it all, or most of it, without . . . that the one
body you've wrapped your arms around . . . the only skin
you've ever known . . . is your own—and that it's dry . . .
and not warm.
　　　(Pause. Back to slightly strained conversational tone)
What will you do, Julia? Will you be seeing Douglas?

JULIA
(Looking at her coffee)
I haven't thought about it; I don't know; I doubt it.

AGNES
Time.
　　　(Pause. They look at her)
Time happens, I suppose.
　　　(Pause. They still look)
To people. Everything becomes . . . too late, finally. You
know it's going on . . . up on the hill; you can see the dust,
and hear the cries, and the steel . . . but you wait; and time
happens. When you *do* go, sword, shield . . . finally . . .
there's nothing there . . . save rust; bones; and the wind.
　　　(Pause)
I'm sorry about the coffee, Edna. The help must hide the
beans, or take them with them when they go to bed.

EDNA

Oooh. Coffee and wine: they're much the same with me--I can't tell good from bad.

CLAIRE

Would anyone . . . besides Claire . . . care to have a drink?

AGNES
(Muttered)

Oh, really, Claire.

CLAIRE

Edna?

EDNA
(Little deprecating laugh)

Oh, good heavens, thank you, Claire. No.

CLAIRE

Julia?

JULIA
(Looks up at her; steadily; slowly)

All right; thank you. I will.

EDNA
(As AGNES *is about to speak; rising)*

I think I hear the men.
(TOBIAS *and* HARRY *appear in the archway, with bags)*

TOBIAS

We'll just take them to the car, now.
(They do so)

EDNA
(Pleasant, but a little strained)

Thank you, Agnes, you've been . . . well, just thank you. We'll be seeing you.

AGNES
(Rises, too; some worry on her face)
Yes; well, don't be strangers.

EDNA
(Laughs)
Oh, good Lord, how could we be? Our lives are . . . the
same.
(Pause)
Julia . . . think a little.

JULIA
(A trifle defiant)
Oh, I will, Edna. I'm fond of marriage.

EDNA
Claire, my darling, *do* be good.

CLAIRE
(Two drinks in her hands; bravura)
Well, I'll try to be quiet.

EDNA
I'm going into town on Thursday, Agnes. Would you like to
come?
*(A longer pause than necessary, CLAIRE and JULIA
look at AGNES)*

AGNES
(Just a trifle awkward)
Well . . . no, I don't think so, Edna; I've . . . I've so much
to do.

EDNA
(Cooler; sad)
Oh. Well . . . perhaps another week.

AGNES
Oh, yes; we'll do it.
(The men reappear)

TOBIAS
(Somewhat formal, reserved)

All done.

HARRY
(Slight sigh)

All set.

AGNES
(Going to HARRY, *embracing him)*
Harry, my darling; take good care.

HARRY
(Kisses her, awkwardly, on the cheek)
Th-thank you, Agnes; you, too, Julia? You . . . you be good.

JULIA

Goodbye, Harry.

CLAIRE
(Handing JULIA *her drink)*
'Bye, Harry: see you 'round.

HARRY
(Smiles, a little ruefully)

Sure thing, Claire.

EDNA
(Embraces TOBIAS)
Goodbye, Tobias . . . thank you.

TOBIAS
(Mumbled)

Goodbye, Edna.

(Tiny silence)

HARRY
(Puts his hand out, grabs TOBIAS', *shakes it hard)*
Thanks, old man.

TOBIAS
(Softly; sadly)
Please? Stay?

(Pause)

HARRY
(Nods)
See you at the club. Well? Edna?
(They start out)

AGNES
(After them)
Drive carefully, now. It's Sunday.

EDNA'S AND HARRY'S VOICES
All right. Goodbye. Thank you.
(The four in the room together. JULIA *and* CLAIRE
have sat down; AGNES *moves to* TOBIAS, *puts her arm
around him)*

AGNES
(Sigh)
Well. Here we all are. You all right, my darling?

TOBIAS
(Clears his throat)
Sure.

AGNES
(Still with her arm around him)
Your daughter has taken to drinking in the morning, I hope
you'll notice.

TOBIAS
(Unconcerned)

Oh?

(Moves away from her)

I had one here . . . somewhere, one with Harry. Oh, there it is.

AGNES

Well, I would seem to have *three* early-morning drinkers now. I hope it won't become a club. We'd have to get a license, would we not?

TOBIAS

Just think of it as very late at night.

AGNES

All right, I will.

(Silence)

TOBIAS

I tried.

(Pause)

I was honest.

(Silence)

Didn't I?

(Pause)

Wasn't I?

JULIA
(Pause)

You were very honest, Father. And you tried.

TOBIAS

Didn't I try, Claire? Wasn't I honest?

CLAIRE
(Comfort; rue)

Sure you were. You tried.

TOBIAS

I'm sorry. I apologize.

AGNES
(To fill a silence)

What I find most astonishing—aside from my belief that I will, one day . . . lose my mind—but when? Never, I begin to think, as the years go by, or that I'll not *know* if it happens, or maybe even *has*—what I find most astonishing, I think, is the wonder of daylight, of the sun. All the centuries, millenniums—all the history—I wonder if that's why we sleep at night, because the darkness still . . . frightens us? They say we sleep to let the demons out—to let the mind go raving mad, our dreams and nightmares all our logic gone awry, the dark side of our reason. And when the daylight comes again . . . comes order with it.
(Sad chuckle)

Poor Edna and Harry.
(Sigh)

Well, they're safely gone . . . and we'll all forget . . . quite soon.
(Pause)

Come now; we can begin the day.

CURTAIN

Box AND
Quotations from Chairman Mao Tse-tung

TWO INTER-RELATED PLAYS

FOR

MAEVE BRENNAN

AND

HOWARD MOSS

FIRST PERFORMED AT THE STUDIO ARENA THEATRE,
BUFFALO, NEW YORK, MARCH 6, 1968

BOX
THE VOICE OF RUTH WHITE

QUOTATIONS FROM CHAIRMAN MAO TSE-TUNG
CONRAD YAMA *as* CHAIRMAN MAO
LUCILLE PATTON *as* LONG-WINDED LADY
JENNY EGAN *as* OLD WOMAN
WILLIAM NEEDLES *as* MINISTER

Directed by ALAN SCHNEIDER

FIRST PERFORMED IN NEW YORK CITY
AT THE BILLY ROSE THEATRE, SEPTEMBER 30, 1968

BOX
THE VOICE OF RUTH WHITE

QUOTATIONS FROM CHAIRMAN MAO TSE-TUNG
WYMAN PENDLETON *as* CHAIRMAN MAO
NANCY KELLY *as* LONG-WINDED LADY
SUDIE BOND *as* OLD WOMAN
GEORGE BARTENIEFF *as* MINISTER

Directed by ALAN SCHNEIDER

INTRODUCTION

While it is true that these two short plays—*Box* and *Quotations from Chairman Mao Tse-tung*—are separate works, were conceived at different though not distant moments, stand by themselves, and can be played one without the company of the other, I feel that they are more effective performed enmeshed.

Even more . . . *Quotations from Chairman Mao Tse-tung* would most probably not have been written had not *Box* been composed beforehand, and *Mao* is, therefore, an outgrowth of and extension of the shorter play. As well, I have attempted, in these two related plays, several experiments having to do—in the main—with the application of musical form to dramatic structure, and the use of *Box* as a parenthesis around *Mao* is part of that experiment.

I may as well insist right now that these two plays are quite simple. By that I mean that while technically they are fairly complex and they do demand from an audience quite close attention, their content can be apprehended without much difficulty. All that one need do is—quite simply—relax and let the plays happen. That, and be willing to approach the dramatic experience without a preconception of what the nature of the dramatic experience should be.

I recall that when a play of mine called *Tiny Alice* opened in New York City a few years ago the majority of the critics wrote in their reviews—such as they were— that the play was far too complicated and obscure for the audience to understand. Leaving to one side the thoughts one might have about the assumption on the part of the critics that what they found confusing would necessarily confound an audience, this reportage had a most curious effect on the audiences that viewed the play. At the preview performances of *Tiny Alice* the audiences—while hardly to a man sympathetic to the play—found it quite clear; while later—after the critics had spoken on it—the audiences were very confused. The play had not changed one whit; a label had merely been attached to it, and what was experienced was the label and not the nature of the goods.

A playwright—unless he is creating escapist romances (an honorable occupation, of course)—has two obligations: first, to make some statement about the condition of "man" (as it is put) and, second, to make some statement about the nature of the art form with which he is working. In both instances he must attempt change. In the first instance—since very few serious plays are written to glorify the status quo—the playwright must try to alter his society; in the second instance—since art must move, or wither—the playwright must try to alter the forms within which his precursors have had to work. And I believe that an audience has an obligation to be interested in and sympathetic to these aims—certainly to the second of them. Therefore, an audience has an obligation (to itself, to the art form in which it is participating, and even to the playwright) to be willing to experience a work on its own terms.

I said before that these two plays are simple (as well as complex), and they *are* simple once they are experienced relaxed and without a weighing of their methods against more familiar ones.

EDWARD ALBEE

BOX

Curtain rises in darkness. Lights go up slowly to reveal the outline of a large cube. The cube should take up almost all of a small stage opening. The side facing the audience is open, but we should see the other five sides clearly, therefore the interior of the cube should be distorted, smaller at the backstage side, for example; also, none of the sides should be exactly square in shape, but the angles of distortion should not be very great—not so great as to call attention to themselves and destroy the feeling of a cube. When the lights are fully up on the cube —quite bright light which stays constant until the final dim-out—there should be five seconds' silence.

VOICE

(The VOICE *should not come from the stage, but should seem to be coming from nearby the spectator—from the back or the sides of the theater. The* VOICE *of a woman; not young, but not ancient, either: fiftyish. Neither a sharp, crone's voice, but not refined. A Middle Western farm woman's voice would be best.*

Matter-of-fact; announcement of a subject)
Box.

(Five-second silence)

Box.

(Three-second silence)

Nicely done. Well put . . .

(Pause)

. . . together. Box.

(Three-second silence. More conversational now)

Room inside for a sedia d'ondalo, which, in English—for that is Italian—would be, is, rocking chair. Room to rock. *And* room to move about in . . . some. Enough.

(Three-second silence)

Carpentry is among the arts going out . . . or crafts, if you're of a nonclassical disposition. There are others: other arts which have gone down to craft and which are going further . . . walls, brick walls, music . . .

(Pause)

. . . the making of good bread if you won't laugh; living. Many arts: all craft now . . . and going further. But *this* is solid, perfect joins . . . good work. Knock and there's no give—no give of sound, I mean. A thud; no hollow. Oh, very good work; fine timber, and so fastidious, like when they shined the bottoms of the shoes . . . *and* the instep. Not only where you might *expect* they'd shine the bottoms if they *did* . . . but even the instep.

(Two-second silence. Grudging, but not very)

And other crafts have come up . . . if not to replace, then . . . occupy.

(Tiny laugh)

4

Nature abhors, among so many, so much else . . .
amongst so much, us, itself, they say, vacuum.

(Five-second silence. A listing)

System as conclusion, in the sense of method as an end,
the dice so big you can hardly throw them any more.

(Some awe, some sadness)

Seven hundred million babies dead in the time it takes,
took, to knead the dough to make a proper loaf. Well,
little wonder so many . . . went . . . cut off, said no
instead of hanging on.

(Three-second silence)

Apathy, I think.

(Five-second silence)

Inevitability. And progress is merely a direction, movement.

(Earnest)

When it was *simple* . . .

(Light, self-mocking laugh)

Ah, well, yes, when it was simple.

(Three-second silence. Wistful)

Beautiful, beautiful box.

(Three-second silence)

And room enough to walk around in, take a turn.

(Tiny pause)

If only they had *told* us! Clearly! When it was clear that
we were not only corrupt—for there is nothing that is
not, or little—but corrupt to the selfishness, to the corruption that we should die to keep it . . . go under
rather than . . .

(Three-second silence. Sigh)

Oh, my.

(Five-second silence)

Or was it the milk? *That* may have been the moment: spilling and spilling and killing all those children to make a point. A penny or two, and a symbol at that, and I suppose the children were symbolic, too, though they died, and couldn't stop. Once it starts—gets to a certain point —the momentum is too much. But spilling milk!

(Two-second silence. Firmly felt)

Oh, shame!

(A little schoolmarmish)

The *Pope* warned us; *he* said so. There are no possessions, he said; so long as there are some with nothing we have no right to anything.

(Two-second silence)

It's the *little* things, the *small* cracks. Oh, for every pound of milk they spill you can send a check to someone, but that does not unspill. That it *can* be *done* is the crack. And if you go back to a partita . . . ahhhhh, what when it makes you cry!? Not from the beauty of it, but from solely that you cry from loss . . . so precious. When art begins to hurt . . . when art begins to hurt, it's time to look around. Yes it is.

(Three-second silence)

Yes it is.

(Three-second silence)

No longer just great beauty which takes you more to ev-

6

erything, but a reminder! And not of what *can* . . . but what *has*. Yes, when art hurts . . .

(Three-second silence)

Box.

(Two-second silence)

And room enough to move around, except like a fly. That would be *very* good!

(Rue)

Yes, but so would so much.

(Two-second silence. Schoolmarmish)

Here is the thing about tension and the tonic—the important thing.

(Pause)

The release of tension is the return to consonance; no matter how far traveled, one comes back, not circular, not to the starting point, but a . . . setting down again, and the beauty of art is order—not what is familiar, necessarily, but order . . . on its own terms.

(Two-second silence. Sigh)

So much . . . flies. A billion birds at once, black net skimming the ocean, or the Monarchs that time, that island, blown by the wind, but going straight . . . in a direction. Order!

(Two-second silence)

And six sides to bounce it all off of.

(Three-second silence. Brave start again)

When the beauty of it reminds us of *loss*. Instead of the attainable. When it tells us what we cannot have . . .

7

well, then . . . it no longer relates . . . *does* it. That is
the thing about music. That is why we cannot listen any
more.

(Pause)

Because we cry.

(Three-second silence)

And *if* he says, or *she* . . . why are you doing that?, and,
and your only honest response is: art hurts . . .

(Little laugh)

Well.

(Five-second silence)

Look! More birds! Another . . . sky of them.

(Five-second silence)

It is not a matter of garden, or straight lines, or even . . .
morality. It's only when you can't come back; when you
get in some distant key; that when you say, the tonic! the
tonic! and they say, what is *that?* It's *then.*

(Three-second silence)

There! More! A thousand, and one below them, moving
fast in the opposite way!

(Two-second silence)

What was it used to frighten me? Bell buoys and sea
gulls; the *sound* of them, at night, in a fog, when I was
very young.

(A little laugh)

Before I had ever seen them, before I had heard them.

(Some wonder)

But I knew what they *were* . . . a thousand miles from

8

the sea. Land-locked, never been, and yet the sea
sounds . . .

(Three-second silence. Very matter-of-fact)

Well, we can exist with *any*thing; with*out*. There's little
that we need to have to go on . . . evolving. Goodness;
we all died when we were thirty once. Now, much
younger. Much.

(Suddenly aware of something)

But it *couldn't* have been fog, not the sea-fog. Not way
back *there*. It was the memory of it, to be seen and
proved later. And more! and more! they're all moving!
The memory of what we have not known. And so it is
with the fog, which I had never seen, yet knew it. And
the resolution of a chord; no difference.

(Three-second silence)

And even that can happen here, I guess. But unprovable.
Ahhhhh. That makes the difference, does it *not*. Nothing
can seep here except the memory of what I'll not prove.

(Two-second silence. Sigh)

Well, we give up something for something.

(Three-second silence. Listing again; pleased)

Sturdy, light . . . interesting . . . in its way. Room
enough for a sedia d'ondalo, which is the Italian of
. . . or for . . . *of*, I prefer . . . The Italian of rocking
chair.

(Three-second silence)

When art hurts. That is what to remember.

(Two-second silence)

9

What to look for. Then the corruption . . .

> *(Three-second silence)*

Then the corruption is complete.

> *(Five-second silence. The sound of bell buoys and sea gulls begins, faintly, growing, but never very loud)*

Nothing belongs.

> *(Three-second silence. Great sadness)*

Look; more of them; a black net . . . skimming.

> *(Pause)*

And just one . . . moving beneath . . . in the opposite way.

> *(Three-second silence. Very sad, supplicating)*

Milk.

> *(Three-second silence)*

Milk.

> *(Five-second silence. Wistful)*

Box.

> *(Silence, except for the sound of bell buoys and sea gulls. Very slow fading of lights to black, sound of bell buoys and sea gulls fading with the light)*

QUOTATIONS
FROM CHAIRMAN
MAO TSE-TUNG

The outline of the cube remains; the set for QUOTATIONS FROM CHAIRMAN MAO TSE-TUNG *appears within the outlines of the cube during the brief blackout.*

CHARACTERS

CHAIRMAN MAO

Should be played, ideally, by an Oriental actor who resembles Mao. However, the role can be played either with makeup or a face mask. In any event, an attempt should be made to make the actor resemble Mao as much as possible. Mao speaks rather like a teacher. He does not raise his voice; he is not given to histrionics. His tone is always reasonable, sometimes a little sad; occasionally a half-smile will appear. He may wander about the set a little, but, for the most part, he should keep his place by the railing. Mao always speaks to the audience. He is aware of the other characters, but he must never look at them or suggest in any way that anything they say is affecting his words. When I say that Mao always addresses the audience I do not mean that he must look them in the eye constantly. Once he has made it clear that he is addressing them he may keep that intention clear in any way he likes—looking away, speaking to only one person, whatever.

LONG-WINDED LADY

A lady of sixty. I care very little about how she looks so long as she looks very average and upper middle-class. Nothing exotic; nothing strange. She should, I think, stay pretty much to her deck chair. She never speaks to the audience. Sometimes she is clearly speaking to the Minister; more often she is speaking both for his benefit and her own. She can withdraw entirely into self from time to time. She uses the Minister as a sounding board.

OLD WOMAN

Shabby, poor, without being so in a comedy sense. She has a bag with her. An orange; an apple, one or two cans: beans, canned meat. She will eat from these occasionally. Her bag also contains a fork, or a spoon, a napkin, and a can-opener. She is aware of everybody, but speaks only to the audience. Her reading of her poem can have some emotion to it, though never too much. It should be made clear, though, that while the subject of her speeches is dear to her heart, a close matter, she is reciting a poem. She may look at the other characters from time to time, but what she says must never seem to come from what any of the others has said. She might nod in agreement with Mao now and again, or shake her head over the plight of the Long-Winded Lady. She should stay in one place, up on something.

MINISTER

Has no lines, and stays in his deck chair. He must try to pay close attention to the Long-Winded Lady, though— nod, shake his head, cluck, put an arm tentatively out, etc. He must also keep busy with his pipe and pouch and matches. He should doze off from time to time. He must never *make the audience feel he is looking at them or is aware of them. Also, he is not aware of either Mao or the Old Woman. He is seventy or so, has white or gray hair, a clerical collar. A florid face would be nice. If a thin actor is playing the role, however, then make the face sort of gray-yellow-white.*

GENERAL COMMENTS

For this play to work according to my intention, careful attention must be paid to what I have written about the characters: to whom they speak; to whom they may and may not react; how they speak; how they move or do not. Alteration from the patterns I have set may be interesting, but I fear they will destroy the attempt of the experiment: musical structure—form and counterpoint. Primarily the characters must seem interested in what they themselves are doing and saying. While the lines must not be read metronome-exact, I feel that a certain set rhythm will come about, quite of itself. No one rushes in on the end of anyone else's speech; no one waits too long. I have indicated, quite precisely, within the speeches of the Long-Winded Lady, by means of commas, periods, semi-colons, colons, dashes and dots (as well as parenthetical stage directions), the speech rhythms. Please observe them carefully, for they were not thrown

in, like herbs on a salad, to be mixed about. I have under-
lined words I want stressed. I have capitalized for loud-
ness, and used exclamation points for emphasis. There
are one or two seeming questions that I have left the
question mark off of. This was done on purpose, as an
out-loud reading will make self-evident.

*The deck of an ocean liner. Bright daylight, that partic-
ular kind of brightness that is possible only in mid-ocean.*

CHAIRMAN MAO

There is an ancient Chinese fable called "The foolish
old man who removed the mountains." It tells of an old
man who lived in Northern China long, long ago, and
was known as the foolish old man of the north mountains.
His house faced south and beyond his doorway stood the
two great peaks, Taihand and Wangwu, obstructing the
way. With great determination, he led his sons in digging
up these mountains, hoe in hand. Another greybeard,
known as the wise old man, saw them and said derisively,
"How silly of you to do this! It is quite impossible for
you few to dig up those two huge mountains." The foolish
old man replied, "When I die, my sons will carry on;
when they die there will be my grandsons, and then their
sons and grandsons, and so on to infinity. High as they
are, the mountains cannot grow any higher and with every
bit we dig, they will be that much lower. Why can't we
clear them away?" Having refuted the wise old man's
wrong view, he went on digging every day, unshaken in
his conviction. God was moved by this, and he sent down
two angels, who carried the mountains away on their
backs. Today, two big mountains lie like a dead weight
on the Chinese people. One is imperialism, the other
is feudalism. The Chinese Communist Party has long
made up its mind to dig them up. We must persevere

17

and work unceasingly, and we, too, will touch God's heart. Our God is none other than the masses of the Chinese people. If they stand up and dig together with us, why can't these two mountains be cleared away?

LONG-WINDED LADY

Well, I daresay it's hard to comprehend . . . I mean: *I* . . . at this remove . . . *I* find it hard to, well, not comprehend, but believe, or accept, if you will. So long ago! So much since. But there it was: Splash!

OLD WOMAN

"Over the Hill to the Poor-House."

LONG-WINDED LADY

Well, not splash, exactly, more sound than that, more of a . . .

(Little laugh)

no, I can't do that—imitate it: for I only *imagine* . . . what it must have sounded like to . . . an onlooker. An overseer. Not to *me*; Lord knows! Being *in* it. Or doing it, rather.

CHAIRMAN MAO

In drawing up plans, handling affairs or thinking over problems, we must proceed from the fact that China has six hundred million people, and we must never forget this fact.

OLD WOMAN

By Will Carleton.

LONG-WINDED LADY

No. To an onlooker it would not have been splash, but a sort of . . . different sound, and I try to imagine what it would have been like—*sounded* like—had *I* not been . . . well, so involved, if you know what I mean. And *I* was so *busy* . . . I didn't pay attention, or, if I did . . . that part of it doesn't re . . . recall itself. Retain is the, is what I started.

OLD WOMAN

"Over the Hill to the Poor-House"—a poem by Will Carleton.

CHAIRMAN MAO

Apart from their other characteristics, the outstanding thing about China's six hundred million people is that they are "poor and blank." This may seem a bad thing, but in reality it is a good thing. Poverty gives rise to the desire for change, the desire for action and the desire for revolution. On a blank sheet of paper free from any mark, the freshest and most beautiful characters can be written, the freshest and most beautiful pictures can be painted.

LONG-WINDED LADY

And so high!

OLD WOMAN

Over the hill to the poor-house—I can't quite make it clear!

19

Over the hill to the poor-house—it seems so horrid queer!
Many a step I've taken, a-toilin' to and fro,
But this is a sort of journey I never thought to go.

LONG-WINDED LADY

I'd never imagined it—naturally! It's not what one *would*.
The *echo* of a sound, or the remembering of a sound
having happened. No; that's not right either. For *them*;
for the theoretical . . . onwatcher.

(Pause)

Plut! Yes!

CHAIRMAN MAO

Communism is at once a complete system of proletarian
ideology and a new social system. It is different from any
other ideological and social system, and is the most complete, progressive, revolutionary and rational system in
human history. The communist ideological and social
system alone is full of youth and vitality, sweeping the
world with the momentum of an avalanche and the force
of a thunderbolt.

LONG-WINDED LADY

Exactly: plut!

OLD WOMAN

Over the hill to the poor-house I'm trudgin' my weary
  way—
I, a woman of seventy, and only a trifle gray—

I, who am smart an' chipper, for all the years I've told,
As many another woman thats only half as old.

LONG-WINDED LADY
And then, with the wind, and the roar of the engines and
the sea . . . maybe not even that, not even . . . plut!
But, some slight sound, or . . . or the creation of one!
The invention! What is that about consequence? Oh, *you*
know! Everything has its consequence? Or, every action
a reaction; something. But maybe nothing at all, no real
sound, but the invention of one. I mean, if you see it
happening . . . the, the thing . . . landing, and the
spray, the sea parting, as it were . . . well, then . . .
one makes a sound . . . in one's mind . . . to, to cor-
respond to the sound one . . . didn't . . . hear. Yes?

CHAIRMAN MAO
Imperialism will not last long because it always does evil
things.

OLD WOMAN
"Over the Hill to the Poor-House."

CHAIRMAN MAO
It persists in grooming and supporting reactionaries in all
countries who are against the people; it has forcibly seized
many colonies and semi-colonies and many military bases,
and it threatens the peace with atomic war.

21

OLD WOMAN

By Will Carleton.

CHAIRMAN MAO

Thus, forced by imperialism to do so, more than ninety per cent of the people of the world are rising or will rise up in struggle against it.

OLD WOMAN

Over the hill to the poor-house I'm trudgin' my weary way—
I, a woman of seventy, and only a trifle gray.

CHAIRMAN MAO

Yet imperialism is still alive, still running amuck in Asia, Africa and Latin America. In the West, imperialism is still oppressing the people at home. This situation must change.

OLD WOMAN

I, who am smart an' chipper, for all the years I've told,
As many another woman that's only half as old.

CHAIRMAN MAO

It is the task of the people of the whole world to put an end to the aggression and oppression perpetrated by imperialism, and chiefly by U.S. imperialism.

LONG-WINDED LADY

Yes. I think so.

CHAIRMAN MAO

Historically, all reactionary forces on the verge of extinction invariably conduct a last desperate struggle against the revolutionary forces, and some revolutionaries are apt to be deluded for a time by this phenomenon of outward strength but inner weakness, failing to grasp the essential fact that the enemy is nearing extinction while they themselves are approaching victory.

LONG-WINDED LADY

I remember once when I broke my finger, or my thumb, and I was very little, and they said, you've broken your thumb, look, you've broken your thumb, and there wasn't any pain . . . not *yet*; not for that first moment, just . . . just an absence of sensation—an interesting lack of anything.

OLD WOMAN

"Over the Hill to the Poor-House."

LONG-WINDED LADY

When they said it again, look, you've broken your thumb, not only did I scream, as if some knife had ripped my leg down, from hip to ankle, all through the sinews, laying bare the bone . . . not only did I scream as only children can—adults do it differently: there's an animal protest there, a revenge, something . . . something other—not

23

only did I scream, but I manufactured the pain. Right then! Before the hurt could have come through, I made it happen.

(Pause)

Well; we do that.

OLD WOMAN

What is the use of heapin' on me a pauper's shame?
Am I lazy or crazy? am I blind or lame?
True, I am not so supple, nor yet so awful stout;
But charity ain't no favor, if one can live without.

LONG-WINDED LADY

Yes; we do that: we make it happen a little before it need.

(Pause)

And so it might have been with someone watching—and maybe even to those who were. Who were watching. And there were, or I'd not be here.

(Pause)

I daresay.

(Pause)

The sound manufactured. Lord knows, if *I* had been among the . . . non-participators I should have done it, too; no doubt. Plup! Plut! Whichever. I'm sure *I* should have . . . if I'd seen it all the *way*, now. I mean, if I'd caught just the final instant, without time to relate the event to its environment—the thing happening to the thing happened *to* . . . then I doubt I would have. Nor would anyone . . . or most.

CHAIRMAN MAO

The imperialists and their running dogs, the Chinese reactionaries, will not resign themselves to defeat in this
land of China.

OLD WOMAN

What is the use of heapin' on me a pauper's shame?
Am I lazy or crazy? Am I blind or lame?

CHAIRMAN MAO

All this we must take fully into account.

LONG-WINDED LADY

But just imagine what it must have been like . . . to be
one of the . . . watchers! How . . . well, is marvelous
the proper word, I wonder? Yes, I suspect. I mean, how
often? ! It's not too common an occurrence, to have it
. . . plummet by! One is standing there, admiring, or
faintly sick, or just plain throwing up, but how often is
one *there. Ever!* Well, inveterates; yes; but for the casual
crosser . . . not too often, and one would have to be exactly in place, at exactly the proper time, and alert! Very
alert in . . . by nature, and able to relate what one sees to
what is happening. Oh, I remember the time the taxi went
berserk and killed those people!

CHAIRMAN MAO

Riding roughshod everywhere, U.S. imperialism has made
itself the enemy of the people of the world and has in-

25

creasingly isolated itself. Those who refuse to be enslaved will never be cowed by the atom bombs and hydrogen bombs in the hands of the U.S. imperialists. The raging tide of the people of the world against the U.S. aggressors is irresistible. Their struggle against U.S. imperialism and its lackeys will assuredly win still greater victories.

LONG-WINDED LADY

Well, it didn't go berserk, of course, for it *is* a machine: a taxi. Nor did the driver . . . go berserk. Out of control, though! The driver lost and out of control it went! *Up* on the sidewalk, bowling them down like whatchama-callems, then crash!, into the store front, the splash of glass and then on fire. How many dead? Ten? Twelve? And I had just come out with the crullers.

OLD WOMAN

I am ready and willin' an' anxious any day
To work for a decent livin', an' pay my honest way;
For I can earn my victuals, an' more too, I'll be bound,
If anybody is willin' to only have me 'round.

LONG-WINDED LADY

The bag of crullers, and a smile on my face for everyone liked them so, and there it was! Careen . . . and dying . . . and all that glass. And I remember thinking: it's a movie! They're shooting some scenes right here on the street.

(Pause)

They weren't, of course. It was real death, and real glass, and the fire, and the . . . people crying, and the crowds, and the smoke. Oh, it was real enough, but it took me time to know it. The mind does that.

CHAIRMAN MAO

If the U.S. monopoly capitalist groups persist in pushing their policies of aggression and war, the day is bound to come when they will be hanged by the people of the whole world. The same fate awaits the accomplices of the United States.

OLD WOMAN

I am ready and willin' an' anxious any day
To work for a decent livin', an' pay my honest way;
For I can earn my victuals, an' more too, I'll be bound,
If anybody is willin' to only have me 'round.

LONG-WINDED LADY

They're making a movie! What a nice conclusion, coming out with the crullers, still hot, with a separate little bag for the powdered sugar, of course it's a movie! One doesn't come out like that to carnage! Dead people and the wounded; glass all over and . . . confusion. One . . . concludes things—and if those things and what is really there don't . . . are not the *same* . . . well! . . . it would usually be better if it were so. The mind does that: it helps.

CHAIRMAN MAO

To achieve a lasting world peace, we must further develop our friendship and cooperation with the fraternal countries in the socialist camp and strengthen our solidarity with all peace-loving countries.

LONG-WINDED LADY

The mind does that.

CHAIRMAN MAO

We must endeavor to establish normal diplomatic relations, on the basis of mutual respect for territorial integrity and sovereignty and of equality and mutual benefit, with all countries willing to live together with us in peace.

LONG-WINDED LADY

It helps.

CHAIRMAN MAO

We must give active support to the national independence and liberation movement in Asia, Africa, and Latin America as well as to the peace movement and to just struggles in all the countries of the world.

VOICE, FROM BOX

Box.

LONG-WINDED LADY

So; if one happened to be there, by the rail, and not too

discomfited, not in the sense of utterly defeated—though that would be more than enough—but in the sense of confused, or preoccupied, if one were not too preoccupied, and plummet! it went by! one, the mind, might be able to take it in, say: ah! there! there she goes!—or he; and manufacture the appropriate sound. But only then. And how many are expecting it!? Well, *I* am. *Now.* There isn't a rail I stand by, especially in full sun—my conditioning—that I'm not . . . already shuddering . . . *and* ready to manufacture the sound.

(Little laugh)

Though not the sound *I* knew, for I was hardly thinking —a bit busy—but the sound I imagine someone else would have manufactured had *he* been there when I . . . WOOOOSSSH!! PLUT!!

(Little laugh)

VOICE, FROM BOX

Box.

OLD WOMAN

Once I was young an' han'some—I was, upon my soul—
Once my cheeks was roses, my eyes as black as coal;
And I can't remember, in them days, of hearin' people say,
For any kind of a reason, that I was in their way!

LONG-WINDED LADY

You never know until it's happened to you.

29

VOICE, FROM BOX

Many arts: all craft now . . . and going further.

CHAIRMAN MAO

Our country and all the other socialist countries want peace; so do the peoples of all the countries of the world. The only ones who crave war and do not want peace are certain monopoly capitalist groups in a handful of imperialist countries which depend on aggression for their profits.

LONG-WINDED LADY

Do you.

VOICE, FROM BOX

Box.

CHAIRMAN MAO

Who are our enemies? Who are our friends?

LONG-WINDED LADY

Do you.

CHAIRMAN MAO

Our enemies are all those in league with imperialism; our closest friends are the entire semi-proletariat and petty bourgeoisie. As for the vacillating middle bourgeoisie, their right wing may become our enemy and their left wing may become our friend.

30

LONG-WINDED LADY

Falling! My goodness. What was it when one was little? That when you fell when you were dreaming you always woke up before you landed, or else you wouldn't and you'd be dead. That was it, I think. And I never wondered why, I merely took it for . . . well, I *accepted* it. And, of course, I kept trying to dream of falling after I'd heard it . . . tried so hard! . . . and *couldn't*, naturally. Well, if we control the unconscious, we're either mad, or . . . dull-witted.

OLD WOMAN

Once I was young an' han'some—I was, upon my soul.

LONG-WINDED LADY

I think I dreamt of falling again, though, but after I'd stopped trying to, but I don't think I landed. Not like what I've been telling you, though that was more seaing than landing, you might say . . . if you like a pun. Once, though! Once, I dreamt of falling straight up . . . or out, all in reverse, like the projector running backwards, what they used to do, for fun, in the shorts.

(*Some wonder*)

Falling . . . *up!*

CHAIRMAN MAO

In the final analysis, national struggle is a matter of class struggle. Among the whites in the United States it is only

31

the reactionary ruling circles who oppress the black people.

LONG-WINDED LADY

Falling . . . *up!*

CHAIRMAN MAO

They can in no way represent the workers, farmers, revolutionary intellectuals and other enlightened persons who comprise the overwhelming majority of the white people.

VOICE, FROM BOX

Seven hundred million babies dead in half the time it takes, took, to knead the dough to make a proper loaf. Well, little wonder so many . . .

LONG-WINDED LADY

Not rising, you understand: a definite . . . falling, but . . . up!

OLD WOMAN

'Tain't no use of boastin', or talkin' over free,
But many a house an' home was open then to me;
Many a han'some offer I had from likely men,
And nobody ever hinted that I was a burden then!

LONG-WINDED LADY

Did I call them crullers? Well, I should *not* have; for

they were not even doughnuts, but the centers . . . hearts is what they called them: the center dough pinched out, or cut with a cutter and done like the rest, but solid, the size of a bantam egg, but round. Oh, they were good, and crisp, and all like air inside; hot, and you'd dip them in the confectioner's sugar. One could be quite a pig; everyone was; they were so good! You find them here and about still. Some, but not often.

OLD WOMAN

"Over the Hill to the Poor-House."

CHAIRMAN MAO

All reactionaries are paper tigers. In appearance, the reactionaries are terrifying, but in reality they are not so powerful. From a long-term point of view, it is not the reactionaries but the people who are really powerful.

VOICE, FROM BOX

Apathy, I think.

LONG-WINDED LADY

My husband used to say, don't leave her next to anything precipitous; there's bound to be a do; something will drop, or fall, her purse, her*self.* And, so, he had people be careful of me. Not that I'm fond of heights. I'm not unfriendly toward them—all that falling—but I have no . . . great affection.

(Little pause)

33

Depths even less.

OLD WOMAN

By Will Carleton.

CHAIRMAN MAO

I have said that all the reputedly powerful reactionaries are merely paper tigers. The reason is that they are divorced from the people. Look! Was not Hitler a paper tiger? Was Hitler not overthrown? I also said that the czar of Russia, the emperor of China and Japanese imperialism were all paper tigers. As we know, they were all overthrown.

LONG-WINDED LADY

All that falling.

CHAIRMAN MAO

U.S. imperialism has not yet been overthrown and it has the atom bomb. I believe it also will be overthrown. It, too, is a paper tiger.

LONG-WINDED LADY

And it became something of a joke, I suppose . . . I suppose. Where is she? Watch her! Don't let her near the edge! She'll occasion a do!

OLD WOMAN

And when to John I was married, sure he was good and smart,

34

But he and all the neighbors would own I done my part;
For life was all before me, an' I was young an' strong,
And I worked my best an' smartest in tryin' to get along.

LONG-WINDED LADY

He was a small man—my husband, almost a miniature
. . . not that I'm much of a giraffe. Small . . . and precise . . . and contained . . . quiet strength. The large
emotions . . . *yes*, without them, what?—all there, and
full size, full scope, but when they came, not a . . . spattering, but a single shaft, a careful aim. No waste, as intense as anyone, but precise. Some people said he was
cold; or cruel. But he was merely accurate. Big people
ooze, and scatter, and knock over things nearby. They
give the impression—the illusion—of openness, of spaces
through which things pass—excuses, bypassings. But
small, and precise, and accurate don't . . . doesn't allow for that . . . for that *impression*. He wasn't cruel at
all.

CHAIRMAN MAO

The socialist system will eventually replace the capitalist
system; this is an objective law independent of man's
will. However much the reactionaries try to hold back
the wheel of history, sooner or later revolution will take
place and will inevitably triumph.

OLD WOMAN

Over the hill to the poor-house—I can't quite make it
clear.

LONG-WINDED LADY

Or cold. Neat; accurate; precise. In everything. All our marriage. Except dying. Except that . . . dreadful death.

CHAIRMAN MAO

The imperialists and domestic reactionaries will certainly not take their defeat lying down and they will struggle to the last ditch. This is inevitable and beyond all doubt, and under no circumstances must we relax our vigilance.

LONG-WINDED LADY

That dreadful death—all that he was not: large, random, inaccurate—in the sense of offshoots from the major objective. A spattering cancer! Spread enough and you're bound to kill *some*thing. Don't aim! Engulf! Imprecision!

VOICE, FROM BOX

When it was *simple* . . .
  (Light, self-mocking laugh)
Ah, well, yes, when it was simple.

OLD WOMAN

And so we worked together: and life was hard, but gay,
With now and then a baby to cheer us on our way;
Till we had half a dozen: an' all growed clean an' neat,
An' went to school like others, an' had enough to eat.

LONG-WINDED LADY

Don't let her near the edge!

CHAIRMAN MAO

Make trouble, fail, make trouble again, fail again . . .
till their doom; that is the logic of the imperialists and all
reactionaries the world over in dealing with the people's
cause, and they will never go against this logic. This is a
Marxist law.

LONG-WINDED LADY

Don't let her near the edge.

CHAIRMAN MAO

When we say "imperialism is ferocious," we mean that
its nature will never change, that the imperialists will
never lay down their butcher knives, that they will never
become Buddhas, till their doom. Fight, fail, fight again,
fail again, fight again . . . till their victory; that is the
logic of the people, and they too will never go against this
logic. This is another Marxist law.

LONG-WINDED LADY

But I hadn't thought I *was*. Well, yes, of course I *was*
. . . but guarded . . . well guarded. Or, so I *thought*. It
doesn't happen terribly often—falling . . . by indirection.

(Pause)

Does it?

OLD WOMAN

An' so we worked for the child'rn, and raised 'em every
one;

37

Worked for 'em summer and winter, just as we ought
to've done;

Only perhaps we humored 'em, which some good folks
condemn,

But every couple's child'rn's a heap the best to them!

VOICE, FROM BOX

Oh, shame!

LONG-WINDED LADY

Not death: I didn't mean death. I meant . . . falling
off. *That* isn't done too often by indirection. *Is* it! Death!
Well, my God, of course; yes. Almost always, 'less you
take the notion of the collective . . . thing, which *must
allow* for it, take it into account: I mean, if all the rest is
part of a . . . predetermination, or something that has
already happened—in principle—well, under *those* conditions *any* chaos becomes order. Any chaos at all.

VOICE, FROM BOX

Oh, shame!

CHAIRMAN MAO

Everything reactionary is the same; if you don't hit it, it
won't fall.

VOICE, FROM BOX

Oh, shame!

38

CHAIRMAN MAO

This is also like sweeping the floor; as a rule, where the broom does not reach, the dust will not vanish of itself. Nor will the enemy perish of himself. The aggressive forces of U.S. imperialism will not step down from the stage of history of their own accord.

VOICE, FROM BOX

The *Pope* warned us; *he* said so. There are no possessions, he said; so long as there are some with nothing we have no right to anything.

LONG-WINDED LADY

And the thing about boats is . . . you're burned . . . always . . . sun . . . haze . . . mist . . . deep night . . . all the spectrum down. Something. Burning.

CHAIRMAN MAO

Everything reactionary is the same; if you don't hit it, it won't fall.

LONG-WINDED LADY

I sat up one night—oh, *before* it happened, though it doesn't matter—I mean, on a deck chair, like this, well away from the . . . possibility, but I sat up, and the moon was small, as it always is, on the northern route, well out, and I *bathed* in the night, and perhaps my daughter came up from dancing, though I don't think

39

so . . . dancing down there with a man, well, young enough to be her husband.

OLD WOMAN

For life was all before me, an' I was young an' strong,
And I worked the best that I could in tryin' to get along.

LONG-WINDED LADY

Though not. Not her husband.

CHAIRMAN MAO

Classes struggle; some classes triumph, others are eliminated. Such is history, such is the history of civilization for thousands of years. To interpret history from this viewpoint is historical materialism; standing in opposition to this viewpoint is historical idealism.

LONG-WINDED LADY

Though not. Not her husband.

CHAIRMAN MAO

No political party can possibly lead a great revolutionary movement to victory unless it possesses revolutionary theory and a knowledge of history and has a profound grasp of the practical movement.

LONG-WINDED LADY

And what I mean is: the burn; sitting in the dim moon, with not the sound of the orchestra, but the *possible*

sound of it—therefore, I suppose, the same—the daughter, *my* daughter, and me up here, up *there*—this one?
No.—and being burned! In that—what I said—that all
seasons, all lights, all . . . well, one never returns from a
voyage the same.

VOICE, FROM BOX

It's the *little* things, the *small* cracks.

OLD WOMAN

Strange how much we think of our blessed little ones!—
I'd have died for my daughters, I'd have died for my sons;
And God he made that rule of love; but when we're old
   and gray,
I've noticed it sometimes somehow fails to work the other
   way.

LONG-WINDED LADY

His scrotum was large, and not only for a small man, I
think, as I remember back—and am I surmising my com-
parisons here, or telling you something loose about my
past?
                    (Shrugs)

CHAIRMAN MAO

Classes struggle; some classes triumph, others are eliminated.

LONG-WINDED LADY

What does it matter now, this late?—large, and not of

the loose type, but thick, and leather, marvelously creased and like a neat, full sack. And his penis, too; of a neat proportion; ample, but not of that size which moves us so in retrospect . . . or is supposed to. Circumcised . . . well, no, not really, but trained back, *to* it; trained; like everything; nothing surprising, but always there, and ample. Do I shock you?

VOICE, FROM BOX

And if you go back to a partita . . .

CHAIRMAN MAO

Such is history.

LONG-WINDED LADY

Do I *shock* you?

CHAIRMAN MAO

The commanders and fighters of the entire Chinese people's Liberation Army absolutely must not relax in the least their will to fight; any thinking that relaxes the will to fight and belittles the enemy is wrong.

LONG-WINDED LADY

That is the last I have in mind. My intention is only to remember.

OLD WOMAN

Strange how much we think of our blessed little ones!

CHAIRMAN MAO

I hold that it is bad as far as we are concerned if a person, a political party, an army or a school is not attacked by the enemy, for in that case it would definitely mean that we have sunk to the level of the enemy.

LONG-WINDED LADY

That is the last I have in mind.

CHAIRMAN MAO

It is good if we are attacked by the enemy, since it proves that we have drawn a clear line of demarcation between the enemy and ourselves.

LONG-WINDED LADY

And the only desperate conflict is between what we long to remember and what we need to forget. No; that is not what I meant at all. Or . . . well, yes, it may *be*; it may be on the nose.

OLD WOMAN

Strange, another thing: when our boys an' girls was grown,
And when, exceptin' Charley, they'd left us there alone;
When John he nearer an' nearer come, an' dearer seemed
    to be,
The Lord of Hosts he come one day an' took him away
    from me!

LONG-WINDED LADY

But, wouldn't you think a death would relate to a life?

43

. . . if not resemble it, *benefit* from it? Be *taught?* In *some* way? *I* would think.

OLD WOMAN

The Lord of Hosts He come one day an' took him away
from me!

CHAIRMAN MAO

Whoever sides with the revolutionary people is a revolutionary. Whoever sides with imperialism, feudalism and
bureaucrat-capitalism is a counter-revolutionary.

LONG-WINDED LADY

Be *taught?* In *some* way?

CHAIRMAN MAO

Whoever sides with the revolutionary people in words
only but acts otherwise is a revolutionary in speech.

LONG-WINDED LADY

I would think.

CHAIRMAN MAO

Whoever sides with the revolutionary people in deed as
well as in word is a revolutionary in the full sense.

VOICE, FROM BOX

And if you go back to a partita . . . ahhh, what when it
makes you cry!?

44

LONG-WINDED LADY

Savage how it can come, but, even more the preparations for it. No, not *for* it, but the—*yes!* they *must* be preparations for it, unless we're a morbid species—that, over the duck one day—the cold duck, with the gherkins and the lemon slices, notched like a cog . . . and the potato salad, warm if you're lucky, somebody suddenly says to your husband, when were you first aware of death, and he's only forty! God!, and he looks, and he says, without even that flick, that instant of an eye to me, odd you should ask me and I'm not even . . . well, I'm thirty-nine, and I've begun, though if you'd asked me two weeks ago, though you wouldn't have, and we saw you then—and it was true; we had; two weeks ago; two weeks *before.* Is it something that suddenly shows and happens at once? At one moment? When we are aware of it we *show* we are? My God!, he said; I hadn't thought of dying since I was twelve, and, then again, *what*, sixteen, *what*, when I wrote those sonnets, all on the boatman, ironic, though. No! And the other man said, no: death, not dying.

VOICE, FROM BOX

And if you go back to a partita . . . ahhhh, what when it makes you cry!? Not from the beauty of it, but from solely that you cry from loss . . . so precious.

OLD WOMAN

Still I was bound to struggle, an' never to cringe or fall—

Still I worked for Charley, for Charley was now my all;
And Charley was pretty good to me, with scarce a word
    or frown,
Till at last he went a-courtin', and brought a wife from
    town.

LONG-WINDED LADY

And another man there—an older man—someone my
family had known, some man we had at parties and once
I'd called Uncle, though he wasn't, some man I think my
sister had been seen to go around with . . . someone
who was around, said, God, you're young! You think of
death when you're knee-high to a knicker, and dying
when your cock gets decent for the first or second time,
and I mean *in* something, not the handy-pan, but when
you think of *dead!* And . . . he was drunk, though . . .
what!—well, my lovely husband looked at him with a
kind of glass, and he was a host then, and he said, with
a quiet and staid that I think is—well, what I have loved
him for, or what is of the substance of what I have
loved him for . . . Straight In The Eye! When I was
young I thought of death; and then, when I was older—
or what I suddenly seemed to be . . . dying . . . with
a kind of longing: Ngggggggg, with a look at me, as if
he could go on . . . and by God!, he slapped away,
and it was the first?, the only gesture I was . . . have,
been . . . even . . . momentarily . . . DON'T TALK LIKE
THAT!!

(Pause)

46

Slapped away with his eyes and said, I am suddenly dying, to which he added an it would seem, and while everybody tried to talk about death he wanted to talk about dying.

CHAIRMAN MAO

We should support whatever the enemy opposes and oppose whatever the enemy supports.

VOICE, FROM BOX

When art begins to hurt . . . when art begins to hurt, it's time to look around. Yes it is.

LONG-WINDED LADY

But, of course, my sister's . . . savior, or whatever you would have it, wouldn't not be still. *He* went *on!* Death!, he said. And then he would lapse . . . for nothing, that I could see, beyond the curious pleasure of lapsing . . . Death! Yes, my husband would say, or *said* . . . *said* this particular time—and Bishop Berkeley will be wrong, he added, and no one understood, which is hardly surprising—I am suddenly dying, and I want no nonsense about it! Death? You stop about death, finally, seriously, when you're on to *dying*. Oh, come on!, the other said; death is the whole thing. He drank, as . . . my sister did, too; she died. I think they got in bed together—took a bottle with them, made love perhaps. CRAP!—which quieted the room some . . . and me, too. He never did that. Death is nothing; there . . . there *is* no death.

47

There is only life and dying.

CHAIRMAN MAO

A revolution is not a dinner party, or writing an essay, or painting a picture, or doing embroidery; it cannot be so refined, so leisurely and gentle, so temperate, kind, courteous, restrained and magnanimous. A revolution is an insurrection, an act of violence by which one class overthrows another.

VOICE, FROM BOX

When art begins to hurt, it's time to look around. Yes it is.

LONG-WINDED LADY

And *I*, he said, *I*—thumping his chest with the flat of his hand, slow, four, five times—*I* . . . am *dying*.

CHAIRMAN MAO

After the enemies with guns have been wiped out, there will still be enemies without guns; they are bound to struggle desperately against us, and we must never regard these enemies lightly. If we do not now raise and understand the problem in this way, we shall commit the gravest mistakes.

VOICE, FROM BOX

Yes it is.

48

LONG-WINDED LADY

And I, he said, I am dying. And this was long before he did. That night he told me: I was not aware of it before. We were resting . . . *before* sex—which we would not have that night; on our sides, his chest and groin against my back and buttocks, his hand between my breasts, the sand of his chin nice against my neck. I always knew I would die—I'm not a fool, but I had no sense of time; I didn't know it would be so soon. I turned; I cupped my hands around his lovely scrotum and our breaths were together. But, it won't be for so very *long*. Yes, he said; I know. Silence, then added; but always shorter.

OLD WOMAN

And Charley was pretty good to me, with scarce a word
   or frown,
Till at last he went a-courtin', and brought a wife from
   town.
She was somewhat dressy, an' hadn't a pleasant smile.

CHAIRMAN MAO

People all over the world are now discussing whether or not a third world war will break out. On this question, too, we must be mentally prepared and do some analysis. We stand firmly for peace and against war. But if the imperialists insist on unleashing another war, we should not be afraid of it.

LONG-WINDED LADY

And I, he said, I am dying.

49

CHAIRMAN MAO

If the imperialists insist on launching a third world war, the whole structure of imperialism will utterly collapse.

LONG-WINDED LADY

But what about *me!* Think about *me!*

OLD WOMAN

She was somewhat dressy, an' hadn't a pleasant smile—
She was quite conceity, and carried a heap o' style;
But if ever I tried to be friends, I did with her, I know;
But she was hard and proud, an' I couldn't make it go.

LONG-WINDED LADY

ME! WHAT ABOUT ME!
(Pause)
That may give the impression of selfishness, but that is not how I intended it, nor how it is . . . at all. *I . . .* am *left.*
(Helpless shrug)
He isn't. I'll not touch his dying again. It was long, and coarse, and ugly, and cruel, and tested the man beyond his . . . beyond *anyone's* capacities. I dare you! I dare anyone! Don't scream! Don't hate! I dare anyone.
(Softer)
All that can be done is turn into a beast; the dumb thing's agony is none the less, but it doesn't understand *why*, the agony. And maybe that's enough comfort: **not** to know why.

(Pause; wistful; sad)

But *I* am *left*.

VOICE, FROM **BOX**

And the beauty of art is order.

CHAIRMAN MAO

We desire peace. However, if imperialism insists on fighting a war, we will have no alternative but to take the firm resolution to fight to the finish before going ahead with our constriction. If you are afraid of war day in day out, what will you do if war eventually comes? First I said that the East Wind is prevailing over the West Wind and war will not break out, and now I have added these explanations about the situation in case war should break out. Both possibilities have thus been taken into account.

OLD WOMAN

She was somewhat dressy, an' hadn't a pleasant smile—
She was quite conceity, an' carried a heap o' style;
But if ever I tried to be friends, I did with her, I know.

LONG-WINDED LADY

Besides, his dying is all over; all gone, but his *death* stays.
He said death was not a concern, but he meant his own, and for *him*. No, well, he was right: *he* only had his dying. I have both.

(Sad chuckle)

Oh, what a treasurehouse! I can exclude his dying; I can

not think about it, except the times I want it back—the times I want, for myself, something less general than . . . tristesse. Though that is usually enough. And what for my daughter—*mine*, now, you'll notice; no longer ours; what box have I got for her? Oh . . . the ephemera: jewelry, clothes, chairs . . . and the money: enough. Nothing solid, except my dying, my death, those two, and the thought of her own. The former, though.

VOICE, FROM BOX

Not what is familiar, necessarily, but order.

CHAIRMAN MAO

War is the highest form of struggle for resolving contradictions, when they have developed to a certain stage, between classes, nations, states, or political groups, and it has existed ever since the emergence of private property and of classes.

LONG-WINDED LADY

(A little stentorian; disapproving)

Where were *you* those six last months, the time I did *not* need you, with my hands full of less each day; my arms.

(Sad, almost humorous truth)

If you send them away to save them from it, you resent their going and *they* want what they've missed. Well . . . I see as much of you as I'd like, my dear. Not as much as either of us should want, but as much as we do. Odd.

VOICE, FROM BOX

. . . and the beauty of art is order—not what is familiar, necessarily, but order . . . on its own terms.

OLD WOMAN

But she was hard and proud, an' I couldn't make it go.
She had an edication, an' that was good for her;
But when she twitted me on mine, 'twas carryin' things
    too fur;
An' I told her once, 'fore company (an' it almost made
    her sick),
That I never swallowed a grammar, or 'et a 'rithmetic.

LONG-WINDED LADY
(New subject)

And there I was! Falling!

CHAIRMAN MAO

Revolutionary war is an antitoxin which not only eliminates the enemy's poison but also purges us of our own filth.

VOICE, FROM BOX

That is the thing about music. That is why we cannot listen any more.
(Pause)
Because we cry.

LONG-WINDED LADY

We see each other less, she and I—my daughter—as I

53

said, and most often on boats: something about the air; the burning. She was with me when I fell. Well: on *board*. When they . . . hauled me in—oh, what a spectacle *that* was!—there she was, looking on. Not near where I came in, exactly, but some way off: nearer where I'd done it; where it had been done. Red hair flying—not natural, a kind of purple to it, but stunning; quite stunning—cigarette; *always*; the French one. Nails the color of blood—artery blood, darker than the vein. The things one knows! Looking on, not quite a smile, not quite not. I looked up, dolphins resting on my belly, seaweed-twined, like what's-his-name, or hers . . . I'll bet all you'll say is Honestly, Mother!

(Slight pause)

And when she came to my cabin, after the doctor, and the welcome brandy, and the sedative, the unnecessary sedative . . . there she stood for a moment, cigarette still on, in her mouth, I think. She looked for a moment. Honestly, Mother!, she said, laughing a little in her throat, *at* it, humor *at* it. Honestly, Mother! And then off she went.

VOICE, FROM BOX

That is why we cannot listen any more.

OLD WOMAN

So 'twas only a few days before the thing was done—
They was a family of themselves, and I another one;
And a very little cottage one family will do,

But I never have seen a house that was big enough for two.

VOICE, FROM BOX

Because we cry.

LONG-WINDED LADY

Where is she now. This trip. Mexico. You'd better chain yourself to the chair, she said to me, later, the day after. You *will* go on deck; put a long cord on yourself. It's not a usual occurrence, I told her; not even for me. No, but you're inventive, she said.

VOICE, FROM BOX

Look! More birds! Another . . . sky of them.

CHAIRMAN MAO

History shows that wars are divided into two kinds, just and unjust. We Communists oppose all unjust wars that impede progress, but we do not oppose progressive, just wars. Not only do we Communists not oppose just wars, we actively participate in them. All wars that are progressive are just, and all wars that impede progress are unjust. The way to oppose a war of this kind is to do everything possible to prevent it before it breaks out and, once it breaks out, to oppose war with war, to oppose unjust war with just war, whenever possible.

OLD WOMAN

But I never have seen a house that was big enough for two.

LONG-WINDED LADY

Mexico; still; probably. I'm in Mexico, in case you care, she said. Four A.M. First words, no hello, Mother, or sorry to wake you up if you're sleeping, if you're not lying there, face all smeared, hair in your net, bed jacket still on, propped up, lights out, wondering whether you're asleep or not. No; not that. Not even that. I'm in Mexico, in case you care.

VOICE, FROM BOX

Look! More birds! Another . . . sky of them.

LONG-WINDED LADY

Oh. Well . . . how very nice. I'm in Mexico, in case you care. I'm with two boys. Sort of defiant. Oh? Well, how nice. Add 'em up and they're just my age; one's twenty and the other's not quite that. Still defiant. Well, that's . . . she lies a bit; she's forty-two. That's very *nice*, dear. They're both Mexican. She sounded almost ugly, over the phone, in the dark. Well . . . They're both uncircumcised, she said, and then waited. When this happens . . . when this happens, she will wait—not those very words, but something she hopes to affect me with, hurt me, shock, perhaps, make me feel less . . . well, I was going to say happy, but I am seldom that: not any more . . . make me feel less even. She'll wait, and I can hear her waiting, to see if I put the phone down. If I do *not*, after a certain time, of the silence, then she *will*. I put it down gently, when I do. She slams. This time, *I* put it down; gently. I've never known which makes her happier . . . if either does, though I suppose one must. Whether she is happier if she makes me do it, or if I pause too long, and she can. I would like to ask her, but it is not the sort of question one can ask a forty-two-year-old woman . . . daughter or no.

VOICE, FROM BOX

It's only when you can't come back; when you get in some distant key; that when you say, the tonic! the tonic! and they say, what is *that?* It's *then.*

OLD WOMAN

An' I never could speak to suit her, never could please her
  eye,
An' it made me independent, an' then I didn't try;
But I was terribly staggered, an' felt it like a blow,
When Charley turned ag'in me, an' told me I could go!

LONG-WINDED LADY

I *do wish* sometimes . . . just in general, I mean . . . I *do wish* sometimes . . .

CHAIRMAN MAO

Some people ridicule us as advocates of the "omnipotence of war." Yes, we are advocates of the omnipotence of revolutionary war; that is good, not bad, it is Marxist.

LONG-WINDED LADY

Just in general, I mean . . . I *do wish* sometimes . . .

57

CHAIRMAN MAO

Experience in the class struggle in the era of imperialism teaches us that it is only by the power of the gun that the working class and the laboring masses can defeat the armed bourgeoisie and landlords; in this sense we may say that only with guns can the whole world be transformed.

LONG-WINDED LADY

I suppose that's why I came this time . . . the Mexicans; the boys. Put an ocean between. It's not as far as a death, but . . . still.

OLD WOMAN

"Over the Hill to the Poor-House," by Will Carleton.

LONG-WINDED LADY

I remember, I walked to the thing, the railing. To look over. Why, I don't *know:* water never changes, the Atlantic, *this* latitude. But if you've been sitting in a chair, that is what you *do:* you put down the Trollope or James or sometimes Hardy, throw off the rug, and, slightly unsteady from suddenly up from horizontal . . . you walk to the thing . . . the railing. It's that simple. You look for a bit, smell, sniff, really; you look down to make sure it's moving, and then you think shall you take a turn, and you usually do not; you go back to your rug and your book. Or *not* to your book, but to your *rug,* which you pull up like covers and pretend to go to sleep. The one thing you do *not* do is fall off the ship!

VOICE, FROM BOX

There! More! A thousand, and one below them, moving fast in the opposite way!

OLD WOMAN

I went to live with Susan: but Susan's house was small,
And she was always a-hintin' how snug it was for us all;
And what with her husband's sisters, and what with child'rn three,
'Twas easy to discover that there wasn't room for me.

LONG-WINDED LADY

Here's a curious thing! Whenever I'm in an aeroplane— which I am not, often, for I like to choose my company: not that I'm a snob, heavens!, it's my daughter who will not see *me*, or, rather, not often. Not that I am a snob, but I feel that travel in rooms is so much nicer: boats and trains, where one can get away and then out again; people are nicer when you come upon them around corners, or opening doors. But whenever I'm up there, closed in, strapped to my seat, with all the people around, and the double windows, those tiny windows, and the great heavy door, bolted from the outside, probably, even when I'm plumped down in an inside seat—or aisle, as they call them—*then!* It's then that I feel that I'm going to fall out. Fall right out of the aeroplane! I don't know how I could possibly do it—even through the most . . . reprehensible carelessness. I probably couldn't, even if I felt I had to. But I'm sure I will! Always! Though, naturally, I never do.

VOICE, FROM BOX
What was it used to frighten me?

CHAIRMAN MAO
Revolutions and revolutionary wars are inevitable in class society, and without them it is impossible to accomplish any leap in social development and to overthrow the reactionary ruling classes and therefore impossible for the people to win political power.

OLD WOMAN
'Twas easy to discover that there wasn't room for me.

LONG-WINDED LADY
Coarse, and ugly, and long, and cruel. That dying. My lovely husband.
(Small pause)
But I said I wouldn't dwell on that.

OLD WOMAN
An' then I went to Thomas, the oldest son I've got:
For Thomas's buildings'd cover the half of an acre lot;
But all the child'rn was on me—I couldn't stand their sauce—

60

And Thomas said I needn't think I was comin' there to boss.

LONG-WINDED LADY

Well! What can we say of an aging lady walks bright as you please from her rug and her Trollope or her James or sometimes her Hardy right up to the thing . . . the railing; walks right up, puts her fingers, rings and all, right on the varnished wood, sniffs . . . that air!, feels the railing, hard as wood, knows it's there—it *is* there—and suddenly, as sudden and sure as what you've always known and never quite admitted to yourself, it is *not* there; there is no railing, no wood, no metal, no buoy-life-thing saying S.S. or H.M.S. whatever, no . . . nothing! Nothing at all! The fingers are claws, and the varnish they rubbed against is air? And suddenly one is . . . well, what would you expect?! One is suddenly leaning on one's imagination—which is poor support, let me tell you . . . at least in *my* case—leaning on that, which doesn't last for long, and over one goes!

VOICE, FROM BOX

. . . a thousand miles from the sea. Land-locked, never been, and yet the sea sounds . . .

CHAIRMAN MAO

War, this monster of mutual slaughter among men, will be finally eliminated by the progress of human society, and in the not too distant future, too.

VOICE, FROM BOX

A thousand miles from the sea. Land-locked.

CHAIRMAN MAO

But there is only one way to eliminate it and that is to oppose war with war, to oppose counter-revolutionary war with revolutionary war, to oppose national counter-revolutionary war with national revolutionary war, and to oppose counter-revolutionary class war with revolutionary class war.

VOICE, FROM BOX

Never been, and yet the sea sounds.

CHAIRMAN MAO

When human society advances to the point where classes and states are eliminated, there will be no more wars, counter-revolutionary or revolutionary, unjust or just. That will be the era of perpetual peace for mankind.

OLD WOMAN

But all the child'rn was on me—I couldn't stand their sauce—

And Thomas said I needn't think I was comin' there to boss.

LONG-WINDED LADY

Over one goes, and it's a long way, let me tell you! No falling *up*; no, siree; or out! Straight down! As straight as anything! Plummet! Plut! Well, plummet for sure, plut conjectural. I wonder why I didn't kill myself. Exactly what my daughter said: I wonder why you didn't kill yourself. Though her reading was special. Had a note of derision to it.

OLD WOMAN

An' then I wrote to Rebecca, my girl who lives out West,
And to Isaac, not far from her—some twenty miles at best;
And one of 'em said 'twas too warm there for anyone so old,
And t'other had an opinion the climate was too cold.

VOICE, FROM BOX

Well, we give up something for something.

LONG-WINDED LADY

I did *not* kill myself, as *I* see it, through a trick of the wind, or chance, or because I am bottom heavy. Straight down like a drop of shot! Except. Except, at the very end, a sort of curving, a kind of arc, which sent me gently into a rising wave, or throw-off from the boat, angling into it just properly, sliding in so that it felt like falling on leaves —the pile of autumn leaves we would make, or our brother would, and jump on, like a feather bed. A gust of wind must have done that. Well . . . something did.

CHAIRMAN MAO

"War is the continuation of politics." In this sense war is

politics and war itself is a political action; since ancient times there has never been a war that did not have a political character. "War is the continuation of politics by other means."

VOICE, FROM BOX
Something for something.

CHAIRMAN MAO
It can therefore be said that politics is war without bloodshed while war is politics with bloodshed.

VOICE, FROM BOX
When art hurts. That is what to remember.

LONG-WINDED LADY
I try to recall if I recall the falling, but I'm never sure, I think I do, and then I think I have not. It was so like being awake and asleep . . . at the same time. But I *do* recall being in the water. Heavens! What a sight! *I* must have been, too, but I mean what I *saw:* the sliding by of the ship, green foam in the mouth—kind of exciting— green foam as the wake went by. Lucky you missed the propellers, they said afterwards. Well, yes; lucky.

CHAIRMAN MAO
Without armed struggle neither the proletariat, nor the

people, nor the Communist Party would have any standing at all in China and it would be impossible for the revolution to triumph.

OLD WOMAN

And one of 'em said 'twas too warm there for anyone so old,
And t'other had an opinion the climate was too cold.

LONG-WINDED LADY

And sitting there! Sitting there in the water, bouncing around like a carton, screaming a little, not to call attention or anything like that, but because of the fright, and the surprise, and the cold, I suppose; and . . . well . . . because it was all sort of thrilling: watching the boat move off. My goodness, boats move fast! Something you don't notice till you're off one.

VOICE, FROM BOX

Then the corruption is complete.

OLD WOMAN

So they have shirked and slighted me, an' shifted me about—
So they have wellnigh soured me, an' wore my old heart out;
But still I've borne up pretty well, an' wasn't much put down,

Till Charley went to the poor-master, an' put me on the town.

LONG-WINDED LADY

And then . . . and then horns, and tooting, and all sorts of commotion and people running around and pointing . . .

(Some disappointment)

and then the boats out, the launches, and dragging me in and hauling me up—in front of all those people!—and then the brandy and the nurse and the sedative . . . and all the rest.

(Pause)

I lost my cashmere sweater . . . and one shoe.

CHAIRMAN MAO

We are advocates of the abolition of war; we do not want war; but war can only be abolished through war, and in order to get rid of the gun it is necessary to take up the gun.

LONG-WINDED LADY

You're a very lucky woman, I remember the chief purser saying to me, the next day; I was still groggy. You're a very lucky woman. Yes, I am, I said; yes; I am.

CHAIRMAN MAO

Every Communist must grasp the truth, "Political power grows out of the barrel of a gun."

VOICE, FROM BOX

Nothing belongs.

OLD WOMAN

But still I've borne up pretty well, an' wasn't much put
down,
Till Charley went to the poor-master, an' put me on the
town.

LONG-WINDED LADY

Then, of course, there were the questions. People don't
fall off of ocean liners very often. No, I don't suppose
they do. Broad daylight and all, people on deck. No; no;
I don't imagine so. Do you think you slipped? Surely not!
Dry as paint. Have you . . . do you cross often? Oh,
heavens, yes! I've done it for years. Have you . . . has
this sort of thing ever happened before? What do you
take me for!? I'm lucky I'm back from this one, I suppose. Then—gratuitously, and a little peevish, I'm afraid
—and I shall cross many times more! And I have—many
times, and it's not happened again. Well, do you . . .
do you think maybe you were—wincing some here:
them; not me—you were helped? Helped? What do you
mean? Well . . . aided. What do you mean, *pushed?*
Bedside nod. Yes. A laugh from me; a young-girl laugh:
hand to my throat, head back. Pushed! Good gracious,
no! I had been *reading*. What were you reading—which
struck me as beside the point and rather touching. Trol-

67

lope, I said, which wasn't true, for that had been the day before, but I said it anyway.
> *(Some wonder)*

They didn't know who Trollope was. Well, *there's* a life for you!

OLD WOMAN

Over the hill to the poor-house—my child'rn dear, good-by!
Many a night I've watched you when only God was nigh;
And God'll judge between us; but I will al'ays pray
That you shall never suffer the half I do today.

VOICE, FROM BOX

Look; more of them; a black net . . . skimming.
> *(Pause)*

And just one . . . moving beneath . . . in the opposite way.

LONG-WINDED LADY

Isn't that *some*thing? You lead a whole life; you write books, or you do not; you strive to do good, and succeed, sometimes, amongst the bad—the bad never through design, but through error, or chance, or lack of a chemical somewhere, in the head, or cowardice, maybe—you raise a family and live with people, see them *through* it; you write books, or you do not, and you say your name is Trollope . . . or whatever it may be, no matter what, you say your name . . . and they have . . . never . . . heard of it. That *is* a life for you.

VOICE, FROM BOX

Milk.

CHAIRMAN MAO

People of the world, unite and defeat the U.S. aggressors and all their running dogs! People of the world, be courageous, dare to fight, defy difficulties and advance wave upon wave. Then the whole world will belong to the people. Monsters of all kinds shall be destroyed.

OLD WOMAN

"Over the Hill to the Poor-House," by Will Carleton.

VOICE, FROM BOX

Milk.

LONG-WINDED LADY

Is there any chance, do you think . . . Hm? . . . I say, is there any chance, do you think, well, I don't know how to put it . . . do you think . . . do you think you may have done it on purpose? Some silence. I look at them, my gray eyes gently wide, misting a little in the edges, all innocence and hurt: *true* innocence; *true* hurt. That I may have done it on purpose? Yes; thrown yourself off.
(Some bewilderment and hurt)
. . . Me?

69

CHAIRMAN MAO

People of the world, unite and defeat the U.S. aggressors
and all their running dogs.

LONG-WINDED LADY

Well; yes; I'm sorry. Thrown myself off? A clearing of
the throat. Yes. Tried to kill yourself.

(A sad little half-laugh)

Good heavens, no; I have nothing to die for.

BOX

(REPRISE)

Perhaps keep the figures from Quotations from Chairman Mao Tse-tung *still and put them in silhouette. Raise the light on the outline of the Box again.*

VOICE

If only they had *told* us! Clearly! When it was clear that we were not only corrupt—for there is nothing that is not, or little—but corrupt to the selfishness, to the corruption that we should die to keep it . . . go under rather than . . .

(Three-second silence. Sigh)

Oh, my.

(Five-second silence)

And if you go back to a partita . . . ahhhhh, what when it makes you cry!? Not from the beauty of it, but from solely that you cry from loss . . . so precious. When art begins to hurt . . . when art begins to hurt, it's time to look around. Yes it is.

(Three-second silence)

Yes it is.

(Three-second silence)

No longer just great beauty which takes you more to everything, but a reminder! And not of what *can* . . . but what *has*. Yes, when art hurts . . .

(Three-second silence)

Box.

(Two-second silence)

So much . . . flies. A billion birds at once, black net skimming the ocean, or the Monarchs that time, that island, blown by the wind, but going straight . . . in a direction. Order!

(Two-second silence)

When the beautiy of it reminds us of *loss*. Instead of the attainable. When it tells us what we cannot have . . . well, then . . . it no longer relates . . . *does* it. That is the thing about music. That is why we cannot listen any more.

(Pause)

Because we cry.

(Five-second silence)

Look! More birds! Another . . . sky of them.

(Five-second silence)

What was it used to frighten me? Bell buoys and sea gulls; the *sound* of them, at night, in a fog, when I was very young.

(A little laugh)

Before I had ever seen them, before I had heard them.

(Some wonder)

But I knew what they *were* . . . a thousand miles from

the sea. Land-locked, never been, and yet the sea sounds . . .

> *(Three-second silence)*

But it *couldn't* have been fog, not the sea-fog. Not way back *there*. It was the memory of it, to be seen and proved later. And more! and more! they're all moving! The memory of what we have not known. And so it is with the fog, which I had never seen, yet knew it. And the resolution of a chord; no difference.

> *(Three-second silence)*

And even that can happen here, I guess. But unprovable. Ahhhhh. That makes the difference, does it *not*. Nothing can seep here except the memory of what I'll not prove.

> *(Two-second silence. Sigh)*

Well, we give up something for something.

> *(Three-second silence)*

When art hurts. That is what to remember.

> *(Two-second silence)*

What to look for. Then the corruption . . .

> *(Three-second silence)*

Then the corruption is complete.

> *(Five-second silence. The sound of bell buoys and sea gulls begins, faintly, growing, but never very loud)*

Nothing belongs.

> *(Three-second silence. Great sadness)*

Look; more of them; a black net . . . skimming.

73

(Pause)

And just one . . . moving beneath . . . in the opposite way.

(Three-second silence. Very sad, supplicating)

Box.

(Silence, except for the sound of bell buoys and sea gulls. Very slow fading of lights to black, sound of bell buoys and sea gulls fading with the light)

74

Edward Albee

Edward Albee was born March 12, 1928, and began writing plays thirty years later. His plays are, in order of composition: THE ZOO STORY; THE DEATH OF BESSIE SMITH; THE SANDBOX; THE AMERICAN DREAM; WHO'S AFRAID OF VIRGINIA WOOLF?; BALLAD OF THE SAD CAFE (adapted from Carson McCuller's novella); TINY ALICE; MALCOLM (adapted from James Purdy's novel); A DELICATE BALANCE; EVERYTHING IN THE GARDEN (adapted from a play by Giles Cooper); BOX AND QUOTATIONS FROM CHAIRMAN MAO TSE-TUNG; ALL OVER; SEASCAPE; LISTENING; COUNTING THE WAYS; THE LADY FROM DUBUQUE; and LOLITA (adapted from Vladimir Nabokov's novel).